Famine in Tudor and Stuart England

Andrew B. Appleby

FAMINE IN TUDOR AND STUART ENGLAND

Stanford University Press, Stanford, California
1978

Stanford University Press
Stanford, California

Printed in the United States of America
ISBN 0-8047-0956-4
LC 77-76151

Published with the assistance of the
Andrew W. Mellon Foundation

To Joyce

Acknowledgments

THIS BOOK IS an outgrowth of my doctoral dissertation written at the University of California, Los Angeles, under the direction of Arthur J. Slavin. His constant encouragement and helpful criticism played a large part in any value the book may have. Others who were kind enough to read and comment on one or another of the drafts the manuscript went through were Robert Brenner, Donald Coleman, Peter Laslett, Roger Schofield, and Geoffrey Symcox. Finally, I would like to thank the helpful staff at the record repositories where I worked, including the Public Record Office, the British Library, the Kendal Record Office, the Lancashire Record Office, the Cambridge Group for the History of Population and Social Structure, and, in particular, the Cumbria Record Office, where Mr. Bruce Jones and his marvelous staff gave me invaluable assistance. Ms. Daira Paulson prepared the maps and the graphs. Needless to say, all errors are my responsibility.

Chapters 7 and 8 appeared in a preliminary form as "Disease or Famine? Mortality in Cumberland and Westmorland, 1580–1640," *The Economic History Review*, 2d ser., 26 (1973), and I would like to thank the editors for permission to reprint extracts from that article here.

A.B.A.

Contents

Famine in Tudor and Stuart England

CHAPTER ONE

The Subject

IN 1587–88, 1597, AND 1623, the northwestern English counties of Cumberland and Westmorland were struck by famine. In those years, thousands of people starved in what appears to have been a series of "positive" Malthusian checks: the population of the region grew to the point where it outstripped the food supply. The disequilibrium between people and food production was brought to a crisis point by harvest failure. At the same time, depression in the clothing industry reduced purchasing power, making it difficult to pay for food from outside to feed the poor. The resulting famines skimmed off the surplus population through starvation aided by disease and emigration. These recurring famines indicate profound weaknesses in the regional economy and the local social structure. This book is an account of these famines in the northwest. Pushing beyond the regional limits of the northwest, I have also provided a cursory examination of famine in all of early modern England. The methodological approach followed here, I hope, will be of help to others studying famine and its effects, either in a historical context or in the world today.

What is famine? It is defined here as a crisis of mortality caused by starvation and starvation-related disease, a crisis measured by the increase in the number of deaths. In many of the localities under consideration, the number of people dying doubled or tripled, compared to an average of deaths in noncrisis years. If the normal death rate in England around the year 1600 was between 30 and 40 per thousand per year, a doubling in any one year meant that another 30 to 40 persons out of every thousand—or 3 to 4 percent of the population—died. A tripling of the death rate meant that 9 to 12 percent of the people died, instead of the usual 3 to 4 percent. These increases may not seem dramatic, but if we keep in mind that the death rate for England and Wales from influenza in the great epidemic of 1918 was three per thousand,[1] perhaps we can gain some idea of the scale of a famine that carried off ten or twenty times that number.

Pierre Goubert, in his study of the Beauvaisis region of northern France, found that the great *crises de mortalité* that ravaged the region toward the end of the seventeenth century and beginning of the eighteenth century were closely tied to the price of grain.[2] As grain prices rose, the number of burials rose too, as starvation, no doubt accompanied by disease, brutally cut back the region's excess population. Our evidence in the English northwest is much thinner and less convincing than Goubert's but suggests none the less that the same cruel correction took place there a century earlier. And the impact of the famine of 1597, although in the south it may not qualify as a crisis, was substantial throughout all England. Goubert found, too, that epidemics unconnected with food shortage had relatively limited effect on the Beauvaisis.[3] The same pattern emerges for the northwest, where the three famines dwarfed any other demographic crisis, completely overshadowing the plague that occasionally invaded the region. The northwest of England was in many ways unlike the Beauvaisis, but both regions—at quite different times—proved vulnerable to famine.

There are two aspects of famine that should be considered here. The first can be termed the physiological—or nutritional—side of starvation and, second, there are those economic and social conditions that allow enough people to starve to qualify as famine, as we have defined it. In this introductory chapter, we will begin with a short account of what is known of starvation—for example, what the symptoms of starvation are and what effect it has on the body. This will be offered as much to help other historians who suspect the presence of famine as to aid us in our attempt to identify famine in early modern England. Our sources too often say nothing about the symptoms of persons dying in the great mortalities and we have to construct our arguments from other evidence. Then, in this same chapter, we will turn to a consideration of the general social and economic conditions that extend individual starvation through a society and lead to famine. These two somewhat theoretical discussions will set the stage for the specific investigation of the famines that struck northwest England in the late sixteenth and early seventeenth centuries. Chapters 2 through 6 describe the growth of population in this region, the local agricultural and industrial economy, and the distribution of the agricultural yield between the landlords and their tenants. Famine can only be understood properly when it is solidly placed in its social and economic context. For this reason—to provide the necessary environment—this book is primarily a regional study. I certainly do not claim that the region was typical of England; indeed, it seems to have been very different from much of the southern portion of that country, although similar in ways to other parts of the north. Chapters 7 and 8 describe the three mortality crises in detail. Here, I attempt to show that these crises were caused by famine rather than disease operating independently of famine. The following chapter, 9, switches focus to a larger scale and attempts briefly to place the two most severe regional crises of 1597 and 1623 within a larger English and European framework and to see to what extent and how severely they afflicted all of England. Chapters 10 and 11 return once again to the regional level to trace the economic and social changes that enabled the northwest to free itself from famine during the course of the seventeenth century. Finally, in Chapter 12, I evaluate the role that each economic and social condition played in the famines of the northwest. The chapter also offers some conclusions and conjectures about the importance of famine in English society in the sixteenth and early seventeenth centuries.

The chapters on famine—7, 8, and 9—are pivotal chapters. Either I successfully show that the demographic crises were caused by famine or I do not. If I fail, the chapters on the pre-conditions of famine and the later chapters on the economic changes that freed the region from famine are of no particular interest. Put bluntly, it is impossible to have pre- and post-conditions without the events in between. For this reason, the reader may prefer to begin with the three chapters on famine, rather than following my arrangement of discussing first the social and economic pre-conditions, then the famines, and finally the post-conditions.

Obviously, human beings need a certain minimum amount of food to survive. If they do not get this minimum, their weight falls, certain changes occur in their appearance and in the condition of their bodily organs, and eventually, of course, they die. The caloric needs of an average adult male weighing 65 kg is approximately 3,000 calories per day, 800 more than the daily needs of an adult female. Males involved in heavy physical labor need somewhat more, as do pregnant and lactating females. Children between the ages of one and three years should have about one thousand calories, and adolescents' caloric demands fall somewhere between the needs of children and those of adults.[4] The specific caloric intake necessary to maintain health is still a subject of debate, and these rough figures are intended as broad guides only. In this study of the famines of the late sixteenth and early seventeenth centuries, such information on caloric needs is of little value, for we have no evidence that indicates what normal caloric intake may have been or how drastically it declined in years of dearth and famine.

In addition to its caloric needs, which can be termed its energy needs, the human body has to have a certain amount of protein. The minimum amount required is also a subject of dispute among nutritionists. It has been suggested that protein deficiency in underdeveloped countries (and, for our purposes, England in 1600 was an underdeveloped country) is rarely found, except in conjunction with caloric deficiency. According to this view, the body incorrectly utilizes proteins when there is a lack of other forms of calories. The protein deficiency can be arrested by increasing the carbohydrate intake, rather than by adding proteins to the diet.[5] Other nutritionists, however, argue that much of the starvation that is found in underdeveloped countries is caused by a lack of protein in a diet that consists almost entirely of carbohydrates. This protein deficiency, they argue, causes certain specific starvation diseases, such as kwashiorkor, which are absent if no food whatever is eaten. Two nutritionists have written recently,

> A little food, of course, is better than no food at all. Yet there is a paradox here. The edema of famine [i.e. swelling of the limbs and stomach] is hardly ever seen in cases of total starvation but develops often in semistarvation. Moreover, a semistarved person's survival time may actually be shortened if he tries to subsist on a diet consisting mainly of carbohydrate and deficient in protein.[6]

It is very unlikely that food, even for the extremely poor, ever gave out all at once in early modern England. More likely, the diet progressively worsened, and the symptoms of famine would have become apparent. Unfortunately, little is known about the diet of the poor, even in the best of times, and what changes took place in that diet as food prices rose is largely a matter of conjecture. Nevertheless, the problem is important enough to warrant an attempt, even though the reader should recognize that any conclusions are open to question.

Judging from the controls and regulations that all authorities throughout Western Europe set to cover virtually every transaction, grain was the core of the diet of the poor.[7] In good years, many small landholders were able to grow enough grain to feed their families; in bad years, when their plots returned less than usual, these smallholders were forced to buy grain on the market. Farm laborers and the city poor customarily bought part or all of their grain on the market. However it was consumed—in wheaten bread loaves in London or in oatmeal cakes in the north—grain of one kind or another was very likely the poor man's single most important expense, far exceeding what he spent on clothing or housing. When the grain harvest failed—and the price of his daily bread began to rise—how did the poor man feed himself and his family? If he lived in the south, where the everyday bread was coarse wheaten bread, he could economize by switching to a lower-priced grain such as rye, oats, or barley, provided these were available. Wheat always tended to be the most expensive grain per measure and this change gave more grain per penny spent.[8] But at best this was a stopgap, for the price of other grains soon followed the price of wheat upward.[9] In much of the north, where little wheat was grown and the mainstay of the diet was oats and barley, even this temporary expedient was unavailable.

Faced with rising grain prices, the poor had no adequate alternative foodstuffs to turn to. They stretched their bread grain with peas and beans and apparently consumed some milk, cheese, and butter in normal years.[10] However, in times of shortage—such as the "dear" years of 1595–97—both beans and peas reached price levels never before seen and dairy products also pushed to a new high, although the increase was not startling from a percentage standpoint. The poor could not afford to replace their usual grain purchases with meat, although cattle and sheep prices usually remained about average during periods of grain shortage. Indeed, the relative price stability of cattle and sheep suggests that they were of minor importance in the diet of the poor. Had they been of any consequence, buying pressure would have forced prices higher.

Perhaps it is worth mentioning that the relative increases in the price of foodstuffs consumed by the poor—barley, oats, rye, peas, and beans—were greater than the increase in the price of wheat during a period of food shortage. For example, wheat prices in 1596 were 2.09 times what they had been in 1593, the year preceding the dearth. By comparison, barley prices were 2.56 times the 1593 level, oats 2.75 times, rye 5.68 times, peas 2.45 times, and beans 2.20 times. (Rye had been unusually cheap in 1593, which helps explain the very high multiple.) These price movements suggest that wheat, which was initially the most desirable and most expensive, soon moved out of the buying reach of the poor, who turned to cheaper alternatives. Their buying pressure, however, pushed up the price of these almost to the price of wheat.

The switch from wheat to lower-priced grains may have brought a slight loss of nutritional quality. Wheat has marginally more protein than does barley, oats, or rye. On the other hand, mixing beans and peas into the bread would have given a better balance of vegetable protein and improved the nutritional quality. Combining different types of vegetable protein enhances the overall protein content.[11]

Less is known about other foodstuffs eaten by the poor in England. Salt fish evidently played an increasing role in their diet during the sixteenth century, although it was not available in quantities sufficient to substitute for grain in times of harvest failure. The poor in the sixteenth century were reported as eating more vegetables than before, but it seems doubtful that either fruits or vegetables were much of a factor in the average diet.[12]

In short, it seems highly unlikely that the poor had any cheap alternative foodstuffs in time of grain shortage. Probably the poor tightened their belts and cut down on all purchases except basic grains stretched with peas, beans, and other fillers. As William Harrison said, the poor were reduced to living on "horsse corne, beanes, peason, otes, tares, & lintels" when the grain harvest failed.[13] If this was the case, they cut back on their consumption of protein (milk, cheese, and butter) to devote their resources to grains and fillers that offered the most calories per penny. As the dearth continued, symptoms of starvation—which are discussed below—must have appeared.

This description of the diet of the poor seems reasonable enough for the poor of the cities and the grain-growing regions of the south. In the pastoral regions of the north and west, symptoms may have been less noticeable because possibly a higher proportion of the diet was protein—the carcasses of dead animals, game birds, perhaps a lamb stolen from an upland pasture.

As food became scarce, the symptoms of starvation would gradually have appeared. What are these symptoms? The most obvious is loss of weight, as first fat and then muscle is consumed to feed the vital interior organs. Other symptoms, gleaned from the literature on starvation in the twentieth century, include the loss of hair on the head and body, a change in skin color and texture to a translucent, parchmentlike gray, an increase in dental decay, and a discernible lassitude. Often the starved person's limbs swell or the stomach bloats, a condition known as "famine edema."

Persons above the age of 45 years and young children are more vulnerable to starvation than adolescents or young adults. Children are particularly susceptible to famine edema. Starvation can also bring a halt to their growth; sometimes starved youngsters are of much smaller frame than normal youngsters. Their lungs are also severely affected; tuberculosis is frequent; emphysema, normally a disease of the aged, is not uncommon. Perhaps the worst effect on children who are starved but do not die is on the brain; the normal number of brain cells is not generated and the child can be permanently mentally handicapped. The younger the child, the more catastrophic are the effects of starvation.[14]

The historian of famine in early modern England searches in vain for any written evidence of these symptoms, although if famine were present, starved youngsters must have been far from rare. Probably—at least in parts of the country—starvation among the children of the poor was too common, too "natural" to elicit any comments. Like disease—which also was seldom reported or described—hunger was one of the inevitable aspects of the life of the poor.

When the available food was completely exhausted, the poor may have—the records are silent—eaten the bark from trees and grass from the fields. Goubert found that the French peasantry, in their extremity, ate unripe grain, roots, grass, and the intestines and blood of animals that had been slaughtered as food for the better-off.[15] At this point, when death faces the starved person, one other symptom appears: bloody diarrhea. Often the starving person has thirty to forty bloody stools a day. These greatly weaken the already debilitated constitution and hasten the approach of death. Although this diarrhea is often reported as if it were an infectious disease, it is simply a result of the intestinal tract becoming nonfunctional.[16] This symptom is important because it is one mentioned in the contemporary account of the famine of 1597, when the vicar of Tamworth, Staffordshire, noted in the parish register that "Dyvers died of the bloudie flixe."[17] Almost certainly this is a reference to the characteristic terminal diarrhea of starvation and not some infectious dysentery that happened to break out in the parish.

One other characteristic of famine is of major importance to the historian. When famine strikes, not only do the burials recorded in the parish registers increase—as starvation and related diseases take their toll—but the recorded baptisms and marriages decline in number. The fall in baptisms can be very marked; in six parishes in the Beauvaisis in 1693–94, Goubert calculated that baptisms fell 62 percent.[18] This same phenomenon has been observed in this century; following the famine of 1944–45 in the Netherlands, the number of births came to only one-third the expected number. In Leningrad, during the prolonged famine of 1941–42, infertility became virtually total. Starvation causes a loss of sexual appetite, and in part the precipitous decline in baptisms can be attributed to less frequent intercourse. The fall can also be in part caused by an increase in spontaneous abortions among starved pregnant women. The bulk of the decline, however, can most plausibly be explained by amenorrhea, an interruption of the female menstrual cycle that makes conception impossible. It is triggered by malnutrition. When food grows short, mature women no longer ovulate—and whatever the level of sexual activity—conceptions decline. This decline in conceptions is then reflected in the number of baptisms nine months later. When the food shortage ends, the amenorrhea disappears and conceptions—and later baptisms—return to a normal level.[19]

The fall in the number of marriages is less striking but was found by Goubert to be very general in the Beauvaisis.[20] The decline probably can be explained by social and economic considerations rather than physiological changes. Perhaps the high price of food ate up the dowry money that fathers had put aside for their daughters; perhaps the prospective bridegrooms had to leave the parish to seek work elsewhere; perhaps money that had been saved for an entry fine into a vacant holding was used to buy food instead.[21] The economic and social dislocation that accompanied famine would have been enough to delay a number of marriages until times were better, making a fall in the number of marriages another indication of famine.

The foregoing discussion of the signs and symptoms of starvation does not explain the economic circumstances that pushed the society to the point of famine. Here we shall consider—again rather theoretically—those conditions that would extend starvation to a sizable portion of the population.[22] In time of famine, the available food—that is, the supply—is insufficient for the consuming needs of all the population—that is, the demand. Neither supply nor demand is absolute; each depends on the other, in a way analogous to the two sides of a balance scale. If the population increases and the supply of food remains constant, the balance tips toward famine. If the population remains constant and the food supply increases, the balance tips toward surplus, with its own social consequences.

Let us look at each side of our imaginary scale in more detail, beginning with population. Unless certain limiting factors come into play, population would endlessly expand. But there are numerous limiting factors that prevent populations from reaching their biologically maximum growth rate. Marriage itself is one of these factors; as J. C. Russell pointed out, it "is designed quite as much to prevent births as to encourage them."[23] There are many other population controls, ranging from a personal decision to delay marriage a few years to natural catastrophes such as a flood, which can wipe out thousands. Institutionalized celibacy, mechanical birth control, abortion, late marriage, infanticide, emigration, war, disease, and famine are a few of the other controls chosen by society or imposed by nature on the natural expansion of population.[24]

On the other side of the balance—the food supply—the picture is as complicated. In a closed, purely agrarian society, food supplies are dependent on what animal and plant foodstuffs can be raised, what fish or game can be caught, and what edible wild fruits, nuts, or vegetables can be gathered. Only in areas of very low population density can people survive exclusively on hunting and gathering; the society must exercise rigorous population limitation or shift its food source from wild to domesticated plants and animals. Of course, even in a developed economy, hunting and gathering may provide important supplemental sources of food, but major reliance will be on cultivated crops and animal husbandry.

Agricultural lands fall roughly into three categories: arable, meadow, and pasture. Arable land is by nature rich land, suited to the planting of grains, pulses, potatoes, other vegetables, and fruits. It also can be left in grass, for animal feed. Meadow is often as rich as arable land and, if it is not too wet, can successfully be tilled, but its grass is extremely valuable as animal fodder, and its special qualities make it a distinct type of land. Pasture is what is left—that land that offers some herbage for animals but is too poor for cultivation. When fixed cultivation is established and relative population density is low, there is some sort of rational utilization of these different types of land. In general, the arable is cultivated and the pasture is left for the animals.

When population grows and presses against the food supply, however, there is a progressive conversion of meadow and pasture to cultivation. In early modern Europe, this cultivated pasture was planted with grain, which—in the short run—made the land yield more calories than it would have in animal production. But land converted from pasture is poor and quickly becomes exhausted. Harvests decline to the point where the seed is not recovered. Then the land must be returned to pasture, even though it may take some years to regain its grass. The temporary benefits are thus erased and food production actually begins to decline. If population growth continues into the period of declining food production, the supply-demand balance is broken, as less food is available to feed more people. Hunger, or famine, follows unless there is some supplemental source of food or unless the people can migrate to an area with a food surplus.

The precarious balance between the food supply and the population is usually first broken by bad weather that destroys part of the crop. In early modern England, heavy summer and fall rains were the most feared; the grains, particularly wheat, rotted in the fields.[25] The effect of summer rain on livestock is mixed; grass benefits from the rain and the available animal fodder increases. On the other hand, sheep are susceptible to liver fluke, which thrives in moist warm weather. Liver rot can deplete the flocks.[26] Once bad weather brings a shortage, the return to normal is slow. In a year of bad harvest, the hungry farmer may eat some of the next year's seed corn, and accordingly his harvest the next year will be diminished, whatever the weather. Thus bad years tend to run as a series.[27]

The introduction of new crops and new agricultural techniques can temporarily ease the pressure of population on the output of foodstuffs. Nitrogen-rich plants, such as clover, when introduced into the crop rotation, prolong high yields and provide animal fodder to supplement the meager grass of the fallow land. Turnips and other root crops can be grown and fed to livestock over the winter when other animal feed is scarce. The meadows can be irrigated to increase the grass and provide more food for more livestock, which in turn produce more manure for the arable land. Seaweed, turf from the moor, lime, and marl can be used to enrich the fields. These, selected from English experience, are but some of the possibilities.[28]

Even more important than these methods of enriching the land and feeding livestock is the diversification of crops available for human consumption. In medieval England, peas and beans were introduced to supplement the ubiquitous grains, and by the beginning of the sixteenth century a sizable portion of the cultivated acreage in certain counties was planted in these legumes.[29] Peas and beans are rich in protein as well as carbohydrates; this innovation brought an improvement in the average diet. The most famous of the "new" foods in England, of course, was the potato. Its use in the eighteenth century—after the period covered by this study—brought an end to the overwhelming dominance of bread grains as the basic food of the poor. Although the potato played no role in the elimination of famine described in this book, it is worth stressing that the potato not only provided more calories per acre than grains but also was an alternative source of food when the grain harvests failed. The diversification of foodstuffs—the growing at the same time of grains, potatoes, other root crops such as carrots and turnips, and green vegetables—provides a cushion that is lacking in any monoculture where blight or harvest failure can destroy the one principal crop.[30] But regardless of the diversification of crops or improvement in agricultural techniques, if no limits are imposed on population growth, famine will merely be postponed, not avoided.

So far in this discussion, population and agriculture have been treated as abstractions, as if all persons have an equal share in the agricultural cake. Obviously this is seldom so. Some men own more land than others, or better land, or have access to roads or the sea.

The word "own" in the preceding sentence is misleading too, for some men have merely rights to a share of the yield of the land they work, while paying rents and taxes to others. When all these inequalities are considered, what we have is not one balance scale, with all the people on one side and all the agricultural production on the other, but rather many scales, each having persons of similar economic position on one side balanced against their wealth on the other. In early modern England there were the following groups, each balanced more or less successfully against their share of the agricultural wealth: cottagers, customary tenants,* freeholders, and lords. (For simplicity I have limited my examples and considered each as a homogeneous economic, not legal, entity.) If famine strikes, certain groups are going to be hit first, others later, some probably not at all. Over time, these groups, and their shares of the wealth, change. Perhaps rents are increased, moving wealth from the tenant to the lord. Perhaps rents are fixed while prices rise, in which case the profits from the price rise accrue to the tenant rather than the lord. Perhaps systems of inheritance break up the holdings of tenants, and they become impoverished as the sizes of their plots of ground shrink, generation after generation. Conversely, perhaps the custom of partible inheritance is abandoned, because too many people divide too little land. Economic difference between family members then replaces a rough economic equality.[31] Whatever form it may take, there is a constant redistribution of the agricultural wealth.

To this point we have been speaking rather generally about a closed agrarian society. But societies are seldom closed or completely agrarian. Our picture becomes further complicated by market exchanges in agricultural and industrial goods between communities. Agricultural and industrial specialization then takes the place of subsistence agriculture and the local, often domestic, manufacture of clothing and farming implements. Crops are tailored to the market and those not grown locally are purchased with the money proceeds of the sale of the cash crop. Land, theoretically, is devoted to

*Tenants who hold land by the custom of the manor will be dealt with in Chapter 5.

the agricultural use for which it is best suited. Economically this is a major advance. The market allows the highland farmer, for example, to devote himself to animal raising and buy his grain on the market with the money realized from the sale of his meat, wool, and hides, rather than try to eke some grain from his own land. In a market economy, the same quantity of land sustains a greater population than in a subsistence economy, because of this more efficient land use. The same market also allows industrial specialization. Weavers, miners, shipbuilders—to name a few—sell their labor and buy necessities with their wages.

The growth of specialization in Europe was a piecemeal affair. In early modern Europe it existed alongside and overlaid the subsistence agricultural base. Agricultural specialists, no matter how large their production for the market, usually maintained some acreage to feed their families and any workers dependent on them. Miners and weavers worked plots or small farms to supply at least a portion of their food. Even the larger cities were full of gardens, tended by the wives of artisans and merchants. But under a market economy the emphasis had changed; a major part of a person's work was expended to produce a marketable commodity; only a minor part went into growing food for immediate subsistence. This shift was gradual in all parts of Europe and left some parts relatively untouched. Even by 1600 much of Ireland and Scotland, parts of France and southern Italy, remained outside a market economy as I have defined it. Pockets of predominantly subsistence agriculture could be found in even the most advanced areas.

The development of a market, although it allowed increased efficiency through specialization of land and labor, contained elements of additional risk. The subsistence farmer had been at the mercy of the weather; the entrepreneurial farmer was at the mercy of both the weather and the market. If either failed him, he was unable to generate a cash income necessary to purchase those necessities he did not grow. The same instability applied to the industrial worker with a small plot of ground. If the weather destroyed the few crops he grew, he could still rely on his wages to buy food. But, with few exceptions, not for long. Usually the bad weather that ruined his garden also sadly reduced the amount of foodstuffs on the market. Food prices rose as supply declined and absorbed more of the purchasing power of all segments of the population. The effect on the industrial worker varied depending on his trade. If he happened to be in the luxury trades, it might have been minimal; his customers had a sufficient economic cushion to allow them to continue purchasing his wares without interruption. But if he happened to be a weaver of common cloth, to cite one example, he would find that the demand for his labor shrank as his customers allocated a larger share of their meager incomes to foodstuffs and a smaller share to all other purchases. Old clothes, even rags, were preferable to empty bellies. So the weaver found himself—one step removed—as dependent on the weather as the agricultural specialist. In his case, however, the crop failure triggered a collapse in the market for his goods. The farmer specializing in new materials for the clothing industries faced the same contracting demand. Wool for cloth and hides for shoes would fall in price, reducing his purchasing power—at the same time that he had to pay higher prices for the grain he bought to feed his family.[32]

The livestock farmer was still not faced with ruin even though the value of his hides and wool had declined. If he could get his beasts to market, he could offset his loss by selling their meat. In time of dearth meat prices followed grain prices upward, although they did not reach the same heights.[33] But there is an important qualification here. The end products of sheep and cattle are mainly wool, hides, tallow, and meat. The first three were relatively easy to transport but the last was difficult. In early modern England most meat moved to market on the hoof. Droving, as differentiated from transhumance, was difficult with sheep, which moved slowly, eating as they went. The more remote a sheep-raising area, the more dependent the sheep farmer was on nonmeat products, such as wool and tallow. Moving cattle was less difficult but the distance to market remained important. The cost of driving the cattle (drovers' wages, tolls, pasture rents) increased proportionately to the distance traveled while the value of the cattle fell (through weight loss and death of part of the herd). Usually, at the end of the drive, the weight loss was made good by rest and fattening before the cattle were sold, but this fattening might be expensive, or even impossible, in time of dearth.

In the same way that distance to market lessened the value of cattle driven to the market, distance increased the cost of imported grain. The buyer's market for grain was not necessarily at the same place as the seller's market for cattle. It may have been necessary to drive the cattle hundreds of miles to market whereas grain could be purchased in a nearby port. But the relationship between the income from meat sales and expenditure for grain purchases progressively worsened, the more remote a region was and the more heavily it relied on livestock, particularly sheep, which were vulnerable to disease and less mobile than cattle.

In this preliminary discussion, we have moved away from a simple land-population balance to the complex interconnections of a market economy. And we have seen that there are potential weaknesses in the market economy, as well as in the simpler subsistence economy. This broad overview has been intended as a rough, preliminary model—an explanatory framework. Unfortunately, as a model it is flawed by incompleteness; it does not include all those forces that can lead to economic collapse, nor does it include all those measures that can be taken to alleviate the distress. Lack of information prevents our completing the model. But it may be a useful guide to the reader to direct attention to certain significant relationships. In the following pages, I hope to show what effects each of these relationships did, in fact, have. In the concluding remarks, certain hypotheses—perhaps conjectures is a better word—will be offered for those aspects of the problem where we have too little evidence for any firm conclusion.

CHAPTER TWO

The Land and the People

THE COUNTIES of Cumberland and Westmorland lie in the northwestern corner of England. Bounded on the west by the Irish Sea, they abut Scotland to the north, Northumberland to the northeast, Durham to the east, Yorkshire to the southeast, and Lancashire to the south. Geographically, the two counties form a distinct subdivision of the north, to an important degree separated from the other northern counties. The Pennine Mountains and the Cheviot Hills stand between them and the coastal plains of the northeastern counties, although the Tyne Gap, running east from Carlisle, allows access through the mountains to Newcastle. The two counties, with the adjoining Furness and Cartmel districts of Lancashire, are partially cut off by Morecambe Bay from the greater Lancashire and Cheshire plains that stretch to the south. At the end of the sixteenth century Cumberland and Westmorland were remote isolated counties, cut off by the sea and the mountains from easy intercourse with the rest of England and the internal market that was developing, with London as its center.

The landscape of Cumberland and Westmorland is dominated by the mass of the Cumbrian Mountains, which lie in the approximate center of the two counties. Here are the highest peaks in England—Helvellyn, Scafell Pike, and Skiddaw—rising more than three thousand feet. This, of course, is the Lake District, one of the scenic glories of England. Today tourists crowd the area in summer, but at the end of the sixteenth century, the lakes and mountains must have seemed forbidding and desolate to the occasional traveler. The mountains themselves are barren, often rocky and almost treeless. Rainfall in the Cumbrians is the heaviest in England; in Borrowdale it averages 130 inches per year.[1] Spring is late in coming; the climate cold and sunless. As Eric Kerridge has remarked, with some exaggeration, "the winter lasted nine months and the rest of the year was cold."[2]

To the east of the Cumbrians, the Eden River flows northwest from Kirkby Stephen in Westmorland, past Appleby, slightly to the east of Penrith and on to Carlisle, to spill finally into the sea at Solway Firth. The valley of the Eden, which gradually broadens toward the north, separates the Cumbrians from the western slopes of the Pennines. These two ranges, together with an edge of the Cheviot Hills, make up the highlands of the two counties. The lowlands, besides the Eden Valley, comprise the Solway Plain, a broad expanse of relatively flat country lying between the Cumbrians and Solway Firth, and the smaller river valleys and narrow coastal plains that divide the Cumbrians from the sea. Among the more important river valleys are the Derwent, coursing from the mountains to the sea at the town of Workington, the Esk, which empties into the sea at Ravenglas, and the Kent, which runs south from Kendal into Morecambe Bay. Rainfall in the lowlands is more moderate than in the Cumbrians, between thirty and forty inches—and the temperature slightly warmer.

Estimating population size and change before the introduction of the regular census inevitably involves a degree of guesswork. Sometimes the materials inspire confidence; sometimes they are obviously faulty. Too often it is impossible to say—they can be neither discarded as worthless nor accepted as true. Each individual bit of evidence must be viewed skeptically. But if we gather together as many pieces as we can, and they reinforce each other, it is possible to offer some tentative estimates of population size and change. This is what I have tried to do here.

In 1563, the Privy Council asked each bishop to report the number of households in every parish and chapelry within his diocese.

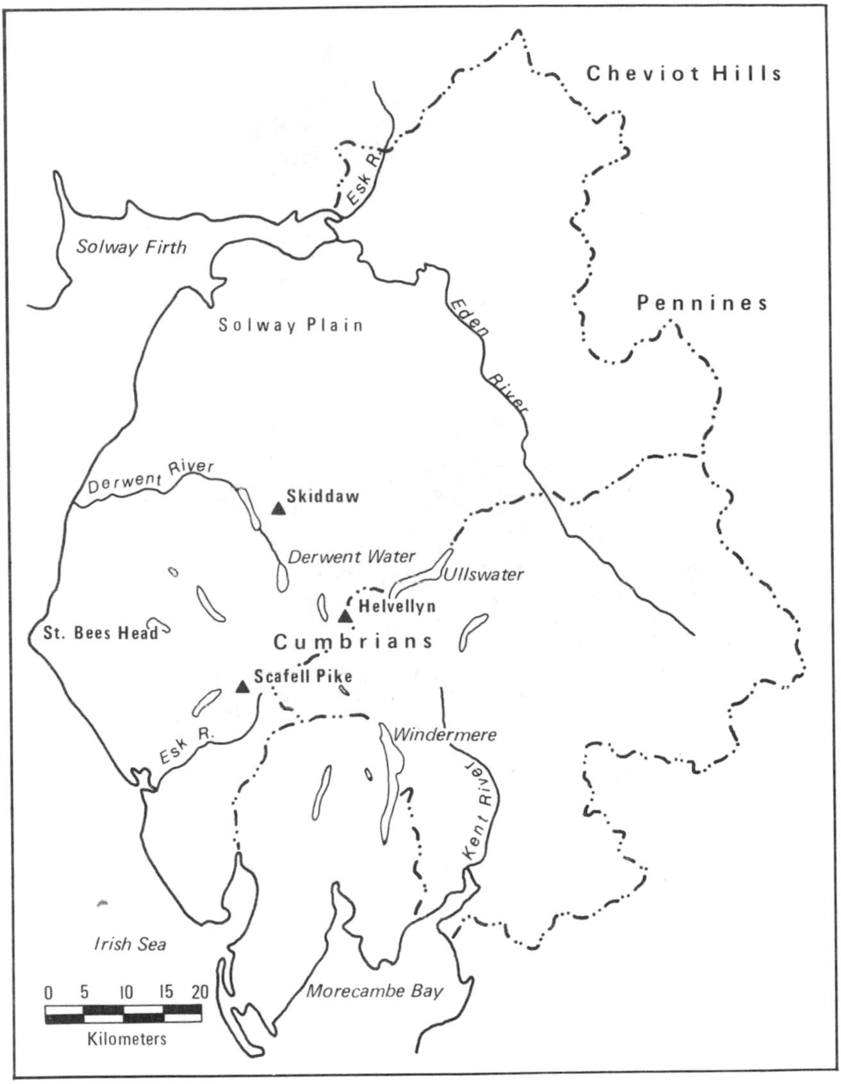

Physical features, Cumberland and Westmorland counties

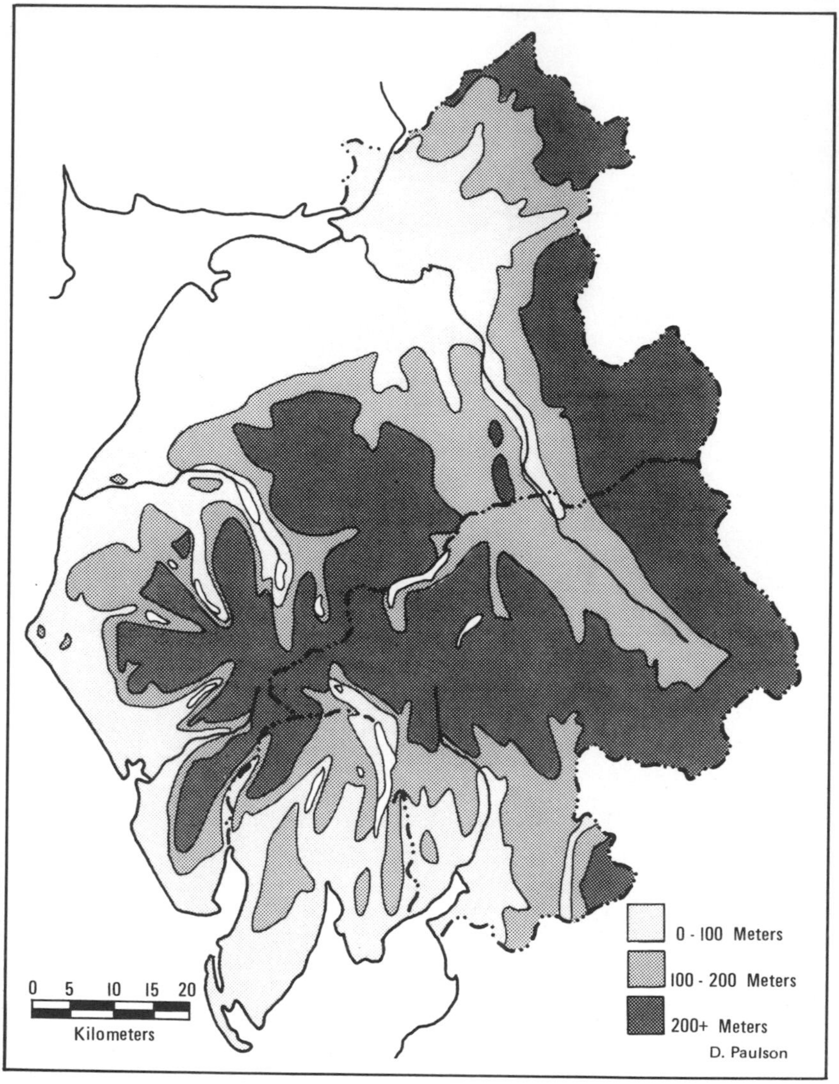

Topographic elevations, Cumberland and Westmorland counties

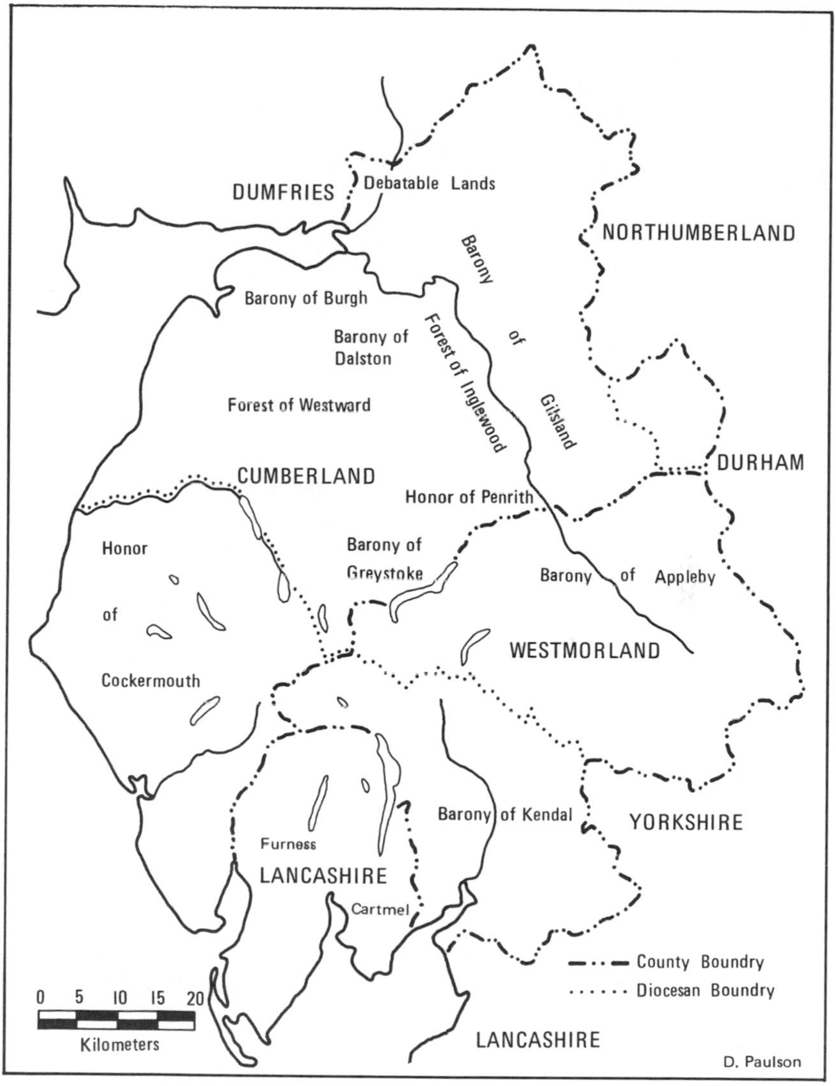

Major political, feudal, and religious divisions, Cumberland and Westmorland counties

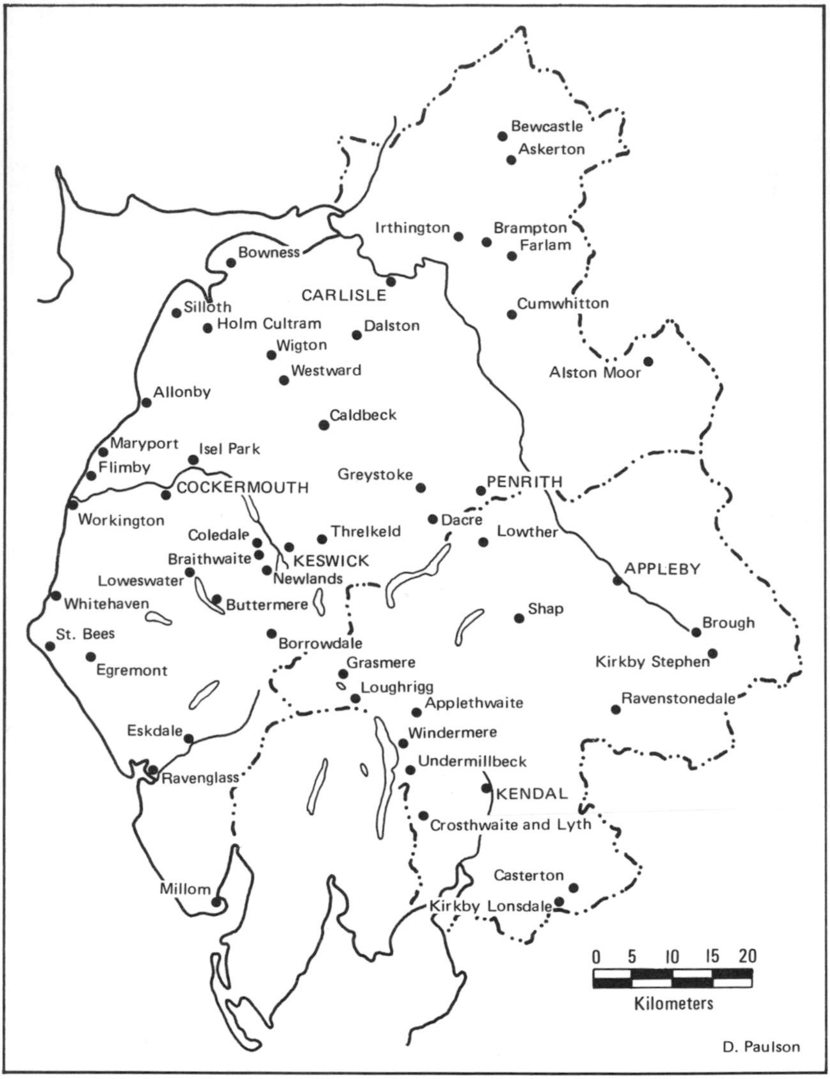

Towns, villages, and hamlets, Cumberland and Westmorland counties

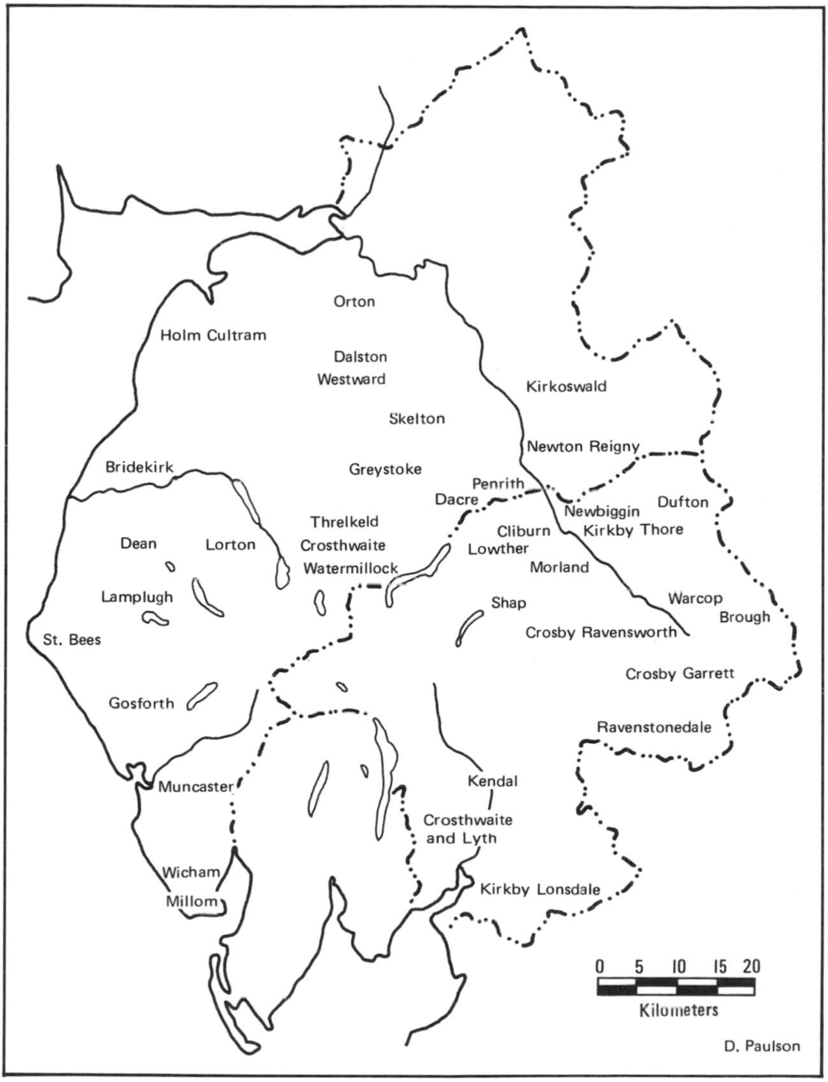

Parishes, Cumberland and Westmorland counties

Except for the Cumberland parish of Alston, which lay in the diocese of Durham, Cumberland and Westmorland were at that time divided between the dioceses of Carlisle and Chester, and the returns from both dioceses survive.[3] Slightly more than a century later, the hearth tax of the 1670's provides a similar household count.* The Westmorland returns are apparently quite complete, with lists of both those charged and those exempt from the tax.[4] The hearth tax returns for Cumberland are unfortunately very fragmentary.[5] However, this shortcoming is made good by an informal census of Cumberland taken in 1687–88 by Thomas Denton, the recorder of Carlisle.[6] Denton gave population, not household, figures for each parish in Cumberland, but all his parish figures are multiples of five, which suggests that he first began with households and then converted to population, using the multiplier of five persons per household. It is an easy matter to reconvert to households. Using these three sources, we then have comparable household counts by parish for both Cumberland and Westmorland for the approximate beginning and end of this study. The 1563 household list precedes the first known famine of 1587–88 by a quarter of a century, while the final household figures follow the last famine by half a century and fall at a time of considerable economic change in the two counties. The individual parish household counts can be found in Appendix A.

All three sets of figures seem generally reliable. The 1563 figures for some parishes are suspiciously round and probably represent estimates rather than careful house-by-house counts. As estimates, however, they do not seem too far off the mark. Although all 32 Westmorland parishes were returned, figures for six out of 102 Cumberland parishes were omitted from the 1563 lists. To facilitate comparisons with later household counts and other censuses, I have estimated the number of households in the six missing parishes; the method used is noted in the appendix, where the figures for the estimated parishes are placed within parentheses. The later figures of 1687–88, too, may have their drawbacks, although all parishes in

*For further discussion of the hearth tax see Chapter 10.

Cumberland were included. Denton certainly did not compile his data but relied on parish clerks to forward him correct counts. As in 1563, some of their totals may have been estimates, although there are fewer suspiciously round figures than in 1563. The Westmorland hearth tax household lists appear to be quite complete, with separate exemption certificates as well as lists of householders assessed and exempted from tax.[7] Unfortunately, the Cumberland hearth tax returns are too confused and fragmentary to permit a thorough parish-by-parish comparison with the Denton households.

According to these lists, Cumberland (excluding Alston) had a total household count of 8,935 in 1563 compared to 13,277 in 1687–88. Westmorland's households totaled 6,417 in 1563, somewhat more than the 5,961 drawn from the hearth taxes of the 1670's. The increase in households in Cumberland was just under 50 percent; in Westmorland, the number of households declined by 7 percent.

To this point, we are on fairly firm ground in comparing numbers of households at one time to numbers of households at another time. But we must push further, onto the quicksands of other censuses of the period, and try to convert all the given figures that we have to population, in an effort to date and measure the change in population between our first and last household counts. We have not yet converted households to population by using a multiplier that, supposedly, represents the average number of persons per household. As we have seen, Denton thought that five persons per household was a good average. We shall use 4.75 here; it seems likely to be more accurate than the Denton multiplier.[8] But there are problems involved in any choice of a multiplier. The number of people per household can vary widely between one locality and another at the same time. For example, in 1787 the Westmorland parish of Brougham had a mean household size of 6.50, while Little Strickland, a chapelry in the adjoining Westmorland parish of Morland, had a mean household size of only 3.63.[9] Household size can change, too, over time, as social and economic factors alter the structure of the household.[10] In short, moving from household figures to population estimates involves risk, but we have no choice but to take the risk, if we are to gain a set of comparable figures.

Using 4.75 as the mean household size, we find that in 1563, Westmorland's population was about 30,500 compared to 28,300 in 1670. Cumberland's population grew from 42,400 at the earlier date to 63,100 in 1688.

In 1603 an ecclesiastical census was drawn up for the diocese of Carlisle. It may provide a clue to the region's population in the early years of the seventeenth century and help us determine the change in population that took place between our first household count of 1563 and the later ones toward the end of the seventeenth century. Unfortunately, nothing similar is available for those parts of the counties in the diocese of Chester. The 1603 census supposedly gives a single, gross figure of all persons old enough to communicate in the diocese of Carlisle, but has no deanery or parish subtotals. The total was 61,847.[11] There is some question about what the "age to communicate" was and consequently some doubt about what portion of the population is represented by the figure. Different dioceses sometimes used different ages in these censuses, and the age generally tended to become somewhat older during the century following the reformation. The most likely age was 14 in the north of England in 1603, and, for the moment, we shall assume that the figure of 61,847 represents all those 14 and older.[12] In an early modern society like the northwest, approximately 35 percent of the people would be younger than 14. The total population was then about 95,000 persons, if the 1603 census was correct and if we have chosen a suitable multiplier to convert the census figure to population.

The 1563 household count for those parishes within the diocese suggests, in turn, a population of 43,100, using the 4.75 multiplier. If the evidence is to be trusted, population more than doubled in the forty years after 1563. A natural increase of this magnitude—about 2 percent per year—is unlikely, but natural growth may have been considerably augmented by the immigration of persons seeking land in the great forests and upland pastures of the region.

The hearth tax and Denton household counts for the later seventeenth century for the same parishes within the diocese, when converted to population by the same 4.75 multiplier, give a population of 58,800. This, in turn, suggests a population decline of almost 37 percent between 1603 and the time of the household counts of the later seventeenth century.

Other highland areas, remote from the growing south, also seem to have experienced a population decline, although not of this degree. In Wales, the number of people old enough to communicate declined by 13 percent between 1603 and 1688, when another ecclesiastical census was taken. The northwest Welsh diocese of Bangor—the most isolated and mountainous in Wales—suffered a drop of 27 percent. Turning from Wales to England, we find that the entire archdiocese of York probably saw a fall in population between 1603 and 1688. Better documented is the population decrease in the dioceses of Lincoln—just over 2 percent—and Worcester—27 percent—both of which were relatively distant from the burgeoning population centers of the south. Unfortunately, we lack specific figures for the most northerly English dioceses—Carlisle, Chester, Durham, and York—in 1688. It seems, however, that the periphery of the country—Wales and the northwest—lost population but that the decline was more than made good by growth in the south.[13]

For the diocese of Carlisle, we have two other sources on population: the Protestation Returns of 1641–42 and the ecclesiastical census of 1676. Perhaps we should briefly discuss each of these. The Protestation Returns were lists of men 18 and over who pledged loyalty to the reformed English church. Those who refused the oath were included separately on the returns. The Returns survive for all 25 Westmorland parishes in the diocese of Carlisle and for 70 of 76 parishes in the Cumberland portion of the diocese.[14] To make these lists of adult males comparable with the other data, I have converted them to population figures by doubling the figures to include adult females and then adding another 80 percent for children. The total estimated population for the 94 extant parishes is 53,800. The population total for these same parishes in the somewhat later hearth tax and Denton lists (again, we multiplied households by 4.75) is 56,230. The fact that these fall roughly in the same range, both in the gross figure and in the individual parish figures which can be found in Appendix A, argues, I think, for their general reliability. The comparison also suggests that population may have been somewhat lower in 1641 than later in the century and may have fallen even more after 1603 than our earlier discussion indicated. If we estimate the population of the missing six parishes—using the parish populations of 1688 for lack of better figures—and add this to the existing returns, we find that the total estimated population of the diocese was 56,400 in 1641–42. This is 41 percent below our estimate for 1603. Such a dramatic decrease seems improbable—but we shall return to this problem shortly.

The 1676 ecclesiastical census for the diocese of Carlisle is less useful, at least for the Cumberland portion of the diocese. Like the earlier census of 1603, it was of all persons "of age to communicate." Unlike the earlier census, however, no total is given for the diocese, but instead individual parish figures are listed, together with a separate listing for "popish recusants," Quakers, and other dissenters. Twenty-one parishes out of 101 were not returned.[15] The instructions to the clergy stated that 16 was the age to communicate. To convert to population, the parish figures should be multiplied by 1.67.[16] But the results are disappointing; the estimated population figures are much too low, so low as to throw doubt on the accuracy of the census. For example, the two parishes that comprised the city of Carlisle—St. Cuthbert's and St. Mary's—had an estimated population of only 1,500 in 1676, compared with 2,600 in 1641 and 4,800 in 1687–88. (Remember, each of these is households converted to population by the use of a multiplier.) The last figure, of 1687–88, is almost certainly fairly accurate because Thomas Denton, the man collecting the data, was recorder of Carlisle. He would not have let grossly inflated household figures for the city parishes slip by. Why should the estimated population for 1676 be so much lower? One would expect the parishes in Carlisle, the cathedral seat, to follow correctly the instructions of the church. A baldly incorrect return, it seems, would have aroused the suspicions of the diocesan officials, just as a similar error would have attracted Denton's attention ten years later. Frankly, it is puzzling.

Carlisle's parishes are not the only ones in the 1676 census that seem unreasonably low. Another 12 parishes in Cumberland are suspicious. Possibly in these parishes only men were counted; the returned figures are usually about one-half what they should have been.[17] Fortunately, the 1676 census is not crucial to our reconstruction of population in the diocese because we have the Denton figures and the hearth tax returns, and we have disregarded it in our main conclusions.

This mass of sometimes confusing, possibly unreliable, and often tedious material suggests the following main patterns of population change for those portions of Cumberland and Westmorland that lay in the diocese of Carlisle. First, population rose by some 100 percent between 1563 and 1603. Second, it then fell by some 41 percent between 1603 and 1641. Finally, it recovered somewhat afterward, growing by less than 10 percent by the time of the tax returns and censuses of the 1670's and 1680's. By these decades, Westmorland's population had not yet regained its level of 1563; Cumberland's comfortably passed the 1563 level, although it was well below the point reached in 1603. Obviously, much depends on the accuracy of the census of 1603; if it was a totally erroneous return, our flimsy reconstruction of population trends collapses, like a tumbled house of cards, and we are left with the beginning and ending household counts plus the Protestation Returns but with no knowledge of population levels at the time of the famines. I have hinted that both the increase in population between 1563 and 1603 and the marked fall in population in the next forty years seem implausible. Both depend on the validity of the 1603 return. Are there any other data we can use to test the reliability of this return?

Our discussion of population change in Cumberland and Westmorland so far has dealt with lists—of households, of persons old enough to communicate, of men 18 and over—that can be converted to estimates of total population by the use of a multiplier. These are the somewhat static points of reference that we have for certain dates, not necessarily the dates we would choose, but the dates that have been given us by the surviving data. We have not yet looked at the parish registers of marriages, baptisms, and burials, nor at other, circumstantial evidence of population change.

The parish registers do not seem to bear out all the conclusions

TABLE 1. *Parish Registrations, Ten-year Averages*

Period	Greystoke		Crosthwaite		Dacre		Dalston	
	Baptisms	Burials	Baptisms	Burials	Baptisms	Burials	Baptisms	Burials
1571–80	42.4	48.5	102.0	69.7	20.6	inc.	42.3	32.7
1581–90	46.0	45.7	92.2	62.6	26.5	24.2	inc.	27.1
1591–1600	inc.	inc.	84.7	103.6	19.1	20.9	36.7	29.2
1601–10	inc.	inc.	91.3	58.3	20.8	14.9	38.9	22.4
1611–20	46.4	37.8	90.8	62.8	inc.	inc.	36.6	29.2
1621–30	inc.	inc.	84.6	inc.	inc.	inc.	30.7	39.2
1631–40	inc.	inc.	78.9	56.5	inc.	inc.	30.2	29.7
1641–50	inc.	inc.	71.0	60.7	inc.	inc.	inc.	inc.
1651–60	inc.	inc.	inc.	inc.	inc.	inc.	inc.	inc.
1661–70	31.4	28.1	inc.	inc.	inc.	inc.	39.4	35.4
1671–80	25.4	35.4	29.9	28.9	inc.	inc.	inc.	20.5
1681–90	24.6	28.4	21.5	27.7	14.8	12.6	29.4	27.4
1691–1700	16.7	29.4	39.5	47.9	17.0	17.7	26.0	31.0

SOURCE: For the date and place of publication (or location) of all parish registers, see Appendix B. I have used the Cambridge Group's transcription of the Dalston register here.

NOTE: Suspicious figures within any decade have not been included but have been marked "inc." for incomplete.

drawn from the various lists we have used. The decadal averages shown in Table 1 for four selected parishes show a decided decline in vital registration figures in the latter half of the seventeenth century, compared to the closing decades of the sixteenth, and support the idea of a population decline during the seventeenth century. They do not, however, suggest that population was growing at a rate anywhere near 2 percent per year during the closing decades of the sixteenth century. Rather, they seem to cast considerable doubt on the validity of the 1603 figure. In certain parishes, population growth had apparently slowed as early as the 1570's. In Greystoke, for example, baptisms were fewer than burials in the twenty years after 1570, indicating that no natural increase took place, although of course immigration may have enlarged the size of the population. In Crosthwaite, on the other hand, baptisms exceeded burials by some 323 in the 1570's, by 296 in the 1580's, and then fell below burials by 189 in the 1590's. If baptisms exceeded burials in the period 1563 through 1570 by the same relative margin as in the 1570's—and the registers are unfortunately incomplete—this would add a further 200, making a total increase of 630 in Crosthwaite's population between 1563 and 1600. According to the 1563 household count, Crosthwaite had a population of 1,520. If another 630 people were added by 1600 (and again our calculations do not include migration), the parish had grown by 29 percent. This seems more reasonable than the enormous increase demanded by the 1603 figure.

Other parishes seem to have enjoyed similar increases. Dalston grew by just short of one hundred in the 1570's and by another 75 in the 1590's. If we assume that the 1580's were like the 1570's, and add another hundred, our increase comes to about 270. Dalston's population in 1563 was 950; another 270 persons would mean an increase of 28 percent. The registers of Brough under Stainmore, Westmorland, are complete for the entire period from 1563 through 1603. They show a surplus of 384 baptisms over burials—on a base population of 665 in 1563, an increase of 58 percent. This is very substantial growth, but hardly comparable to the supposed doubling that the 1603 figure suggests.

Analysis of other registers would, I fear, make this account even more unreadable than it is now. The problem, though, is clear: the 1603 figure appears much too high, when compared with the experience of the individual parishes. Should we discard the 1603 figure as worthless? Certainly it is unlikely that the diocese doubled its population in forty years, in view of the growth we can trace in the individual registers. It is still more questionable if we keep in mind that in many parishes the 1590's were a decade of net loss, because of the crisis of 1597–98, and the doubling would have had to take place between 1563 and 1590, an even shorter period of time. The 1603 figure either is worthless, it seems to me, or is, indeed, a count of the *total* population, not merely those old enough to communicate. This would bring us back into the plausible range. If population grew from 43,100 in 1563 to 61,847 in 1603, it increased 43 percent, a range much closer to that found in the individual parishes.

Such an assumption—and it is an assumption, because we do not know exactly how the 1603 figure was compiled—also accords better with the decline that came in the seventeenth century. According to the Protestation Returns, population was 56,400 in 1641–42. If the population figure of 95,000 is used for 1603, this amounts to a decline of 41 percent in less than forty years. Despite the severity of the 1623 famine, this is unlikely. Much more reasonable would be the 9 percent decline from 61,847—using the 1603 figure as total population—to 56,400.

The individual parish registers confirm this decline in those four Cumberland parishes we have chosen as examples. Three of the parishes whose baptismal and burial data are given in Table 1 lie in southern Cumberland, not far from the center of the two counties. Dalston is a rural parish not far south of Carlisle. Although their registers are flawed at various points, the pattern of declining registration indicates that population was less at the end of the seventeenth century than a century earlier. This rural depopulation was perhaps typical of many country parishes. Part of the apparent decline is no doubt illusory; the growth of nonconformity makes the registers less valuable as a record of the entire population. But even allowing for substantial nonconformity—such as 5.5 percent of the population of Greystoke in 1676, according to the ecclesiastical census of that year—the picture is one of falling rural population.[18]

On a very few manors, it is possible to trace the increase in the number of tenants in the sixteenth century. At Irthington, in the Barony of Gilsland, there were 25 customary tenants in 1502. By 1536, the number had grown to 33, the same as in 1567. The manor had 46 tenants in 1604, 50 in 1611, and 48 in 1626.[19] If we assume that the various lists of tenants were made in a roughly comparable way, we can say that the number of tenants more than doubled between 1502 and 1611, with most of the growth taking place after 1567. The slight decline in the figures from 1611 to 1626 probably can be explained by the great mortality of 1623. The nearby manor of Cumwhitton experienced similar growth: 29 tenants in 1502, 52 in 1575, and 60 in 1603.[20] A survey taken in 1571 of the Crown manor of Penrith uncovered 62 "bondage" tenants, although there were supposed to be no more than 34. By 1619, the numbers of bondage tenants had risen to 91.[21] These increases in the tenantry support the other evidence of demographic expansion.

On certain manors, the number of tenants remained quite constant during the supposed period of growth. Four surveys, dated 1538, 1573, 1604, and 1649, for Holm Cultram, a large Crown manor on the Solway Plain, show 368, 361, 361, and 387 tenements, respectively.[22] If population increased at Holm Cultram—and the household counts of 1563 and 1687 show an increase of more than 50 percent—where did the new families live? Evidently some lived on lands that had been sold off after the dissolution of the monasteries had brought the manor into Crown hands. Before dissolution, for example, seven houses had been located on Silloth Grange, then part of the manor. The Grange was sold, however, to one Robert Wheatley. He, in turn, rented it out, and his new tenants built twenty additional houses there.[23] The demesne lands of the manor were leased by the Crown to neighboring gentry, who then located subtenants on the land.[24] The surveys of Holm Cultram do not include any of these subtenants on the lists of customary tenants. As this example shows, population increased even where there was no increase in the number of customary tenancies.

Not everyone could be accommodated on the existing manors, as additional customary tenants or squatters or subtenants on the demesne. Some men found land in the great Forests.* A commission in 1578 reported 178 different encroachments within the Forest of Inglewood, a vast, ill-defined Crown property that stretched north from Penrith almost to Carlisle. These encroachments were enclosures, by means of a stone wall or a hedge, that converted Forest land to individual use. The majority of the encroachments were very small, an acre or less, and appear to have been held by poor squatters who had no other land. The tenants of manors abutting on the Forest had also encroached, to add a bit of land to their holdings. The local gentry had made other, larger encroachments, which they then rented to poor men. Mr. William Skelton, for example, had an encroachment with six houses on it, each rented to a separate family. Ten families lived on land enclosed by Mr. Thomas Denton. With the exception of the encroachments by tenants of neighboring manors, all the encroachments seem to have ended up in the hands of poor men, who had no other holdings.[25] By providing vacant land, the Forest absorbed part of the excess population of the region.

In 1619, a survey of the Forest revealed 757 different encroachments, including 602 houses.[26] Some of these had been reported by the 1578 commission but many others were more recent. Although the surveyors in 1619 arranged their data somewhat differently than the 1578 commissioners, a comparison of the two documents indicates that many more people inhabited the Forest in 1619 than forty years before. The pattern of the holdings remained the same: many squatters, some customary tenants of adjoining manors who encroached to enlarge their other holdings, and local gentry who sublet their encroachments.

Clearly, the Forest provided a haven for part of the surplus population in the latter half of the sixteenth century. It seems that little encroachment took place early in the century. A survey of 1540 shows very few encroachments of Forest land.[27] A survey taken in

*Forests were legal geographic entities and did not necessarily have trees on them.

1665—toward the end of our period—cannot be directly compared with the 1619 survey but it suggests that encroaching had continued after 1619. This survey unfortunately does not indicate whether the encroachers were customary tenants of nearby manors, who had enlarged their holdings by pushing out into the Forest, or whether the encroachments were squatters' holdings. Apparently encroachment continued—but it may not reflect the search for land by a surplus population.[28]

The Forest of Inglewood was enclosed piecemeal through the initiative of individuals, many of them squatters. On the other hand, enclosure of a large part of the Forest of Westward, a Percy holding, was accomplished at one time, in 1569, and appears to have been initiated by the steward of the Forest. By 1570, 94 tenements and six cottages were established in the Forest.[29] In the Forest of Inglewood, much of the land had been encroached by landless squatters, and other land had been encroached by gentry who then sublet it to poor men. The latter process seems to have predominated in Westward, although local customary tenants shared with the gentry in receiving land and then renting it out again. But whatever the process, most of the new encroachments were settled by poor, otherwise landless men.

The moors and fells of the highlands played a role similar to the Forests of the lowlands. A squatter could carve a few square yards of land out of the common pasture, throw up a rude cottage, and try to scratch a living out of the inhospitable soil. Occasionally squatters appear on a survey; more often they were probably admitted as tenants or cottagers on the manorial rolls and are reflected by the increase in the numbers of tenants. The survey of Cumwhitton, made in 1575, shows 52 tenants, of whom eight hold only land encroached from the common pasture.[30] They are listed as tenants and no doubt in time would be indistinguishable from the other tenants, but apparently initially they were excess people, younger sons or outsiders, who were permitted to squat on the pasture. The established tenants rarely objected to the loss of pasture; the upland commons were vast, largely unsuitable for cultivation, and the chances slender that enough land would be converted to private use to seriously reduce the herds and flocks pastured there.[31] Many customary tenants themselves encroached—a few yards here, to straighten a wall there—and opposition to a poor squatter may have seemed inconsistent. The lords, too, seem to have tolerated or encouraged encroachments, provided they were done with the lords' permission. The encroachments meant additional rent at no expense to the lords. The great landlords of the region—the Crown, the Percys, the Dacres—were either absentees or held their land in a traditional way, drawing their revenues from rents and entry fines. They were not directly involved in the exploitation of either their demesne lands or the great pastures. Had they been runners of sheep or cattle or large-scale grain producers, it might have been in their interest to prevent encroachment on the demesne and the pastures. But instead they depended on rents—and encroachment swelled their rent rolls.[32]

The population of the two counties was predominantly rural in the sixteenth century. Towns were unimportant, villages small. The most populous town was Kendal, with 338 households in 1606.[33] At this time, it was probably slightly larger than Carlisle, which had 320 households within the city walls in 1597.[34] These were the two major towns—but with perhaps 1,500 people each, they were little more than large villages. Penrith parish, which included the town of Penrith, had 140 households in 1563 and the same number of households was shown for the Cockermouth chapelry.[35] On the Cumberland coast, the largest village was Workington, with 30 households in 1566.[36] Whitehaven, which became an important port city in the eighteenth century, had just six households in 1566.[37]

The population increase in Cumberland and Westmorland—whatever its precise dimensions—was part of the general demographic surge that took place in Western Europe during the sixteenth century, only to slow or stop sometime between 1600 and 1650.[38] If our assessment of population change in the two counties is correct, population grew by about 43 percent between 1563 and 1603. It then declined by some 9 percent in the early seventeenth century when the overall population of England was growing slightly. This decline seems to have been more or less typical of the decline that took place in Wales or in other regions of the north of England. The evidence of encroachment on the great common pastures of the highlands and the forests of the lowlands suggests that in the sixteenth and the early years of the seventeenth centuries the surplus population stayed on the land, rather than migrating south toward London, that great sponge that helped soak up England's excess people.[39] In part, this reluctance to migrate may be traced to the vacant land—forest or pasture—that still remained in the two counties, however marginal this land may have been from an agricultural point of view. In part, too, people no doubt stayed because the region was remote, without established seaports and with only rudimentary overland routes to the outside. Perhaps this latter point should not be overemphasized—sixteenth-century people were surprisingly mobile—but the isolation would have tended to retard migration.

We have partially explored the population/food supply problem. Our evidence—unsatisfactory as it sometimes is—creates a mosaic that leaves little doubt that population increased in the sixteenth century, then declined in the early seventeenth, to finally make a partial recovery toward the end of the century. Several questions remain: Did food production expand to match the growth of population? Was the population decline brought about by what Malthus would call a "positive" check, that is, a correction in existing overpopulation? If so, was the correction caused by failing food supplies that brought starvation or so weakened the poor that they easily succumbed to disease? Or, conversely, was the correction caused by some epidemic disease (plague, for instance) that had no relation to malnutrition? It is to the first of these questions that we now turn, to attempt an assessment of agriculture and industry in the two counties.

CHAPTER THREE

The Agricultural Community

In the sixteenth and early seventeenth centuries, Cumberland and Westmorland were overwhelmingly agricultural counties. As we have seen, cities were few and insignificant. Most people lived on the land and drew their livelihood directly from it. If economic weakness led to famine, it would most likely appear in the agricultural sector. In this and the following two chapters, I shall describe rural settlement, offer a few remarks on field systems and indicate what crops and animals predominated, and then pass on to the problems facing the average tenant: the size of his holding, the productiveness of the land, the availability of markets, and the level of rents and entry fines he paid his lord.

It is convenient to draw a distinction between the highland and lowland agricultural zones.[1] The highlands—the Cumbrians, the western slopes of the Pennines, and the Cheviot Hills—were characterized by limited arable land along the narrow valley floors and extensive rough pasture on the adjoining mountain fells. The inhabitants lived in small hamlets of a few houses alongside the arable fields, which the husbandmen either cultivated in common—as in the Cumbrian manors of Braithwaite, Buttermere, Lorton, Threlkeld, and Wasdale Head—or in separately held enclosures—as in Eskdale, Ennerdale, Loweswater, and Keswick.[2] Where the fields were farmed in common—that is, shared by the inhabitants and planted and harvested at the same time—there is no evidence of a systematic rotation of crops, as in the classic three-field rotation of the Midlands. Rather, the fields seem to have been regularly sown in the spring with the same white grain—either oats or barley—and then opened after the autumn harvest to the stock which grazed on the stubble. It is not clear whether the usual custom was to occasionally allow the land to lie fallow or whether it was constantly cultivated. Even though it benefited from the dung dropped by the stock during the winter, cultivation year after year must have contributed to soil exhaustion and meager returns on the seed. With the coming of spring, the stock were taken to summer on the fell pastures and the arable land was again sown with oats and barley. Many of the inhabitants evidently went along to the fells, to watch over the stock. These stockherds lived in rude huts, quickly thrown up, called sheilings, on the great pastures.[3] After the grain harvest in the autumn, the stock was again brought back to winter in the valleys.

In such a setting, the natural emphasis was on cattle and sheep, not on sown crops. The farmer grew what corn he could on his limited arable and relied on the seemingly endless pasture to maintain his livestock. And he hoped that the proceeds from the sale of his animals or their hides, wool, woolfells (or woolskins), tallow, and meat would enable him to buy grain if his own arable holding did not produce enough to feed his family. The probate inventories left by highland farmers reflect this emphasis on livestock, rather than on sown crops. Thomas Birsted, of Crosthwaite parish, had 200 sheep, nine cows and calves, and two horses at his death in 1570. Hay appeared among his effects but no grain and no plow. Possibly Birsted did not cultivate any arable land whatever and bought the grain he needed. Birsted was well-off; the value of his estate was £46-8-8.[4] David Bell of Ousby, whose inventory was compiled in 1614, had 60 lambs but no adult sheep. His estate, like Birsted's, included neither grain nor a plow. Judging from his goods, Bell was a fattener of lambs, buying them after weaning and pasturing them on the Ousby common or his own holdings until they were ready for sale.[5] The 1614 inventory of John Birkhead of Crosthwaite included 79 sheep, 13 cattle, and two horses. He also had 13 bushels of unspecified seed and one skep (12 bushels) of bigg (an inferior northern barley) as well as 40*s*. worth of oatmeal. In all, his grain was worth £7-5-0, compared with a value of £20 for his sheep and £20-10-0, for his cattle. His farm implements included a plow, a wagon, and two carts.[6] The inventory suggests that his grain production may have been sufficient to supply the household needs, without outside purchases.

Henry Bell of Farlam, in the Pennine foothills, in 1614 owned a plow and grew rye, something of a rarity in Cumberland or Westmorland. However, his sheep and cattle represented about two-thirds the value of his total estate.[7] The inventory of John Gaskerth of Crosthwaite, drawn up in August of 1565, shows unharvested haver (oats) and bigg worth 46*s*. 8*d*. His cattle were valued at £2-2-0 and his sheep at £6-8-4. His four horses, rather a large number, were listed at £4-12-4.[8] Crosthwaite is a mountainous parish, lying close to the center of the Cumbrians, but the valley floor around Keswick contains extensive level land suitable for arable tillage. Keswick vale is probably the largest such area in the Cumbrians, and grain cultivation may have been more important here than in the narrower valleys.

Not all Crosthwaite inventories reflect the affluence of the men we have so far used as examples. Edward Dowthate, on his death in 1614, owned one-half of a cow and a calf. His estate also included 10*s*. of corn in the fields (the inventory date was August 1, two months or so before the harvest) and a few other items, including a frame, which was probably a weaver's frame. He owned no animals, other than his calf and the cow he shared with someone else.[9] It is conjecture, but he may have earned a poor living as a weaver or a farm laborer, stretching his wages with the yield of a small plot of ground. Slightly less precarious was the economic condition of Richard Kyd of Addingham, in the Pennine foothills. His inventory, dated October 1565, lists one cow, a mare and her foal, four "old" sheep and two lambs, four bushels of bigg, three of haver, and some hay and straw. At his death Kyd left a wife, three sons, and three daughters.[10] The seven bushels of grain and the few animals must have offered them a slender barrier against hunger, after the necessary deductions were made for seed corn, rent, and the inevitable entry fine and heriot his heir would pay.

The degree of dependence on livestock is sometimes quite surprising, even considering the geography of the highlands. Perrybell Dod, of Croglin parish, left a comfortable estate of £48-8-8 in 1614, but his inventory shows only three bushels of oats and no plow or other husbandry gear. However, he owned 13 cattle and 81 sheep.[11] Dod evidently bought all his grain and limited himself to animal production. In a small way, he was an entrepreneur, a specialist in the production of animals and animal products for market.

Thanks to a series of manorial plans drawn up to accompany a survey of the Barony of Gilsland made in 1603, it is possible to describe in some detail the pattern of settlement and landholding in several manors to the east of the Eden Valley, in the Pennine foothills and uplands.[12] In Upper and Nether Denton, in the Pennine uplands, some dwellings are grouped together, in clusters of three or four, but the majority of the houses are placed singly, a hundred yards from any other dwelling. In the manor of Brampton, to the west of the Dentons, the houses in the market village of Brampton are grouped together but others in the manor are scattered separately, as in the Dentons. There is no evidence of common fields in Brampton; all arable and meadow land apparently was held in separate closes. Settlement in Askerton was similar to that in the Dentons: single homesteads or at most two or three together, surrounded by closes but without common fields. The Barony of Gilsland ran for more than ten miles, roughly north to south. The manors we have mentioned were in the northern portion of the Barony. In the southern part, most of the inhabitants lived in hamlets, although occasional isolated farmhouses are found. In the southern manors, too, common arable fields seem to have been more usual than in the northern part of the Barony. Most of the houses in the hamlets of Cumrew and Newbiggin lay in a line, facing the village street. Common arable fields adjoined the hamlets. The badly faded plan of Cumwhitton shows at least six separate groupings of houses in the manor, in three distinct enclosed areas, which, in turn, are separated from each other by the common pasture. It is not clear whether each hamlet had a common field. In Hayton, which lies to the north of Cumwhitton on the eastern edge of the Eden Valley, there were at least four separate hamlets and some 28 different common fields. It seems that the large number of fields was dictated by the topography of the land and does not indicate any intricate system of rotation.

The hamlet–common field pattern apparently predominated in the south and west part of Gilsland, whereas the north was given over to isolated farmhouses, each on its own enclosure. The plans give the impression that the northern manors may have been settled later than the southern ones and may never have adopted common field cultivation, whereas the more southerly manors retained it from some past time. Within the common field manors, the isolated farmsteads with their own closes may have represented newer holdings, established some time after the older common field holdings.

Whichever system of settlement prevailed—hamlets or single dwellings—the unit of settlement was small. Except for Brampton, a market village, and Castle Carrock, the hamlets of Gilsland had no more than a few houses. This settlement pattern for the highlands is important; I will argue in a later chapter that diffused, separated settlement would have inhibited the spread of epidemic disease.

In the lowlands of the Solway Plain and the Eden Valley, villages were more common, although the hamlet remained the typical form of settlement, judging by the manorial surveys. All the lowland manors studied by the historical geographer R. S. Dilley had common arable fields, except Millom and perhaps Greystoke. Usually each hamlet within a manor had its own field or fields.[13] As in the highlands, the presence of more than one arable field does not indicate that any system of crop rotation was followed. Rather, the same land seems to have been cultivated constantly, planted year after year in spring oats or barley. This constant cultivation is suggested by the pattern of landholding. A tenant did not necessarily hold land in more than one of the hamlet's fields, and if the field was fallowed, it seems that he and his family would have starved. It seems likely, therefore, that the arable was permanently under cultivation, even when it became exhausted. The manor of Bowness was an exception; there the tenants' holdings were fairly equally divided between one large and two small fields.[14] Crops may have been rotated and the fields occasionally fallowed.

A few lowland settlements, Dilley found, had "infield, outfield" systems, in which the portion called the infield received all the available fertilizer and was kept under constant cultivation. The outfield was never manured and was tilled until it became exhausted, when it was returned to grass to regain its fertility.[15] This field system does not, indeed, seem much different from the ones we have already discussed; they seem to have been infield, outfield systems without the outfield.

With more arable land, the lowlands enjoyed greater agricultural diversity than the highlands. Haver (oats) and bigg (barley) remained the basic crops, as they were in the highlands, but other grains were also cultivated by lowland farmers. Rye was grown on the Cumberland coast—at Millom, Whitbeck, Holm Cultram, and in the region around Carlisle. It was also grown in the Eden Valley.[16] Wheat is not often found in the probate inventories; in general it was grown only by the better-off gentry for their own tables.[17] In Heversham parish, in southern Westmorland, however, "March" wheat, that is wheat sown in the spring, was being grown in 1600.[18] Occasionally peas and beans appear in the inventories, but neither seems to have been important in the sixteenth century.[19] Hemp was grown on the Cumberland coast, along the Eden Valley, and in the Kent Valley in Westmorland.[20] Flax appears in a few inventories.[21] Poultry was more common in the lowlands than in the highlands.[22] Swine, too, appear in the inventories from the lowlands more frequently, although they do not seem to have been common anywhere in the two counties in the sixteenth and early seventeenth centuries.[23] In many manors, the number of swine that could be kept was limited by manorial court rulings. Everywhere, they had to be ringed to prevent their rooting and destroying grain crops.[24] The lowland farmer, like his highland neighbor, was primarily concerned with his livestock. Cattle and sheep made up the bulk of most men's estates, although the balance between the value of a man's grain compared to his livestock was closer than in the highlands.

Consider some examples, drawn from the probate inventories. John Dalton, of the parish of Crosby on Eden, just northeast of Carlisle, owned various cattle worth £25-4-0 in 1614, plus two mares valued at £5, and £15 worth of corn and hay. Dalton evidently kept no sheep.[25] The inventory of Richard Baron, of St. Cuthbert's parish, Carlisle, lists cattle worth £12, two "nags" worth 50*s*., one sheep, and "the whole crop growing upon his tenement," which was valued at £14.[26] The value of his grain just edged the value of his cattle. The area around Carlisle specialized in cattle and grain, not sheep, it seems. The same appears to have been true in Holm Cultram, on the Cumberland coast, although sheep appear more prominently in the inventories. Mabel Beby of Holm Cultram in 1614 had 21 cattle, six horses, and 13 sheep, worth together £54-10-0. Her grain—bigg and oats—was valued at £26-6-8, less than half the value of her livestock.[27] Fifty years earlier, the estate of Robert Saull, also of Holm Cultram, included eight horses, 20 cattle, and ten sheep, valued at £19-16-8. His oats, bigg, a bushel each of wheat and rye, and three bushels of peas were together valued at £9-15-0.[28] Five years later, John Chambers of the Holm left oats and bigg worth £15-12-0, compared to livestock of all types worth £27-5-0. His sheep were worth £3-0-4.[29] All the persons so far given as examples were comfortably off—but others were not. John Sybson of Holm Cultram in 1565 owned a nag worth £1, two oxen and two kine valued at £2-13-4, and oats and bigg worth 23*s*. His total estate was £6-7-0, less debts of £4-6-6.[30] Edward Stubb, of Wigton, left an estate valued in 1599 at £5, made up of two oxen, two kine, and two "old" sheep.[31] Thomas Stoddart, of the adjoining parish of Aikton, owned one cow, five sheep, and seven and one-half bushels of grain worth, all told, £6-2-6 at his death in December 1600.[32] These few examples indicate that the lowland farmer was less dependent on livestock, particularly on sheep, than the highland farmer. But throughout the two counties, animal raising was more important than sown crops.

In his study of English farm laborers, Professor Alan Everitt found that a very high percentage of Cumberland and Westmorland laborers owned some livestock, even though their landholdings were miniscule, in most cases only a cottage with a croft or garden. Everitt's definition of "laborer" is not entirely satisfactory for the northwest, although it may be suitable for other regions of England. Everitt calls all persons laborers who held fewer than five acres of land or who were exempted from the hearth tax in the 1660's and 1670's. In the northwest, too great a percentage of the population fits into one or another of these categories. In upland, pastoral regions, without much demand for agricultural labor, it might be better to simply call these people cottagers, although undoubtedly the cottagers of the northwest took what work they could get. The term laborer implies some degree of regular employment, which may not have been forthcoming in the northwest. This quibble aside, Everitt's analysis shows how dependent the poorer elements in society were on livestock.[33]

At the other extreme on the economic scale were the great sheep and cattle magnates, who ran thousands of sheep and hundreds of cattle. Alan Bellingham, of Kendal and Heversham parishes in Westmorland, left 4,224 sheep valued at £573-11-6 at his death in 1579. His cattle numbered 223, with a declared value of £286-13-4.[34] Sir Richard Lowther, of Lowther parish, Westmorland, ran 1,045 sheep in 1578. By the turn of the century, his flocks had declined to between eight and nine hundred,[35] perhaps as a result of poor demand for wool, perhaps owing to losses from diseases. In 1566 Sir Richard kept 192 cattle, including 24 oxen. In 1599, the Lowther cattle numbered 108 and in 1600, 114.[36] The reason for the decline is obscure. Certainly demand for meat and cattle products remained strong toward the end of the century. Probably the culprit was disease, but conceivably the Lowthers had reduced their herd by converting some of their pasture to plowland.

The household accounts of the larger landowners indicate the uses to which the various grains were put. In the Lowther household, wheat was baked into bread and pastry and, in 1576, fed "to the horse," presumably Lowther's personal riding horse. The servants were not as fortunate as the horse; they made do with bigg, the coarse barley that was also given to the poultry and swine, and baked into bread for the household. Oats were made into oatmeal, for the use of the household, and given to strangers, the horses, poultry, and swine. "Skilling"—probably hulled oats—was ground into oatmeal and also fed as groats to the servants and the horses.[37] Both oats and bigg were malted in the Lowther household. The malt was then used in brewing and fed to the horse and given to the servants. There was little differentiation made between the two main grains—oats and bigg. Peas were used in the kitchen and given to the servants. The Lowthers apparently made little use of rye, although it appears occasionally in small quantities in their account books.[38] Lord William Howard's accounts show the same types of grains, used in the same manner. Beans also appeared in the Howard accounts; they were fed to the riding horses. Wheat was purchased at Brampton, Carlisle, and Penrith for the use of the Howard household. After 1628, it was grown on the demesne at Corby. The Howard household also consumed vast numbers of game birds, fish, and deer, as well as apples, pears, plums, and cherries.[39]

The variety of foodstuffs in the Howard accounts in no way reflects the diet of the average north country farmer. He and his family probably subsisted on a monotonous diet of oatcakes, oatmeal, barley cakes, oat and barley bread, and beer, occasionally supplemented by some fruit. Peas and beans appear too infrequently in the records to have been common fare. It is hard to estimate the amount of meat in his diet. Despite the general agricultural emphasis on livestock, the smaller farmer may have conserved his beasts; they were his capital, and their sale was his only source of cash to pay his rent and to buy grain when his own store was exhausted. This was probably the attitude at least toward cattle, which could be driven to market. Sheep, however, are hard to drive. Those in the more isolated highland regions may have sold the wool and woolfells and eaten the old or diseased sheep, rather than undertake the thankless task of moving them to market. In other localities, such as Lowther, the proximity of a market in the town of Penrith made the fattening of sheep for the sale of their meat profitable. Whether it ate much meat or little, the small-holding family probably supplemented its basic grain and fruit diet with an occasional domestic or wild fowl, perhaps some herring from the Irish Sea, and milk and cheese. Cheese rarely appears on the inventories, which seems odd for a region with many cows. Perhaps it was too insignificant to list, but if so, it was for domestic consumption only. The absence of cheese presses also suggests that only soft cheese was made—if indeed *any* cheese was made. Milk may have been drunk fresh and not preserved as cheese.

The inventories indicate a high level of borrowing in these rural communities. Quite often debts owed by or to the deceased were larger than the value of any single item on the inventory. Almost without exception, the debts are expressed in money—and the majority appear to be money loaned, rather than money owed in payment for some service. For example, William Sleddalle of Natland in the parish of Kendal had goods worth £8-7-4 at his death in 1598. He was owed £19-3-0, however, and he owed others £2-8-6.[40] Gilbert Stainbancke of the same parish, who died the same year, left goods worth £7-13-6, minus debts of £6-18-0. His estate, then, came to less than one pound.[41] The amount of money a man might have out in loans could be substantial. Christopher Stainton of Crook, also in Kendal parish, had £48 in goods plus debts owing to him of £162 in 1598. In all, some forty names appear on the inventory as his debtors.[42] The greater part of the £57 estate of George Benson of Greystoke parish was made up of debts owed to him.[43] These men may have been unusual, but examples of lesser local lenders appear regularly in the records. Occasionally men owed more than the value of their goods. For instance, John Atkynson of Holm Cultram left goods worth 26*s*. 10*d*. when he died in 1570. He owed £3-4-10, plus several bushels of grain. The grain was specified separately from the money and apparently was advanced to him as grain.[44] Robert Browne of Wigton left goods valued at £6-10-8 in 1570 but his debts came to £7-2-3.[45]

What does this borrowing signify? Any answers must be conjectural, until an exhaustive, careful study of all the financial dealings within a village has been made. But possibly it is not too hazardous to conclude that the economy of the two counties was more of a money economy than might be expected. There was no indication—aside from the occasional entry like Atkynson's grain—that goods were borrowed, or that bargains were struck for the exchange of goods for services. The north has been called chronically specie-poor, but the inventories' constant use of money values makes one wonder. The admittance rolls, the rentals, all the surveys reflect the same money payments. Never, in the documents I have seen, were payments made in kind for a customary tenant's rent or entry fine.

Aside from this, any generalization drawn from the presence of the borrowing is of doubtful validity. But certain questions come to mind. Was lending the way to accumulate wealth in sixteenth-century Cumberland and Westmorland? In the case of Stainton, with four-fifths of his estate in loans, one is inclined to say yes. But was the money lent at interest? If so, what rate of interest? What was the risk involved? The manorial courts handled many disputes over debts, and enforcing repayment, particularly in years of harvest failure, must have been difficult. Were men like Stainton professional moneylenders, but, on the other hand, were most of the loans merely one neighbor helping out another who was in a pinch? Although the loans were expressed in monetary terms, they may not have been what we would call "economic" transactions. No interest rate was shown, nor were dates indicating when a loan was made or due. An interest rate might have been assumed, but without beginning or ending dates it would have been impossible to compute what interest was due. Alan Macfarlane has suggested that this type of interest-free loan was used to strengthen ties with other villagers; such a loan paid "social" interest, as it were, rather than economic interest. Placing money out on loan to various neighbors was also less risky than keeping a large sum in one's home.[46] The subject deserves further study.

The agricultural community that slowly becomes visible from the manorial plans, the studies of field systems, and the probate inventories was one primarily given over to the raising of livestock.

Cattle were more important than sheep in the lowlands; in the highlands, the opposite was the case. The major sown crops were oats and barley, both suitable for the poor soils of the region. Agricultural diversity was at a low level; peas, beans, swine, and poultry were not common and appear to have been found usually in the inventories of the better-off, rather than as aids to the poor cottager. The people lived in hamlets, for the most part, although small villages were found in the lowlands and numerous isolated farmhouses existed in the highlands. Despite its rural nature, the local economy was a money rather than a barter economy. And lending and borrowing—apparently of specie—was common.

From this evidence it is hard to see if the region was poor. Some men were well-off, some were not, but the relative size of the economic groups within the rural communities remains unclear. We will now try to determine the size of the "average" man's agricultural holding, how productive his land may have been, and what proportion of his yearly production he retained and what part went to his lord.

CHAPTER FOUR

Size of Holdings

THE FAILURE of the rebellion of 1569 marked the end of the effective power of the great magnates in the border counties. The leaders of the abortive uprising—the earls of Northumberland and Westmorland and Leonard Dacre—had fled to Scotland, and the north was again loyal to the Queen. The Crown, however, was left with two problems: the defense of the border against a possible invasion from Scotland and the endemic lawlessness that marked the region. Without a standing army, the Crown relied on the armed tenantry of the northern counties to protect the border. But toward the end of the sixteenth century, musters were turning out fewer men equipped with horse and armor than in the middle years of the century. In 1580, the West March (Cumberland and Westmorland) mustered 520 horsemen, compared with 580 at the last preceding muster of 1552.[1] The correspondence from the North to the Privy Council during the 1580's and 1590's referred repeatedly to the "decay" of armed men.[2] One of the reasons given was the tiny size of the average holding; the impoverished tenant could not afford horse and armor. It was also recognized that the other local problem—lawlessness—stemmed in part from the same condition. In mid-century, Sir Robert Bowes wrote that "there be mo[r]e inhabitants . . . than the . . . countryes maye susteyne . . . they cannot uppon so smalle fermes . . . live . . . but by stealing in England or Scotland."[3] Bowes was speaking of the region immediately adjacent to the border. It was here that banditry flourished, not in the interior of either Cumberland or Westmorland.

This extreme parcelization of land along the border evidently arose from the custom of partible inheritance. In Tyndale and Liddesdale, "if a man have issue ten sons, eight, six, five or four, and sits on a holding of but 6s. rent, every son shall have a piece of his father's holding."[4] As a result, all the heirs were ruined. An act for the "fortifieng of the Borders towardes Scotland" (23 Elizabeth, c. 4), offered the same explanation: the "Inhabitauntes themselves have demynished their owne Strength, by deviding their Howses and Farmes which were mete onely for one able Householder and Famelye into the occupac[i]on of sondrye p[er]sons commonlye being the Children or other Kinsfolkes."[5] A 1604 survey of Bewcastle, not far from the Cumberland-Scotland border, suggests that partible inheritance was practiced there.[6] This survey gives the name of each customary tenant and also the name of the person from whom the tenement descended. Within the same small hamlets, several tenants with the same surname traced their titles to a person with the same given and surname. For example, in Bailey, where the name Routledge predominated,[7] there were, in 1604, seven customary tenants named Routledge who had received their tenements from John Routledge. It is, of course, possible that there were seven different John Routledges in the previous generation, but it seems more likely that there were only one or two, and that at least some of the 1604 Routledges were brothers, each holding a tenement that came down from a common father.[8] This does not necessarily indicate partible inheritance; the father may have purchased lands for his sons—other than the one inheriting the "home" tenement—before his death. But the effect would have been the same; the father's wealth was divided, and each son left with a small, probably almost marginal, piece of land. The largest Routledge holding was 18 acres of poor arable and meadow; the smallest just 5.5 acres.[9] In all, 42 tenants shared 530 acres, an average of 12.6 acres per tenant.

Just to the north of Bewcastle lay the Debatable Lands, which abuted the border and were dominated by the ferocious Graham clan. The 1604 survey lists each tenant in the Debatable Lands, and records the numbers of persons in each tenant's household, the number of servants in the household, the number of cottagers dependent on the tenant, and finally the number of acres of land—presumably arable—held by each tenant. For example, there were ten persons in William Graham of the Rose Tree's household, plus ten servants. There were also 120 cottagers, who lived in 21 cottages. This little community, headed by Graham, held 165 acres, or just over one acre per person. According to the survey, a total of 1,065 persons in the Debatable Lands held some 1,219 acres of land. In all, the Debatable Lands totaled 7,403 acres; if the remainder of the land was pasture, each person on the average enjoyed one acre of arable and six acres of pasture. It is difficult to see how these people could have survived, without stealing from their neighbors.[10]

A historian of Westmorland has found the same fragmented land holdings in that county. "The wretched parcels left after generations of sub-division" were too small to provide a living to the inhabitants of Grasmere.[11]

These examples of partible inheritance—or any system of providing all the sons with land—are drawn from northeastern Cumberland and the parish of Grasmere in Westmorland. Each of these areas had peculiar social and economic structures that may have favored partible inheritance. On the northern border of Cumberland, a clan family would have been strengthened in its disputes with other clans by keeping all its sons at home, although the individual members might be too poor to make much of a showing at a muster. If the clan was aggressive—like the Armstrongs or the Grahams[12]—its members shared the booty from cattle thieving or blackmail, thus supplementing the poor returns from the small farms and limited flocks. If the clan was weak—like the Routledges[13]—maintaining their numbers may have been the only way to avert ruin at the hands of their stronger neighbors. Lawlessness may have been the cause, as well as the result, of the division of a man's lands among all his sons. Whatever the rationale, the clans were concentrated along the border, and their inheritance patterns would not necessarily have been practiced elsewhere in the two counties. In Grasmere parish, on the other hand, there was an extensive cottage woolen industry,[14] which offered additional income to those whose farms were too small to support a family. Extreme subdivision of holdings would not have been totally uneconomic as long as demand for weaving and spinning remained high. Clothing manufacture, however, was important in only three Westmorland parishes—Grasmere, Windermere, and Kendal—and, here again, inheritance customs practiced there need not have prevailed elsewhere.

Certain communities permitted only impartible inheritance. In Holm Cultram the number of tenants remained remarkably stable between 1538 and 1649. Four different surveys taken within that period show a remarkable similarity in the number of customary tenants, indicating that tenements were rarely or never split by inheritance or sale. Until the dissolution of the monasteries, Holm Cultram had been abbey land and impartible inheritance may have been imposed at an early date by the church. In 1571 it was confirmed that "no ten[a]nte maie divide by graunte or surrender his ten[emen]te."[15]

In the numerous disputes over fines and the right to inherit that took place between tenants and lords on many manors, there was no hint that partible inheritance was widely practiced at the end of the sixteenth century. It seems reasonable, as Joan Thirsk has suggested, that partible inheritance was at some earlier time the general custom throughout the two counties, but that it was dying out early in the sixteenth century,[16] except along the northern border and perhaps in the clothing parishes of Westmorland. The available arable land simply could not be divided indefinitely. Certainly there was an effort during Elizabeth's reign to halt further division of customary holdings on Crown lands in the north. The Queen's tenants in the parish of Crosthwaite and Lyth, Westmorland, agreed in 1579 that "no Tenement shall hereaft[e]r be brokine or severyed." The same agreement stipulated that the holder could will his tenement to "w[hi]ch of his sonnes as it pleaseth him."[17] Similar agreements were drawn up between the Crown and the tenants in Furness, in the adjoining part of Lancashire.[18] By the time of the Parliamentary surveys of 1649–50, impartible inheritance* apparently was practiced everywhere on the Crown estates.[19]

*Inheritance customs were not always specified, but heirs were spoken of in the singular in references to entry fines payable on the death of the previous tenant.

Size of Holdings

Whatever the role partibility played in the division of customary holdings, contemporaries stressed the small size of the holdings, although it was usually supplemented by the right of pasture on the commons. Edmund Hall and William Homberston, who surveyed the possessions of the attainted Thomas Percy for the Queen in 1570, summed up the condition of the land and the tenantry of the great Honor of Cockermouth as follows:[20]

> The Countrie consists most in wast[e] ground [i.e. common pasture] & is very Cold hard & barren . . . yett it is very populous & breadeth tall men & hard of nature whose habitac[i]ons are most in the Vallies & Dales where every man hath a small porc[i]on of ground w[hi]ch albeith the soile bee hard of nature yett by continuall travell is made fertile to their great releif and comfort for their greatest gaine consists in breeding of cattle w[hi]ch are noe Charge to them in the Somer by reason they are pastured & fedd upon the mountaines & waste.

Two generations later, a report from Westmorland noted that "the people of this Countie keping . . . smale tenant rights' not able to maintain a plow, but 3 or 4 joining together the husband wife and children doth till the litle tenement . . . their little tenant rights, not suffacunt for a family."[21]

An analysis of landholdings in various manors confirms these observations in some localities but not in others. The 1603 survey of Gilsland, a contiguous group of 15 manors on the slopes of the Pennines, gives tenants' holdings in statute acres.[22] Within the Barony, the size of customary holdings varied considerably. On the manor of Askerton the tenants held large blocks of land; the tenants were in no way land-poor, and no cottages were built on the waste to accommodate the landless.[23] In Cumwhitton, on the other hand, there were numerous small holdings. As we have seen, cottages were built on the waste and some men appear to have held only tiny pieces of land adjoining their cottages.[24] The distribution of tenant holdings, by size, for Askerton and Cumwhitton appears in Figure 1. The Cumwhitton graph shows that medium-size holdings were uncommon, whereas both poor and well-off tenants were relatively numerous. In Askerton, on the other hand, the majority of the tenants held over fifty acres of land each. In part, this difference in the size of the typical holding can be explained by the location

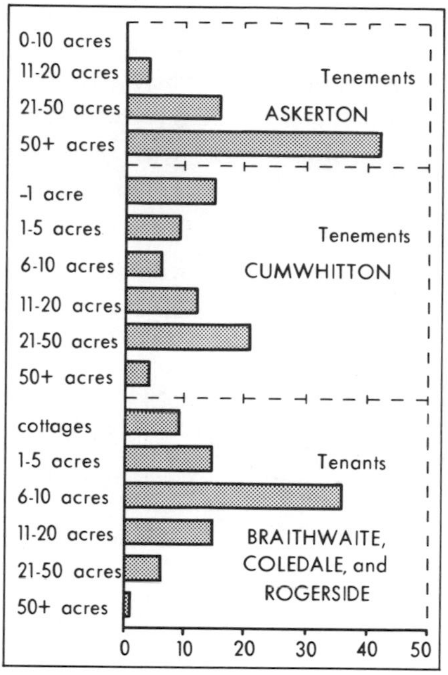

Fig. 1. Landholdings in various manors.

of the two manors. Cumwhitton was a lowland manor on the eastern side of the Eden Valley, whereas Askerton was a sparsely settled, northern upland manor. In Askerton, where the soils were poorer than in Cumwhitton, a householder may have needed much more land to survive. The landholding pattern in these communities close to the border is not entirely clear. In the narrow valleys of the borders, small holdings seem to have been typical, as we found in the case of the Routledge clan; in a fell manor such as Askerton, with little or no valley land, a larger holding may have been necessary.

The survey of 1603 was unusual in that it gave the size of the holdings in statute acres. More often, the surveys showed customary acres. R. S. Dilley has found four different customary acres in use in Cumberland at this time, ranging in size from 1.19 statute acres to 1.67 statute acres.[25] He also found that successive surveyors of an area were not consistent in their use of any one customary

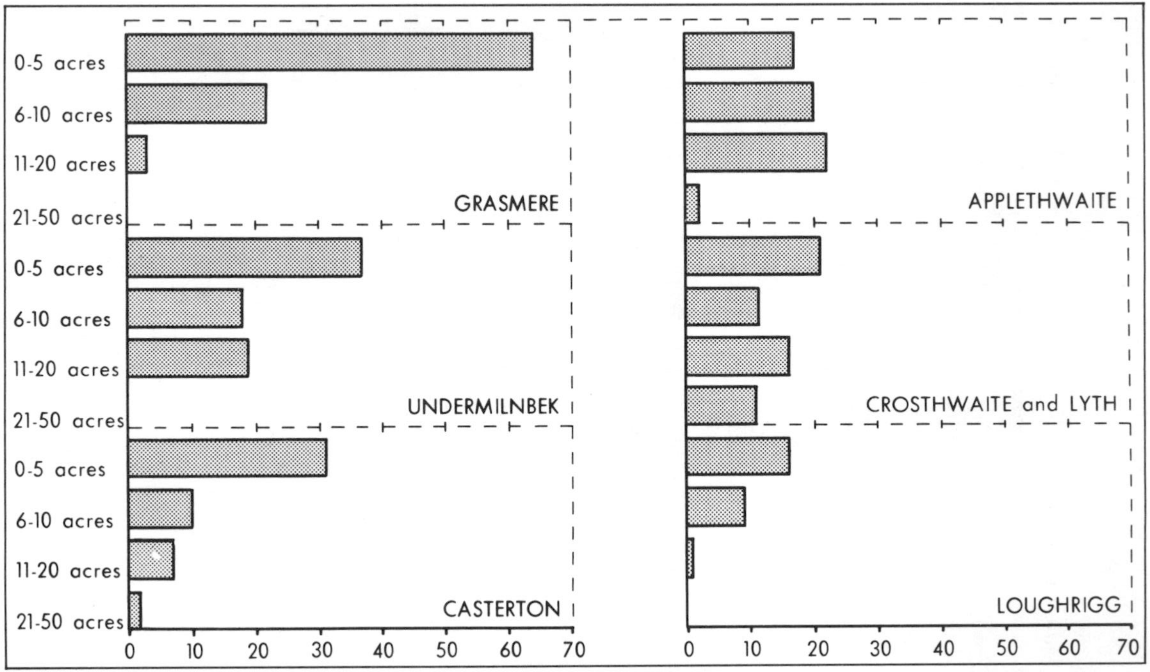

Fig. 2. Size of landholdings and number of tenements in various Westmorland manors, 1574.

acre. The exact modern equivalent, then, of the various tenant holdings in Cumberland is not known but probably falls within the range Dilley indicates. (It is possible, of course, that other local variations were used, in addition to those he uncovered.) A breviate of a 1589 survey for Gilsland, in customary acres, showed that the 627 tenants together held 3,342 acres of arable land, 3,081 acres of meadow and pastureland, and about 10,000 acres of waste, or common pasture.[26] This works out to just over five acres of arable per tenant, just under five acres of meadow, and about 16 acres of common. Multiplying by one and one-half to convert roughly to statute acres gives each tenant seven and one-half acres of arable and the same of meadow, plus 24 acres of common. Averages obscure the number of smallholders, as the analysis of Askerton and Cumwhitton shows, but the size of the average holding appears quite modest.

In the village of Greystoke, in the Cumbrians, the typical customary tenant held 14 customary acres of arable land in 1589. Some tenants held ten acres, others less.[27] The majority of the customary tenants on the nearby manor of Stainton held 14 acres of arable and one-half acre of meadow.[28] In Matterdale, within the same parish, the usual holding was eight acres of meadow and one of "pasture," which usually means, on these manors, an enclosed parcel of the common pasture.[29] Farther to the west lay the Percy manors of Braithwaite, Coledale, and Rogerside.[30] The distribution of land, by size and in customary acres, appears in Figure 1. These manors adjoined one another, and some tenants held land in two or all three manors, so the holdings have been combined and set forth in a single graph. On these manors, the largest group of tenants held from six to ten customary acres. Across the Derwent Fells, in Buttermere, many tenants had no arable land, merely a few acres of meadow.[31] Even for a highland manor, Buttermere had an extreme location, sandwiched between high fells to the east and west, and lakes to the north and south. Only a small rectangle of valley floor remained for cultivation.

The size distribution of customary landholdings in various Westmorland manors is shown in Figure 2.[32] These are all dated 1574, and in each case the original acreage has been multiplied by 1.4, on the assumption that the areas were given in customary acres.[33] In all these manors, with the possible exception of Applethwaite, there were a large number of marginal holders. Those holding the smallest parcels, from one to five acres, would have been forced to rely on outside employment, as farm laborers, weavers, or spinners, to feed themselves even in good years. Those holding between six and ten acres would have been unable to produce enough food in a poor harvest year. On another manor, Troutbeck, the sizes of the 56 largest customary holdings were not given, only the sizes of the 13 smallest. Of these, 12 were of less than one and one-half statute acres.

In these highland manors, some of the tenants held a single piece of land with a dwelling on it—what might be termed a "unitary" holding. For example, William Scott of Braithwaite, Cumberland, had a tenement with a house and six acres of arable land; that was the extent of his holding, as shown on the 1570 Percy survey. Other customary tenants had a similar tenement with a dwelling, plus another parcel of land or two. William Studard had a tenement with eight acres in Rogerside and a plot of land taken from the common pasture (*vasti de novo incremento*) in Braithwaite. The holdings of still other customary tenants were composed of numerous separate pieces of land, resembling a crazy quilt spreading out from their dwelling. Richard Nicholson of Egremont, where the highlands meet the narrow coastal plain, held three "garths" containing a total of one rood (one-quarter acre) of land, six closes—all listed separately in the Percy survey of 1578[34]—with 15.5 acres, another close of 2.5 acres, a little meadow close with no area indicated, and two "improvements," that is land taken in from the common pasture, of two roods. In all, Nicholson held 14 different pieces of land, with a total area of 19.75 acres.

In our examples, both Studard and Nicholson had recently taken in or converted a small part of the common pasture. Nicholson's intake was just half an acre; Studard's too small to be recorded. Why did the two men desire these tiny additions to their lands? Not to pasture livestock, for both already had free pasture on the common, and they had to pay rent for their new intakes. Nor would it have been to improve the breed of their livestock, for segregating animals at breeding time was not yet practiced. In Studard's case, he may have wanted a fold, where he could collect his beasts at night, off the commons, in order to gather their dung in the morning. But Nicholson already had several closes; another seems superfluous. Probably, both men wanted the intakes to grow grain, either for their own use or for sale. With population expanding, and all fertile arable land already under cultivation, enclosing bits of the common may have been the only way to increase grain production. Even the marginal lands of the common pasture would yield a crop or two before they became exhausted. They then could be returned to grass until they regained their fertility. Perhaps this is what happened to Nicholson's other closes before; carved out of the common, they had been planted for a few years, and then allowed to revert once again to pasture.

These intakes or enclosures of parts of the common pasture by established customary tenants appear throughout the 1570 and 1578 surveys of the Percy highland manors. In Chapter Two, we noted encroachments on the common by squatters, who had no other place to settle, and also the enclosure of parts of the common by gentlemen, who then sublet the land to landless men. Coupled with this was constant conversion of common pasture in the highlands to the private use of the customary tenants, who probably planted it in grain. In some manors, encroachments were relatively few, in others, numerous. For example, in the manor of Rogerside, nine of the 29 customary tenements contained land taken from the waste.[35] In Buttermere, out of 21 tenements, 12 were partly made up of converted common pasture.[36]

In the foothills of the Eden Valley, the same encroachments can be found in the hamlet of Soulby, part of the manor of Dacre. The size of the holdings of the customary tenants all increased between a survey taken in 1567 and another taken in 1604. Holdings that had been 14 acres at the earlier date grew to 18 or 20 by the latter date; those that were 13 acres grew to 16 or 17.[37]

If we shift our attention to the lowlands, we find the same pattern of small customary holdings in arable and meadow and the ubiquitous right of pasture. And we find analogous encroachments on the common pasturelands. In the Barony of Wigton,[38] the customary tenants held six, eight, or ten acres of land in Wigton, and one-half or one acre of meadow in either "Colmyre" or "Grenmyre," which apparently were two large expanses of meadow situated apart from the arable. A tenant's holdings were not necessarily as small as they appear at first glance. Wigton was surrounded by other manors, and many Wigton tenants seem to have held land in one or more of these in addition to their Wigton holdings. John Adamson, for example, held a cottage, a croft of one acre, and one-half acre of meadow in Wigton. The survey shows that a John Adamson also held a tenement and five acres three miles away in the manor of Woodside, with a half-acre of meadow in Colmyre attached to this tenement. Are there two John Adamsons, or only one? The evidence suggests that it was the same man. In Wigton and the surrounding manors, extremely small pieces of land—half an acre or an acre—appear frequently in the survey. Almost invariably, on a nearby manor, a man with the same name appears, this time holding a parcel of land with a dwelling on it. The impression is that the man held one "home" tenement and various other pieces of land scattered about in that and adjoining manors. To take other examples, Bartholomew Adamson appears in the 1570 survey three times, holding in all three acres of meadow in Colmyre and four acres of arable in Woodside. John Ayket held one tenement in Wigton, another in Kirkland, and two parcels in Colmyre, a total of 14 acres of arable and one of meadow. John Barnes held two tenements in Waverton, containing together three acres, plus a parcel of meadow in Aikhead. These two manors are about one and one-half miles apart. Richard Ismay held 11 acres in Rosewain and one-half acre of meadow in Colmyre. William Ismay had a tenement with six acres of land at Wigton and a cottage with one acre in Westward, some two miles away. John Messenger, Jr., held a tenement with eight acres in Waverton, one acre in Woodside, and one-half acre in Wigton. From Waverton to Woodside, the distance is something over five miles. These examples are typical of those who held land in more than one manor.

As these examples show, the combined holdings of individuals were—with rare exceptions—still fairly small, even if the area was given in customary acres. The parcels must have been difficult to farm efficiently, since they were scattered over two or three manors, miles apart. In the highlands, the mountainous terrain discouraged a man's holding pieces of land in several different manors, although we have examples from Braithwaite, Coledale, and Rogerside where one man held land in more than one manor. Usually, the highland farmer expanded his holdings at the expense of the common pasture within the manor. Without the barrier of the mountains, a lowland tenant could work scattered holdings, even though it proved inconvenient. Occasionally, pieces of land held apart from the "home" manor were designated on the survey as land taken in from the common pasture. In the lowlands, however, pasture was not as extensive as in the highlands, and continued encroachment quickly reduced the number of animals that could be pastured. On most manors, therefore, the number of new intakes was small. Other areas, however, appear to have been opened to tenants who settled on previously unoccupied land. This process can be seen clearly in the Forest of Westward, which lies three miles southeast of Wigton. All the lands in the 94 customary tenements and six cottages are designated *de antiquo improvamento* or *de novo improvamento*. A close look at the names of the tenants reveals that many of them already held lands and tenements in the Percy manors to the north and west—Waverton, Wigton, Woodside, etc. For example, John Adamson, who was mentioned above, held a tenement with four acres of land in Westward in addition to his lands in Wigton and Woodside. Other tenants apparently held no other land outside the Forest. The enclosure of the Forest meant more tillable land for established customary tenants, such as Adamson, and opened lands to otherwise landless men. It also enhanced the Percy rents by £32-16-11.

The enclosures had a negative side, as well. According to the Bishop of Carlisle, some three hundred poor families in the adjoining Barony of Dalston depended for their livelihood on the pasture in the Forest. When it was closed to them in 1569, they forcibly entered and pulled down the new enclosures.[39] On the surface, the dispute appears to have been between the inhabitants and lords of the Baronies of Wigton and Dalston, over jurisdictional rights to the Forest. But perhaps at heart the conflict was between the established customary tenants, who wished to expand their grain cultivation, and the landless poor, who made a precarious living by pasturing a few beasts on the previously free commons, and were unable to pay the rent demanded by the Percy steward. At least this interpretation is suggested by the fact that the rioters included some inhabitants of Wigton.

The pattern of widespread but scattered landholding by some of the customary tenants, such as John Adamson, raises another question. Did they work all these lands themselves, or did they let some of them to others, at rents above what they had to pay? Unfortunately, the survey is silent about who worked the land, revealing only the name of the person legally holding it. With the subsistence type of agriculture practiced in the lowlands, and the considerable distance that sometimes separated a man's holdings, subletting would seem to have been more profitable than working the land directly. Without more evidence, it is largely speculation, but perhaps there was a class of customary tenant who enjoyed a type of partnership with his lord. When Thomas Percy wished to enclose the Forest of Westward, to increase his rents, he let some of the newly enclosed land to established customary tenants, who, in turn, subleased them to lesser men at higher rents. This muted the opposition of the tenantry, by passing part of the profits off to some of them. All the tenants were hurt by the loss of pasture, but these favored tenants gained more than they lost. Only the smaller tenants and the landless, who saw their pasture disappear and gained nothing in return, suffered. Without pasture to sustain them, the landless were forced to take a sublease, at the rent demanded. Perhaps this was why the Wigton poor joined in the riot and pulled down the enclosures of their better-off neighbors.

Such sharing of the profits was a well-established practice on the Percy estates. One of the landowners in the Forest of Westward was John Briscoe, a gentleman, who held 30 acres of newly enclosed land. He also held extensive lands in Kirkland and Rosewain. Another member of the gentry holding land in the Forest was Anthony Barwis, who had freehold tenements in Wigton and Woodside and other lands throughout western Cumberland. In 1570 Barwis was steward of the Honor of Cockermouth and Feodary of all Percy lands within the Honor. He was a man "of great wor[shi]pp in those p[ar]tes."[40] Both Briscoe and Barwis had benefited from their Percy connections to obtain land in the Forest; loyal servants were often rewarded in this way. Neither man worked his land directly but rented it to subtenants, profiting by the spread between what they received and what was due Thomas Percy.[41]

The landholding pattern suggests that there were four broad economic types in these lowland manors. First, there was the large landholder, who had, either in customary or freehold lands, a number of tenements, some of which were farmed by others. Within this landowning category was a powerful local lord such as Barwis; also within it, although far below Barwis on the economic scale, was John Adamson, who had at most one or two subtenants. Second, there was the customary tenant with one tenement and perhaps another parcel or two of land, all of which he worked himself. Third, there was the cottager, who appears on the surveys with his little plot of ground alongside his cottage. Fourth, there was the subtenant—the renter of land from the large holder—who is individually lost to historical view. The last two were the most vulnerable to economic dislocation; the cottager because of his minuscule holding and the subtenant because each year he made a new rental bargain with his landlord. As population grew and competition for land became intense, the subtenant would very likely have been pushed down toward subsistence.

Taking the two counties together, extreme division of the land—into parcels too small to support a family—appears to have centered in the clothing parishes of Westmorland and along the northern border of Cumberland. These were the same localities that practiced partible inheritance. Elsewhere lands were not so fragmented, but everywhere (except Askerton) there was a large proportion of smallholders. In the lowlands around Wigton, in addition to the smallholders, there were strong indications of a sizable group of subtenants, holding at the sufferance of customary tenants or freeholders. Everywhere enclosures had pushed onto the old common pasturelands as men sought to bring more land under cultivation. It is worth noting that this type of enclosure did not lead to depopulation, as it did where arable was enclosed for sheep runs, but to overpopulation. The availability of extensive common pasture, coupled with the practice of allowing parcels of it to be enclosed, held out to every man the hope that he could somehow gain a living locally, rather than migrate south or east to an uncertain future. Like partible inheritance, enclosure tended to create marginal smallholders.

From what little evidence is available, it seems unlikely that high crop yields offset the smallness of many of the holdings. As in other parts of early modern England, the yield per acre is obscured by uncertainty about both the size of the acre and the size of the measure—skep, bushel, or peck—used for grain. There is, however, some indication of seed-yield ratios. On the Denton lands at Cardew, southwest of Carlisle, 156 bushels of oats were harvested in 1591 from 54 bushels of seed, a ratio of 2.9 to 1 (expressed hereafter as 2.9:1). The yield ratio in the same year was 4.8:1 for bigg; the following year oats yielded 3.7:1 and bigg 3.8:1.[42] There is no way of telling if these are typical yields for the lands, but in England generally, 1591 was a good year for both oats and barley and 1592 was an abundant year,[43] so these may represent above-average returns on the seed planted. Cardew, it should be mentioned, had good loam, and later all types of grain grew well there.[44] The productivity of these lands was perhaps as high as any within the two counties.

On the demesne lands at Lowther, yield ratios are available for the harvest years 1598–99 to 1604–5, inclusive.[45] English grain harvests during that span were average to good, except for a poor harvest in 1600.[46] Table 2 shows the grains sown on the Lowther estates, the amount harvested, and the corresponding seed-yield ratio. By way of comparison, the seed-yield ratio at Hitsum in the Netherlands in 1570–73 was: wheat, 13.6:1; barley, 7.5:1; oats, 4:1. In Somerset in 1583, the yields were: wheat 8:1, and barley, 6.6:1.

TABLE 2. *Seed-Yield Ratios, Lowther, Westmorland*

Period	Crops	Bushels sown	Bushels harvested	Yield ratio
1598–99	Wheat	39	120	3:1
	Bigg (barley)	32	75	2.3:1
	Oats	106	236	2.2:1
1599–1600	Wheat	32	168	5.3:1
	Bigg	30	120	4:1
	Oats	116	216	1.9:1
1600–1601	Wheat	30	145	4.8:1
	Bigg	24	128	5.3:1
	Oats	117	192	1.6:1
1601–2	Wheat	26	47	1.8:1
	Bigg	29	91	3.1:1
	Oats	97½	313	3.2:1
1602–3	Wheat	36	90	2.5:1
	Bigg	36⅙	100	2.8:1
	Oats	125	440	3.5:1
1604–5	Wheat	34	139	4.1:1
	Bigg	29	60	2.1:1
	Oats	113	308	2.7:1
Average	Wheat	197	709	3.6:1
	Bigg	180⅙	574	3.2:1
	Oats	674½	1705	2.5:1

At Walkenried, Germany, in the years 1603–6, the yields were: wheat, 4:1; barley, 5.5:1; oats, 2.5:1.[47] The yields at Lowther and on the Denton lands appear substantially below those in the Netherlands and Somerset but roughly comparable with or slightly inferior to the German example. The major grain, oats, performed relatively the best, compared to the other areas, but its seed-yield ratio was lower than the yield ratio for the other two grains. Another English example puts northern agriculture in a worse light. Robert Loder, characterized as a "conservative-minded farmer of little experience," was returning 12:1 in wheat and 8:1 in barley for the years 1612 to 1620.[48]

The examples of seed yields that we have for Cumberland and Westmorland very likely were not typical of the average tenant. As we have noted, the Denton lands were fertile, certainly far more productive than the average arable land in the highlands. The Lowther lands benefited from vigorous management and awareness of the value of keeping seed and harvest records, from which the ratios have been compiled. Of course, the same could be said of the figures we have for comparison. But in Cumberland and Westmorland, the smallholder would have had no plow or draft animals, no access to the farming literature that was then appearing, little capital to improve his holding, and, perhaps most important, no economic cushion to allow him to fallow his lands when they became exhausted. If, as I have suggested, the land that was being taken from the waste was planted in grain, it probably barely returned its seed after a year or two under the plow.

To summarize briefly, at the end of the sixteenth century the economic position of many of the poorer husbandmen in both Cumberland and Westmorland seems to have been precarious. According to the surveys, many individual landholdings were very small, often smaller than the four acres considered by Elizabeth's government to be the minimum necessary to support a farm laborer and his family.[49] Indeed, the surveys may convey an unduly favorable impression; if subtenants worked parts of the surveyed holdings of others, land was even more fragmented than our sources indicate. It is impossible to generalize on the acreage necessary to support a single family. Too many other factors influenced a family's economic position. If the husband worked regularly as a farm laborer—which was unlikely in a largely pastoral region—or the family was engaged in weaving or some other employment, a cottage and a croft may have enabled them to survive, particularly if the family had a cow or two on the common pasture. Because the beasts had to be wintered on the holding of the cottager, however, his livestock was always limited by the size of his holding. To make matters worse, the cottager's small parcel of land was usually not good arable, but had been enclosed from the great pastures. Such land was of questionable fertility; after a few years it probably became exhausted, necessitating another enclosure—with additional money going for rent. In short, by the end of Elizabeth's reign the growth of population had created large numbers of impoverished cottagers and subtenants who scratched out a marginal existence on small plots of poor soil.

CHAPTER FIVE

Lord and Tenant

TO THIS POINT the economic structure of Cumberland and Westmorland has been studied in a horizontal manner. I have attempted to show the pressures of population on the land, stressing the unproductiveness of agriculture, the small size of many holdings, and the progressive conversion to tillage of parts of the common pasture. But I have no more than alluded to the vertical structure—the lord, the state, and the church—that shared in the agricultural yield through rents, taxes, and tithes. It is to this division of the "profits and issues" of the land that we now turn, to see if the lord, the state, or the church contributed to the impoverishment of the average tenant and helped bring about the famines of the end of the sixteenth and beginning of the seventeenth centuries. As before, attention will be directed primarily toward the smallholders, in particular the most numerous group of smallholders, the customary tenants. Along with a few small leaseholders and tenants at will, the customary tenant sat at the bottom of the visible rural economic pyramid. (The various types of landholding tenants are described below in detail.) Aside from the farm laborer and the subtenant—both of whom remain historically obscure—only these smallholders would be threatened in the three great famines.

Taxes played an insignificant role in the life of the average customary tenant. Until 1603 lay subsidies (other than alien subsidies levied on foreigners) were not collected in the border counties in compensation for the armed service on the border demanded of all the inhabitants.[1] Except on those lands immediately adjacent to Scotland, border service seems to have been only an occasional chore, which indeed might have returned more in booty than it cost in time lost to farming. After subsidies were resumed in 1603, they were small, falling only on the larger landowners and landlords.[2] The exactions of the church, in tithes, were constant, varying little from one end of the period to the other. Most great tithes were impropriated and fell into the category of another fiscal levy by the landlords. There were tithe disputes, usually about whether payments were to be made in specie or in kind, and if in kind, what measure was to be used.[3] By far the tenant's most important obligation—dwarfing the other two—was the one he owed his landlord. The struggle between the tenants and their lords over rents, entry fines, and work obligations ran through the entire 150-year period. It is a confusing, complex affair, unsuitable for quantification. However, I will suggest certain broad trends, at the same time trusting that the reader will recognize that any generalization need not have applied to every one of the hundreds of manors within the two counties.

Before the union of the Crowns in 1603, each customary tenant in Cumberland and Westmorland had two tenurial ties, one to his manorial lord and another directly to the Crown. The first obligated him to pay various rents and fines, contribute labor services called "boon days," attend the manorial courts—in short, to perform the myriad services and make the payments commonly demanded of tenants throughout England. These will be discussed in detail shortly. The second tie—the one directly with the Crown—obligated all adult males, not only customary tenants, to serve in defense of the border. Specifically, the customary tenants were

> upon one howers warning [to] serve upon the said borders of Scotland with ther Armour & furniture [i.e. arms, horse, etc.] within ye wardenry of the westmarches at ther owne costes & charges from tyme to tyme during the pleasure of the Lord Warden of ye said marches. . . . And when any service is to be done without ye Realme & in ye realme of Scotland then upon warning given by fyring of a becon, post or p[ro]clmac[i]on from the Lord-

warden of the said marches . . . your said subiectes do serve by the space of Eight dayes in the said realme of Scotland at their owne costes & charges.[4]

Despite the burden this placed on each tenant, border service was commonly referred to, at least by the customary tenants, as the "anncient & lawdable custom of tenant right," for it provided them with a weapon in their disputes with their manorial lords. The Crown, anxious to protect the northern frontier, did not wish to see the inhabitants of the counties so impoverished that they could not provide themselves with horses and arms. If they were, the defense of the border would break down, and England would be open to invasion. Under Elizabeth, the customary tenants could—and did—appeal to the Crown for protection against the exactions of their landlords. And the Crown often took their side.

Before we trace the disputes between lords and tenants, it would be worth while to define the various manorial tenures commonly found in the two counties. A summary of a 1608 survey of all Crown manors in Cumberland and Westmorland divided the tenants into these categories: freeholders, leaseholders, tenants at the will of the lord, copyholders, and customary tenants.[5] First, the freeholders—or more precisely the free tenants—included those holding by knight service, by socage, and by burgage. The holder by knight service or by socage had economic advantages, generally holding a manor or a number of tenements. The surveys seldom indicated the extent of his holdings, except in general terms, because the free tenant was beyond the control of his overlord, if he met his obligations and paid his usually nominal rent. Burgage tenure was a variety of socage, limited in the two counties to some of the inhabitants of boroughs chartered by the King or by one of the local magnates, such as the Earl of Northumberland.[6] As a group, the free tenants need not particularly concern us. Second, there were the leaseholders, or tenants by indenture, as they were often called. These were numerically relatively unimportant before 1603, but as we shall see, they increased after that date. The leasehold tenants held their lands for a specified number of years, often 21, or of lives. A leasehold might be let, for example, to a man, his son, and his grandson, for as long as any one of them might live. This would be for three lives. In the sixteenth century, leaseholds were often given on advantageous terms to gentry followers of the great lords.[7] Other leases were taken up by men who held no other land. Third, there were the tenants at will. Usually these were tenants who occupied the lords' forests and demesnes without a specific lease, although they paid rent. They could be put off whenever the lord wished, retaining only a right in what crops were growing at the time of their eviction. Economically these ranged from the poorest sort, with a cottage in the forest, to important gentry who were given lands at low rents as a reward for loyalty.[8] This latter form of "good-lordship" was similar to the leases, which were used in the same manner. Fourth, there were the copyholders, who can be considered a subgroup of the customary tenants. They held by the custom of the manor but had the additional security of a copy of the court roll that recorded their admittance to their tenement.

Last, there was the most numerous group—the customary tenants. Or at least the tenants considered themselves "customary," holding both by the customs of the particular manor where they lived and by the custom of tenant right that prevailed throughout the two counties. However, the lords usually referred to their tenants as tenants at will, literally unprotected by either the customs of the manor or the broader custom of tenant right. On the surveys, the language was ambiguous, referring almost interchangeably to customary tenants and tenants at will.[9] No doubt the surveyors recognized the correct legal position, that a customary tenant was "a tenant at will who could not be ejected at will . . . ; the will of the lord was not a free will, but a will subjected to the custom."[10] That the lords cared to recognize this limitation to their will is less certain.

The obligations of the tenants, under what they claimed was the manorial custom, varied greatly from one manor to the other. Perhaps a single example, drawn from the manor of Threlkeld, will roughly indicate the rights and duties of the tenants throughout the two counties.[11] In Threlkeld the customary tenants were divided into two groups, holders of tenements and cottagers. Legally their positions were the same, but services owed by one group varied slightly from those owed by the other. All the tenants enjoyed the right to dig peat, gather stones, cut "underwood" (i.e. hazels, willows, alders, thorns), and pasture all animals they had on their customary holdings on the common.* They were to receive enough wood to keep their dwellings in repair. On the death of a tenant, his wife was to have the entire tenement,[12] as long as she was "Chaste."† On her death it passed to the male heir. In the event that the heir, on his father's death, was underage, the lord did not have the right of "tuition," i.e. wardship. Failing a male heir, the descent of the tenement to the eldest daughter was preferred.

The tenants, for their part, were obliged to pay suit of court to the court leet and the court baron. They were to have their corn ground at the lord's mill, paying a fortieth part of the corn for the service. On the death of the lord or the tenant, or on the alienation by the tenant of the holding, the new tenant was to pay, within six months, a fine amounting to four years' ancient rent.‡ The holder of a tenement was also to provide, once every two years on reasonable notice by the manorial bailiff, a horse and a man to lead it, to carry a load of the lord's goods for a distance of no more than 12 miles. Cottagers were obliged to carry "a reasonable Burthen," or tend a horse once every two years. The customary tenants were to repair the lord's mill, to grease and shear the lord's sheep, and to dig peat for the lord. Every customary tenant owed a half-day plowing the lord's demesne every year and had to supply the plow, the plow horses, and the men to tend them. Cottagers, who evidently were assumed to have no plow, owed one day's harrowing on the demesne. Each tenant was to give one day mowing grass and another reaping corn. For each day's boon services listed above, the lord was to supply the tenants with food and drink.

These boon services, suits of court and mill, and entry fines may

*This was to prevent the tenants from pasturing other men's animals for a fee, and thus overcrowding the commons.

†Or, as it was commonly expressed, as long as she neither "married nor miscarried."

‡As we shall see, the tenants paid for the setting of fines at this relatively low level.

appear onerous, but by Cumberland and Westmorland standards they were very moderate. In particular, entry fines of four times the old rent were low. Customarily entry fines throughout the counties were arbitrary, to be agreed on between the lord and the tenant. However, the lords, like their peers throughout Europe, sought ways to extract more revenue from their tenants—and the arbitrary entry fine proved an excellent way.[13] The old rents were seldom questioned by the lord; here the custom of the manor was allowed to stand. Perhaps the lord recognized that his rentals and surveys would be strong evidence against him in the event of litigation, since they recorded the customary rents. But entry fines were more amenable to upward manipulation, because they had not been firmly established at any multiple of the rent. Nor, in some instances, had the "change" of lord been defined, and tactics were devised to switch the ownership of the manor, and accordingly demand another fine from each tenant. The Queen's surveyors, Edmund Hall and William Homberston, noted the change that had taken place by 1570 on the vast Percy holdings in Cumberland. The customary tenants of the Honor of Cockermouth held their lands by copy of court rolls (which technically made them copyholders), paying fines "at the Lords will after the death alienac[i]on or exchaunge of every Lord & ten[a]nt wh[ic]h custome hath heretofore beene by the Lorde . . . reasonablie used." The surveyors went on to note that formerly the customary relationships were so easy, that

> the ten[a]nts thought themselves well pleased & in good estate & albeit their ffermeholds were but small yett the Comons were great & large soe as the Ten[a]nts were well able to live to mainteine themselves & their families . . . ; till nowe of late yeares the greadines of the Lordes hath beene such & their practices soe horrible by making Conveyance & devises of their Lande to cause the poore ten[a]nts to make ffine sometimes once in two three or ffoure yeares or more [and] the poore ten[a]nts are soe raunsomed as they are neither able to live & mainteine their families. . . . That Custome wh[ic]h heretofore they most desired is now become soe odious unto them as they are not able to endure it.[14]

The mechanism of "Conveyance & devises" of the land, to force the tenants to pay a fine, is not clear from the context. It is also not clear just who the "Lordes" were, that is, whether the reference is to the Percys or to lesser lords holding from the Percys.

A complaint lodged in the Court of Requests in 1594 against Sir Edward Herbert and his wife Mary by their tenants in the manors of Loweswater, Brackenthwaite, and Thackthwaite provides clarification. The tenants claimed that the Herberts had twice sold the manors within the previous 14 years and feared that they would continue to sell them in the future, each time demanding a general fine.[15] Evidently the sales were collusive, a transfer of the land on a pretended sale to another gentleman who then "sold" the manors back again. Collusive sales of this type seem to have been a commonplace among the gentry of the Honor, although nothing indicates that the Percys used the subterfuge on their own numerous manors. We do not know how the tenants fared in their suit, but in 1597 Chancery ruled that a general fine was not owed if a lord sold a manor. Sir Edward Coke, writing of this decision, noted that the change of the lord "ought to be by Act of God, otherwise no fine can be due," or else the tenants "may be oppressed by multitude of fines."[16] Perhaps this principle had not yet been established. The intent of the lords in the Honor of Cockermouth is clear, however; they wanted to milk their tenants, and, if the Queen's surveyors were correct, some at least had been successful.

Complaints about higher fines were frequently heard toward the end of the century. In the Herbert case, mentioned above, the tenants also objected to paying ten years' old rent for a fine. Before the manors descended to Lady Mary from her father, they claimed, fines were set at two years' old rent. The great and frequent fines, the tenants alleged, would "utterly undoe and beggar" them and they would be unable to do their border service.

In 1589 the Bishop of Carlisle was a defendant in a suit brought in Requests by one of his tenants in Dalston, George Blaymyre, who said that his ancestors had always paid a fine of two years' old rent but the Bishop was now demanding a "great intollerable and unaccustomed ffine." Blaymyre had refused to pay the fine and the Bishop was seeking to evict him by an action of *ejectio firma* at common law. Blaymyre went on to say that he could not plead his tenure of tenant right as a defense in a common law action because tenant right was peculiar to the northern counties and not "common" to all of England. His only recourse, he added, lay in a court of equity. He had turned to Requests because he could not expect a fair hearing in the Council of the North, since the Bishop was a member.[17]

These same themes run through the bulk of cases heard in the Courts of Chancery and Requests. The fine demanded by the lord was "extreame & outragious . . . utterly contrary to the ancient custome" and would cause the "utter undowing & impov[er]yssh-ing" of the tenants. Because their tenure was peculiar to the north, they had no defense against common law eviction actions and had to seek equitable justice. All the tenants' pleas emphasized that they would be unable to defend the border if the lord's demands were not moderated.[18]

It is clear that the equity courts were at times sympathetic to the tenants' complaints.[19] Exactly how often it is impossible to say. But there existed a modicum of protection for the customary tenant if he could bring his case before an equity court. No doubt the court decisions were often compromises, raising the fine somewhat but keeping it "reasonable" and, it was to be hoped, leaving the tenant prosperous enough to meet his obligations to defend the border. London was far away, however, the tenants poor, and even equity proceedings time-consuming and expensive. Probably only the most flagrant cases were heard and perhaps adjudged in the tenants' favor.

Pleas in court cases are naturally biased; the tenants' description of their dismal lot has to be accepted skeptically. However, their complaints were substantiated by other reports from the north. An unsigned letter in 1591 to the Privy Council gave the following reasons for the decline in the number of horsemen available for border service. First, the "Principall cause" was that Cumberland lords exact "as greate or greater fynes than they doo in the Southe, besides the contynuall services they doo putt their Ten[a]nts unto for all mannor of . . . worke whatsoev[er]." Second, the estates formerly occupied by gentlemen are now held by "meane men" who so squeeze their tenants "as they are scant able to finde themselves and their families meate and drinke." Third, Crown lands are leased to men who "take so unreasonable fynes as they [i.e. the tenants] are not able to buye a good horse, or havinge one is not able to keepe him." Leasing a manor to such a man "does beggar all the Ten[a]nts therein."[20]

The picture was not uniformly bleak, however. Customary tenants on Crown estates apparently fared considerably better than their fellows on private estates, despite the adverse comment quoted above. In 1568, Elizabeth confirmed her Cumberland tenants on the payment of a fine of two years' old rent and in 1571 urged the local lords to follow her example.[21] In the various manors of the Richmond Fee, part of the Barony of Kendal, fines in 1574 were either one or two years' old rent, depending on the particular manor.[22] A customary tenant on the Crown manor of Castle Sowerby paid a fine of one year's rent on the alienation of his holding, but no fine or heriot was paid by his heir after his death.[23] The tenants of Borrowdale paid one year's old rent on the death of the tenant or the alienation of the holding and "one godes penny" on the death of the lord.[24] The change of either lord or tenant called for a one-year fine in the manor of Holm Cultram, and each customary tenant also paid a fixed fine every five years—called a "running gressum"—which amounted to approximately three times the old rent.[25] These examples are drawn from Crown estates, but certain lords also made no effort to push up fines. The Percys may have been easy toward their tenants, at least until the ninth Earl of Northumberland began to improve his estates in the 1590's.[26] If the evidence can be trusted, the Dacres asked fines of but two or three years' old rent on their extensive holdings—the baronies of Burgh, Gilsland and Greystoke—even though the fines were arbitrary.[27] The Dacres may have been the last of the old breed of great northern magnates, who saw their tenants as armed retainers rather than as mere entries on a rent roll. There is even a hint that the Dacres explicitly demanded tenant loyalty in return for low fines.[28] The Dacre lands reverted to the Crown in 1570, but fines remained low until the estates were returned to private hands.

Whatever the typical tenants' true condition on Elizabeth's death, the 1603 union of the Crowns clearly undermined the tenants' legal protections. Their defense against unreasonable fines had been tenant right—the obligation to serve on the borders—and it had proved a useful plea in the distant equity courts. Now even this slender protection disappeared, for the borders no longer needed defending. The lords soon moved to nullify customary tenure and to force their tenants to take leases or else to pay a lump sum for the confirmation of their customary estates and holdings.* The Crown, in a reversal of Elizabeth's moderate attitude toward her tenants in the northwest, made the first important move against the tenants. In the Court of Exchequer, June 15, 1610, tenant right tenures in the Cumberland manors of Dacre, Blackhall, Lazonby, Staffield, Glassonby, Ainstaple, Irthington, and West Farlam were set aside and forty-year leases substituted.[29] The following year, Lord William Howard, who had become lord of Gilsland in the right of his wife, a Dacre, moved against his tenants. Noting that previous Chancery decrees[30] had voided tenant right as a defense in equity, Howard "offered to make unto [his Gilsland tenants] estates for lives by warrante . . . or some other goode estates in law beinge unto them much better for theire profitts." At least this was Howard's description of the offer. His tenants saw it in a different light; they remained unconvinced that their welfare was his sole concern. As in most Star Chamber cases, it is difficult to reconstruct what actually took place. The complaint, answers, and depositions give very different accounts. The complaint alleged that certain disaffected local gentlemen, playing on the tenants' fears, had urged them to meet together and oppose Howard with force. These gentlemen, who were the actual defendants in the case, denied this, and the tenants deposed that the meeting had been peaceful, designed merely to discuss legal ways to seek confirmation of their customary estates. Very likely the tenants did fear that Howard "intended to extirpat them their Wives and Children out of their Tenem[en]ts and livings

*These "leases" appear to have been really a method of extracting lump-sum payments from the tenants to confirm for forty years their ancient customs. Under the confirmed customs, they continued to pay the old rents, fines, etc.

and to plant strangers in their Roomes . . . and their Widdowes should be w[i]thout their thirds to support them in their widdowhood and their Children should begg w[i]thout releife or succor."[31] In any event, Star Chamber found the defendants guilty and fined them,[32] but the question of the tenants' right to customary, inheritable estates remained open.

On the Percy estates, the customary tenants were pressured to become leaseholders at triple the old rent. They refused, evidently feeling that their right to inherit was defendable at law.[33] Seeking an alternative way to increase his revenues, the Earl of Northumberland in 1616 wrote his representative in the Honor of Cockermouth, Sir Wilfred Lawson, and complained that the entry fines of twenty years' old rent that Lawson was demanding of the tenants were not large enough. The Earl's letter has not survived and we do not know what he thought the tenants should pay. In his answer, Lawson defended twenty-year fines, noting that they were "more than double so much as your lordship hath formerlie taken, if the bookes of ffines be looked into."[34] The correspondence stops here and does not tell us if the Earl continued to press for higher fines, or was content with twenty years' old rent. The letter shows clearly, however, that entry fines on the Percy lands took a sharp jump upward in the years after 1603.

In 1619 Charles, the Prince of Wales, successfully proved that his tenants in the extensive Barony of Kendal had no customary inheritable estates. In return for a payment of £2,700, Charles agreed to confirm his tenants' estates of inheritance, fix fines at two years' old rent on the death of the lord and three years' on the change of tenant, and otherwise confirm the rights of the tenants. They agreed and thus obtained a satisfactory, if expensive, settlement.[35]

While this compromise was being thrashed out, King James issued a proclamation against tenant right. Published in 1620, it stated,[36]

> Whereas it hath beene oftentimes, by Decrees and Judgements at Law declared and setled, That Tenant-rights, since the most happy Union of these two renowned Kingdomes . . . are utterly . . . extinguished and abolished

> . . . And yet neverthelesse divers Suits are continually raised and prosecuted . . . grounded upon the said claime of Tenant-right, or Customarie estate of Inheritance, under that pretence, whereby . . . both parties doe sustaine needlesse charge, and impoverishment . . . [and] may also . . . open a way to turbulent and seditious attempts: Wee . . . have both recommended . . . to all Our Judges, to surpresse and surcease strifes and suits of this nature, And have [ordered our officers to] let all Estates, whether for Lives or Yeeres, be it for Fine or improvement of Rent, by Indenture onely.

The proclamation then asked all the lords of the counties to follow the Crown's example by leasing their lands, and commanded that there be no further mention of tenant right or customary estate for border services. In conclusion, the proclamation expressed the hope that "good and dutifull" tenants would be treated considerately by the lords. If they were not, the equity courts were to "over-rule" the lords.

Despite the proviso that the equity courts would find against any landlord that was excessively hard on his tenants, the proclamation probably appeared to many landlords as license to raise rents, convert to leases, or whatever they wished, and to evict those tenants unable or unwilling to meet their terms. Certainly this is what the tenants expected. Within a few months of the proclamation, tenants on non-Crown manors in the Barony of Kendal assembled to raise money for a common defense against their lords. The tenants sought to petition either the King or Parliament, asking that the lords be directed to confirm their customary tenure and fix their fines and obligations in return for some reasonable payment, as Prince Charles had done. The lords claimed that the assemblies were riotous, seditious, and in opposition to the King's proclamation, and the Crown hailed the tenants before Star Chamber.[37]

By bringing the tenants before Star Chamber, the lords apparently wished to show them in the worst possible light, and to crush once and for all any further opposition to leaseholds or arbitrary fines. But the tenants—or their counselors—shrewdly argued that although they had been obligated to serve on the borders, they had been admitted as tenants in the various manors by the custom of the manor, paying such rents and fines as the manorial custom dictated.

And nowhere did the pre-1603 manor court rolls say that they held by border service. In short, they claimed they held by double tenure; border service and custom. But by custom they were entitled to their estates. It is interesting to recall that prior to 1603 the tenants had argued just the opposite; then their other tenure, based on border service, was used to protect them from excessive fines. At that time the lords, not wishing to emphasize border service, had omitted it from their admittance rolls. The tenants also argued that if they had forfeited all rights to their holdings by the termination of border service, had not the lords forfeited their estates as well? The lords, too, had been obligated for border service; should not their lands return to the Crown?

James himself pressed the Court to resolve the question of the tenants' titles,[38] and Star Chamber accordingly named a panel of judges to "consider of the title and claim of both sides . . . that there may be absolute peace." In 1625 the panel made its recommendations. The disputes in all the manors within the Barony of Kendal were the same, the judges said, and were reducible to two: first, did the customary tenants have an inheritable estate, and, second, were fines fixed by custom or arbitrary at the will of the lord? The judges found for the tenants on the first; their estates were essentially copyholds of inheritance, even though they lacked "divers formalities" found in copyhold of inheritance in the south. The judges also found that border service "was no special part of their services," but a duty demanded not only of them but of all freeholders and lords as well. Nor was there "ever any mention of their border service in their admittances." On the second point of dispute, the nature of the fines, the panel declined to offer an opinion, saying that this would exceed the instructions given them. However, they strongly urged Star Chamber to adjudicate the matter. If left unresolved, they feared, disputes over fines would cause "endless suits."[39]

It is not known if Star Chamber ever settled the problem of fines. Probably it did not, for litigation continued. In fact, the two questions—of the right of inheritance and the size of the entry fine—are inseparable. As R. H. Tawney said, if the heir could not pay the fine, he effectively lost his father's land, whatever the legal niceties.[40]

During these years the tenants of a number of manors in Cumberland and Westmorland were contracting with their lords for confirmation of their estates and the setting of fixed fines and obligations in return for a lump sum payment to the lord. But even on the manors where agreement was reached, there still remained the possibility of misunderstanding or abuse. For example, the tenants of Bassenthwaite had paid eight years' old rent in 1607 for confirmation of their estates by their lord, John Irton. The parties had also agreed on fines of nine years' old rent, on the change of the lord or tenant. Sometime after the agreement had been signed, however, Irton managed to get hold of the tenants' copy. He then began to demand fines greater than stipulated in the agreement. Without their copy of the contract, the tenants had no remedy at common law, and turned to Chancery for relief.[41] On other manors, apparently there was no breach by either party. The tenants at Threlkeld paid Sir John Lowther £1,360 for confirmation of their estates and the custom in 1635. Many particulars of this agreement have already been given here, but one other provision deserves attention. The agreement stipulated that the lord could distrain and then sell a tenant's personal property if the tenant failed to pay his rent or fine, to grind his corn at the lord's mill, to fulfill his boon services, and so on. But the tenant did not forfeit his customary tenement or the right of his heir to inherit; these were forfeitable only for treason or felony. Evidently the tenants wished to forestall any possible dispute that would cause them to lose their beloved land. This agreement, like others drawn at that time, called for a decree in Chancery and a private bill in Parliament, to register the terms of the contract.[42]

The tenants had reason to be suspicious of their lords. Some (like John Irton) went back on their agreements. At least one lord, Joseph Huddleston, simply refused to abide by the decrees of the courts. In 1632 Huddleston brought an action in the Court of Exchequer claiming that his tenants at Hutton John had not paid their fines and hence held only at his sufferance. The Exchequer decree in 1635 determined that the tenants must pay a forty years' fine, but henceforth each fine was to be four years' old rent, and ordered Huddleston to confirm the tenants' customary estates. The payment of forty years' rent appears to have included some rent arrears and a sum for confirmation, so it was not, strictly speaking a fine. Huddleston refused to accept the tenants' payments, and would not confirm their estates. The dispute dragged on in various courts until 1716, when it was finally resolved in favor of the tenants.[43] By that time Huddleston was long dead and everyone, except the lawyers, was poorer.

Huddleston was no doubt unusually irascible, but the tendency was toward greater burdens on the customary tenants—unless of course they contracted with their lord for fixed fines and obligations. After the Star Chamber opinion in 1625, little effort was made to deny the tenants their inheritance rights and convert them to leaseholders,[44] but pressure for heavier fines continued. We have already seen that fines were increased on Percy manors, and on many other manors fines of twenty or thirty years' rent were assessed.[45] On still other manors, "running" fines were instituted and added to the general fines the tenants paid. The tenants of Hensingham, for example, paid a running fine of seven years' old rent every seven years, or what amounted to a doubling of the old rent. They also paid fines of from 18 to thirty years' old rent on the death of the lord.[46] On still other manors, fines remained arbitrary, the lord demanding what the tenant could bear.[47] On the manor of Calder, the tenants had obtained a decree in Exchequer "in the late queene Elizabeths tyme" setting their fines at four years' old rent, but this was overturned about 1621 and the tenants ordered to pay arbitrary fines.[48] By the end of the century, fines as high as 96 times the old rent were demanded in the manor of Leversdale, in the barony of Gilsland, although most fines there ranged from twenty to thirty years' rent.[49]

On Crown manors, fines tended to remain modest, perhaps because the tenants found the Crown willing to agree to low, certain fines if a lump sum was paid, in a manner similar to the settlement on the Kendal lands.[50] Toward the end of the century, increasing numbers of private lords followed the Crown precedent and contracted with their tenants to make fines certain or even to allow the tenants to convert their tenancies to freehold.[51] Economically, these agreements were of long-term benefit to the tenant, although it may have been a considerable short-term strain to raise the necessary cash.

The trend toward fixed obligations, however, was incomplete as late as the end of the eighteenth century. William Hutchinson, writing about Cumberland in 1794, deplored the "most numerous and strong remains of vassalage and servility retained in the customs of the manors within this county, that are to be found in any part of England." He noted that "the miserable tenant, who is to pay an arbitrary fine and a heriot, is perpetually impoverished," adding that "those customary tenures are a national grievance. From this tenure is chiefly to be attributed the vast and dreary wastes that are found in Cumberland."[52]

A short summary of the evidence seems in order here. It appears that landlords gradually increased the entry fines demanded of their tenants during the sixteenth century. Some lords were more grasping, some less, but the general trend was toward higher fines. The Crown, however, stood in the way of extreme exploitation, fearing that this would lead to a breakdown of border defense. The Crown also treated its own tenants with moderation. But after 1603 the Crown led the way in demanding greater payments from its tenants, although usually in the form of a single settlement payment. Private landlords followed suit and demanded higher fines or the substitution of leasehold for customary tenure. The Star Chamber ruling of 1625 established that a customary holding was an estate of inheritance, but left the problem of fines unresolved. And fines continued to creep up, in amount and diversity, unless the tenants were willing to make a contractual settlement with their lord that permanently fixed fines.

Were the increased fines excessive? Did they impoverish the tenants, by shifting away the profits of the land to the lords? It is impossible to say—because we do not know what the profits of the holdings were and whether or not the increased fines were so burdensome that many tenants were kept on the edge of mere subsistence. It seems doubtful that the landlords' push toward higher fines —particularly after 1603—had much to do with the disastrous famines the area suffered. The timing is wrong. Fines rose more after 1603, that is, after two of the famines. And they continued to rise, here and there, after the last famine, that of 1623. If the pressure of rents and fines had been crucial, it seems that other famines would have followed. None did. But I shall have more to say on this subject in the final chapter.

CHAPTER SIX

Communications, Trade, and Industry

GEOGRAPHICAL ISOLATION contributed to the economic backwardness of sixteenth-century Cumberland and Westmorland. Communications were poor, both inside the region and reaching to the outside. The Tyne Gap, which permitted access to the northeastern counties, has already been mentioned. This must have been a well-traveled route at the end of the sixteenth century, over which grain and other goods were brought from Newcastle in exchange for raw wool and cheap woolens produced in the two counties.[1] Another link to the east was the road from Penrith, south past Appleby, then east to Brough and on eastward to Bowes in Yorkshire, finally intersecting the highway between London and Newcastle at Darlington. Other roads of importance ran to the south. One went from Carlisle along the Eden Valley to Appleby and then south to London.[2] Another, which also ended in London, made its way from Cockermouth to Keswick, then south through the Cumbrians to Kendal and on to Lancaster over the sands of Morecambe Bay.[3] Local roads, probably mere trails in many places, connected the various towns and hamlets of the counties. In general, overland communications must have been poor. A soldier from Norwich, traveling in 1634, described his journey between Penrith and Kendal as "through such wayes as wee hope wee never shall againe, being . . . nothing but a most confus'd mixture of Rockes and Boggs."[4] As late as 1698, the road that connected Cockermouth, Keswick, and Kendal was said to be "as bad as anything in England, being very hilly, stony and moorish."[5]

Travel by water was, if anything, more difficult. The rivers of Cumberland and Westmorland were not navigable and the Cumberland seaports remained undeveloped by 1600, despite the long coastline and several potential harbors. A royal commission inquiring into the ports of Cumberland in 1566 revealed that Workington, then the largest port, harbored only three vessels, called "pickerdes," of seven or eight tons each, that carried herring to Chester and Liverpool and returned with salt. Only one vessel, the *Bee* of nine tons burden, sailed from Whitehaven, also to Chester and Liverpool, carrying herring and returning with cattle. Farther south, Ravenglas was a hamlet of ten households, the home port for four vessels, each manned by four fishermen, which engaged in the same limited trade.[6] Maryport was not mentioned in this inquiry. In 1582, a survey of shipping and mariners in Cumberland indicated that there were only 12 small vessels in the entire county, and 198 seamen, many of whom never navigated anything larger than an open boat.[7]

The unimportance of the Cumberland ports during the sixteenth century can be seen from their absence on various customs documents. In 1585 Sir Francis Walsingham was granted the farm of the customs and subsidies of the outports. No port in Cumberland or Westmorland was named in the list of outports.[8] The renewal of his lease in 1588 again omits any mention of ports in the two counties.[9] A 1594 list of fees paid to custom officials in various outports recorded no payments to any official at Carlisle, Workington, or Whitehaven.[10]

The earliest surviving port books for Cumberland, dating from 1611, show a slight increase in trade at Workington and Carlisle. In the first six months of 1611, a total of 34 ships called at Workington, loading coal from the mines nearby, and copper, no doubt from the mines outside Keswick. Imports were primarily herring, along with small quantities of linen yarn and linen cloth, alum, flax, and clothing. The imports to Carlisle came overland from Scotland. The most important items in this trade were Scottish woolens and linens, woolfells, herring, and cowhides. Scottish cattle also entered England at Carlisle, to begin their long journey to the south.[11] This trade was old, having existed intermittently during the sixteenth century, but had been hampered by numerous prohibitions and interruptions. With the accession of James to the English throne, the trade began to grow.[12]

The insignificance of coastal trade or commerce with Scotland in these years is undeniable, but some commercial and industrial activities existed that depended on outside markets. In Westmorland, there were the remnants of a formerly prosperous cloth industry. Particularly in the parishes of Grasmere and Kendal, cheap, coarse cloths called "cottons" were woven from the rough northern wools. They seem to have been popular with the London poor and had also been exported from Southampton. But decline had set in after the middle of the sixteenth century.[13] As usual with economic changes, it is hard to date the decline with any precision. As late as 1607 Kendal may have still been prosperous; Camden described it in that year as "a towne of very great trade . . . the inhabitants have great trafficke and vent of their wollen clothes throughout all parts of England."[14] A generation later, Richard Brathwaite wrote of a "late" decrease in the woolen trade in Kendal, noting that now the town is "no lesse penurious than populous . . . so . . . such Inhabitants as formerly . . . were able to give an almes at their doore, are now forced to begge their almes from doore to doore."[15] Quite likely Brathwaite believed that the severe depression of the early 1620's was the decisive blow to the woolen manufacture, but the market had been softening for some time before. Only a small part of the local wool was woven at Kendal or Grasmere; most was packed to clothiers in the West Riding or in Lancashire.[16] The wool of Cumberland and Westmorland was so coarse that it was traditionally exempted from regulations limiting wool sales to cloth manufacturers or staplers. Anyone could deal in the wool, and merchants of Newcastle were permitted to export it to the Continent without license. The cloth made in Westmorland—the cogwares, kendals, and cartmells—was also exempt from regulation, allowing the manufacturers to determine the length, width, and weight of their cloth.[17] The total lack of regulation suggests that both the wool and the woolens of Cumberland and Westmorland were marginal, from a national point of view. They were allowed to find what markets they could, without interference and without taxation, because they were unimportant other than as a source of support for the inhabitants of the two counties.[18]

At the end of the sixteenth century, coal and copper mining provided some employment for the inhabitants of the two counties. The great coal deposits around Whitehaven were not worked at this time, but mining was carried on at Clifton and coal was exported from the nearby port of Workington. The port books for 1611 show that shipments from Workington for six months totaled a meager 443 tons.[19] This may have been untypically low—the trade fluctuated from season to season and year to year—because other sources indicate that 2,641 tons were shipped from Workington to Scotland and Ireland and 92 tons to the Isle of Man in the year ending October 29, 1605.[20] In 1616, 3,000 tons were carried to Ireland, 600 tons to Scotland, and 150 to the Isle of Man. Ten years later, approximately 4,500 tons were exported, mostly to Ireland.[21] By this time it was apparent that a profitable market existed in Ireland, but disputes between freeholders who worked the mines and the Curwens, who controlled the port of Workington, hampered any further expansion of output.[22]

Coal was also mined on the Earl of Northumberland's lands in Westward and Bolton before the turn of the century. The bailiff's accounts for the years 1594 to 1597 show average revenues at Westward of just under £64 per year.[23] Either these sums were gross rather than net or the mines declined in value, for they were leased in 1615 for 21 years at £15 per year.[24] It is possible to gain an idea of the scope of the mining at Westward from the colliery accounts for 1603–4.[25] A total of seven miners were employed: three "haggars" (the men hewing the coal from the face of the seam), two "drawers" (presumably those pulling the coal baskets along the tunnel to the bottom of the shaft), and two "winders" (who hoisted the coal to the surface). A haggar was paid 6*d.* per day, a drawer 3*d.*, and a winder 5*d.*, and each man was allowed an additional 1*d.* for drink. In addition to the miners, other workmen were employed to dig the numerous shafts, which ranged from 18 to 42 feet in depth. These multiple shafts suggest inadequate tunneling and a rather low level of technology, by early seventeenth-century standards, although adits—underground drainage tunnels—were dug to carry off water from the pits by 1615.[26] The mines were not worked continuously; in 1603–4 they operated for only 83 days. Most of the coal was used to smelt copper ore mined at Keswick,[27] and perhaps the amount needed at the smelter was too small for full-time mining at Westward. Or perhaps the miners were customary tenants who only mined coal when work was lacking on their own holdings.

In eastern Cumberland, coal was mined in the Barony of Gilsland. Lord William Howard let his mines there and received a royalty on each ton mined.[28] The records do not say where the Gilsland coal was sold. Near Egremont, in southwestern Cumberland, the Earl of Northumberland in 1616 renewed a lease on a mine to a William Fletcher, who used the coal in salt-panning.[29] In this process, sea water was poured into a large, flat, iron pan,[30] which was then heated over a coal fire until the water had evaporated and only salt remained. There was a ready local market for salt among the herring fishermen of the Cumberland coast, who previously had imported salt from the panners of Lancashire and Cheshire.

Although copper had been mined in the Keswick region of the Cumbrians as early as 1475,[31] a systematic attempt to exploit the copper ores in Cumberland, Westmorland, and across the Lancashire border in Furness was undertaken only in the 1560's. In 1563, the Crown gave Daniel Höchstetter, a member of one of the most prominent banking and mining families of Augsburg, permission to survey the mineral resources of England.[32] Höchstetter was in Keswick in June of the following year and must have realized the potential for copper mining in the region, for shortly thereafter, in December 1564, the Queen empowered him to mine and smelt all ores in the northwest. In return, the Queen was to receive one-tenth of all gold and silver and one-twentieth of all copper produced.[33] In July 1565, a partnership was formed to finance and manage the mining operations. The major partner, with 11 of the 24 shares outstanding, was Haug, Langnauer and Company, an Augsburg mercantile and banking company with mining interests in the Austrian Tyrol and northern Hungary. Höchstetter acted as Haug, Langnauer's agent in England and was responsible for the direct management of the operations. Two and one-half shares in the partnership were held by Thomas Thurland, the Master of the Savoy, who also was active in the management of the partnership. Two shares went to Sir William Cecil and another two to the Earl of Leicester, to ensure the support of the Privy Council for the undertaking.[34] It seems that Haug, Langnauer contributed all the initial capital for the venture. Three years later, in May of 1568, the partnership was changed to a corporation called the Company of Mines Royal.[35]

In October 1565, some fifty men were at work constructing a smelting house on the Greta River outside Keswick.[36] Mining began the next year to the southeast of Keswick in the Newlands Valley, where a rich vein of copper ore had been discovered at a place later known as Goldscope.[37] The first copper was smelted at Keswick in the autumn of 1567.[38] Because the English lacked the necessary skills in mining and smelting, both these operations were performed by Germans, many of whom had been recruited in the Tyrol mines. Before mining got under way, Höchstetter had written the Privy Council that he would need three to four hundred Germans for the operation, but the actual number who came to England in the years the mines were operating seems to have been closer to 150.[39]

The Keswick venture experienced difficulties from the start. The copper mine at Newlands was located on land granted to the Earl of Northumberland by Queen Mary and he claimed the output as rightfully his. On May 12, 1567, three of his gentleman retainers in Cumberland arrived at the mine and ordered that no further mining be done and also demanded that the ore previously dug was to stay in the county.[40] The Crown—which of course had authorized the mining—took a different position, arguing that all ores that contained precious metals within the kingdom legally belonged to it, not to the holder of the land. As the owner of the metals, the Crown stated, it could grant mining rights to whomever it wished.[41] The dispute went to Exchequer, which early in 1568 decided in favor of the Crown.[42] The question of legal title was settled and the mining continued. Before the decision, however, the Earl seems to have stirred up local feelings against the miners. In 1566, a German was murdered in Keswick, apparently beaten to death by a mob.[43] This atrocity was not repeated, but there seems to have been tension between the local people and the Germans until the Exchequer decision of 1568. Then relations eased, some of the miners married local women, and the Germans were accepted in the community.

Another problem facing the company was the local shortage of timber. Timber was needed initially for the construction of the buildings, particularly the smelthouse, and wood was also necessary as fuel for the smelter. There was, however, a "great lack" of woods in the county, although both Lady Catherine Ratcliffe, the lord of the manor of Keswick, and the Earl of Northumberland owned woods not far from the smelthouse.[44] Timber for building construction was obtained from these two, but local wood supplies seem to have been inadequate to fuel the smelter. Plans were made to build a wharf at Workington and import timber from Ireland, but this seems to have come to nothing, probably because of the cost and inconvenience involved.[45] Instead the company substituted coal and peat for wood in much of the smelting process. Smelting required four distinct cookings before the ore was converted to copper. In the first two, coal and peat were used as fuel. In the third step, peat alone was used. Only in the fourth cooking was wood, together with peat, used as fuel. The copper was then fined with charcoal, which is a wood product. The use of coal and peat greatly reduced the need for wood, and the local supplies seem to have been sufficient for the charcoal and the final cooking of the ore. The switch to coal and peat demanded some experimentation, because the Germans were accustomed to smelting with wood, and at first this somewhat slowed the smelting of the ores.[46] The coal burned in the smelter came from the mine at Bolton mentioned above; the peat was dug on the great fells of the Cumbrians. Charcoal was brought from Isel Park, on the Derwent River to the northwest of Keswick, and also from the Furness region of Lancashire.[47]

The isolation of the mines and the distance from suitable port facilities must have added to the difficulties and expense of operating the mines. Supplies that could not be obtained locally were brought overland, usually from Newcastle, despite the distance and bad roads. Workington, although it was much closer, was apparently too primitive to be used consistently. The company account books show that wine, oranges, candles—even artichokes—were purchased in London and shipped to Newcastle, where they were then carted or packed the seventy or so miles to Keswick.[48] The accounts show that the company bought substantial quantities of iron, for use in the Keswick smithy. Although the northwest was rich in iron ore and later developed an important iron industry, all the iron used by the company seems to have been bought in London and brought north, rather than purchased locally.[49]

In addition to the mine at Goldscope in the Newlands Valley, copper ore was dug at Caldbeck, Borrowdale, and Grasmere. All the ores were carried to the smelter at Keswick. In the 1590's, mining also began at Coniston, in Lancashire, and this ore was smelted at Keswick. Considerable amounts of ore were mined and as much as sixty tons of copper was smelted yearly in the 1570's.[50] However, the operation never returned a profit. By 1576, costs had exceeded revenues by £22,000.[51] The next year Haug, Langnauer withdrew from the company because of the mounting losses and other business reverses that the firm suffered in Germany. Höchstetter, however, remained in charge of the Keswick operation until his death in 1581.[52] Because of the poor returns, the company was unable to find further capital, and in 1580 it leased the entire operation to Höchstetter and Thomas Smith, a wealthy London merchant. After Höchstetter's death, his place in the operating partnership was taken by his son Emmanuel and his son-in-law Mark Steinberger. These three—Smith, Steinberger, and the younger Höchstetter—continued to operate the mines until 1597, when Steinberger died and the lease ended. The company then made one final attempt to make the mines pay, but their further investment of £700 was quickly eaten up as the operation continued to lose money. In 1601, the company again leased the mines, this time to Emmanuel and Daniel Höchstetter. The two operated the mines until 1614, when Emmanuel died and was replaced by Jospeh Höchstetter. Under the Höchstetter lease, less copper—about 21 tons a year—was made than in the first optimistic years of the company's operation.

Apparently the Höchstetters had a good idea of the limited demand for copper and curtailed production to satisfy but not exceed that demand. The Höchstetters also expanded the silver output of the Caldbeck mine. Between 1614 and 1624 the Caldbeck mine produced an average of £435 of silver a year, compared to copper worth about £2,300 and lead worth between £300 and £400 a year. The Höchstetters' expenses are not known but they seem to have operated at a profit.[53]

On lease to the Höchstetters, the mines continued in operation until the early 1640's, when they finally were closed down. The smelthouses and the other buildings that "were so numerous as they looked like a little Towne" fell into disrepair, and by 1671, not one of them still stood.[54] After almost eighty years, the Keswick mining and smelting venture had come to an end.

During its lifetime, the mining operation had a considerable impact on the regional economy, particularly at first when the buildings were being constructed and then for some years when the mines were in full production. All the skilled mining and smelting was done by Germans, although the account books indicate that some Englishmen were trained as apprentices.[55] But there were many less-skilled jobs—such as sorting the ore after it had been mined—that English men and women could fill. The smelthouse and the stamphouses—where the ore was crushed after it had been sorted—were built by local carpenters, probably with the assistance of the Germans and certainly under their direction. More important than direct employment in the mines or in building construction was the employment arising out of the demand for fuel. Trees were felled, charcoal was burned, peat was dug, and coal was mined—and all these had to be brought to the smelter. The accounts of 1571 list 54 men who brought peat to the smelter. These names, of course, would not include all the persons digging peat for the smelter; many of these men may have employed others whose names do not appear. Another twenty men and women are named as carriers of copper ore from the Newlands mine and the Caldbeck mine to the smelter. The accounts contain the names of 18 men who brought charcoal from Isel Park. A further 53 persons brought charcoal from

Furness and Borrowdale. And still others were employed as stone and slate carriers, lime carriers and boatmen. The 1571 accounts indicate in some instances the home parish or township of the carriers, and it is clear that men and women from many localities in southern Cumberland, Westmorland, and Furness sought work carrying fuel and building supplies for the mining operations.[56] Although their names do not appear on these accounts, other packhorse men and carters were hired to bring in supplies from Newcastle and also to carry the finished copper to that port, where it was shipped to London. In sum, the mining operations provided needed employment to many persons from communities throughout the northwest and may have brought a degree of prosperity to Keswick. As we shall see in the next chapter, the mortality crisis of 1587–88 affected only very slightly the parish of Crosthwaite, where the town of Keswick is located. Perhaps the mines—and the employment they gave—moderated the effects of harvest failure that year.

The greatest copper production came in the years 1570 through 1584; in a good year, sixty tons of copper were smelted. Then production declined slightly to the end of the century. Under the Höchstetter lease, an average of about 21 tons was made each year between 1601 and the early 1640's.[57] If we assume that employment—in all its forms—followed production, employment declined after 1584 and—by the first decades of the seventeenth century—leveled out at possibly one-third of what it had been in the booming 1570's. Although the mines were operated for almost eighty years, their contribution to the local economy was largely concentrated in the early years.

Copper from the Cumbrian mines provided one tie with a larger national market; the cattle trade also was part of a trade network reaching to the south. Cattle from Cumberland and Westmorland were driven south to various provincial markets or, after changing hands two or three times, to the London market. In increasing numbers after 1603, cattle from western Scotland—which had been driven over the borders near Carlisle—joined the locally raised animals for the long trek south. The most northerly great fair in England for these Scottish and locally raised animals was at Brough-under-Stainmore in eastern Westmorland. Brough was one of the great cattle exchanges of the north, visited by buyers from the eastern and southern counties. From Brough the animals were driven across the Pennines to Bowes in Yorkshire and then south, often ending up in Norfolk, where they were fattened for the London market.[58]

The economic isolation of the two counties was thus a partial rather than a total isolation. The area knew three levels of commercial activity. First, there was a local economy based on the manor, the parish, and the small market villages, such as Brampton and Wigton. This economy was largely subsistence, although the extra steer sold in the local market for rent money might, of course, end up as part of a herd being driven south to London. Second, there were commercial contacts with neighboring counties, which included the coastal trade to Lancashire and Cheshire, the overland trade with Newcastle, and the sale of wool to the clothiers of Yorkshire and Lancashire. Third, there was some limited integration into a national economy in copper, cattle, and perhaps Kendal woolens. Distance hindered a further involvement in a national market; the overland routes were long and difficult, and trade by sea remained largely undeveloped.

By the beginning of the seventeenth century the signs of another trade became apparent—an international trade with Ireland and Scotland. By 1611 coal was being shipped in small quantities to Ireland, and the northern border had been opened to the Scottish cattle trade. The next sixty years would see this trade mushroom into a regional market of importance, tying together northwestern England, western Scotland, and eastern Ireland into one market, linked by the Irish Sea. But this was in the future.

At the close of the sixteenth century the people of Cumberland and Westmorland remained largely dependent on local resources and a moribund woolen trade. As we shall see in the next chapter, these provided inadequate protections against the famines that marked the end of the sixteenth and the beginning of the seventeenth centuries.

CHAPTER SEVEN

Famine and Disease, 1587–1588

BETWEEN 1550 AND 1700 Cumberland and Westmorland experienced three severe demographic crises. In the years 1587–88, 1597–98, and 1623, burials in many parishes rose two, three, or four times the normal number.[1] These years of crisis can be seen at a glance in the graphic representation of the registers of Brough-under-Stainmore, which lies in eastern Westmorland. (See Figure 3.) Although Brough is only one example, it is typical of most parishes in the two counties. Perhaps there were other bad years preceding these years of crisis; 1557 may have been a year of terrible mortality,[2] but the parish registers are too few and too unreliable for any satisfactory analysis. Historians have long recognized the severity of the three crises in the northwest but have usually attributed the excessive deaths to plague or typhus.[3] Famine has been seen as slightly contributing to the death toll either by lowering resistance to the epidemic agents that were present or by forcing infected beggars onto the roads, which in turn helped spread the infection, but the historical accounts of these catastrophes minimized the role of starvation in Cumberland and Westmorland. Some years ago Michael Drake studied the mortality in the West Riding of Yorkshire for these same years and concluded that starvation was a major case of death in each of these crises.[4] A recent study of the crisis of 1623 in Lancashire has come to the similar conclusion that starvation was the primary cause of death there that

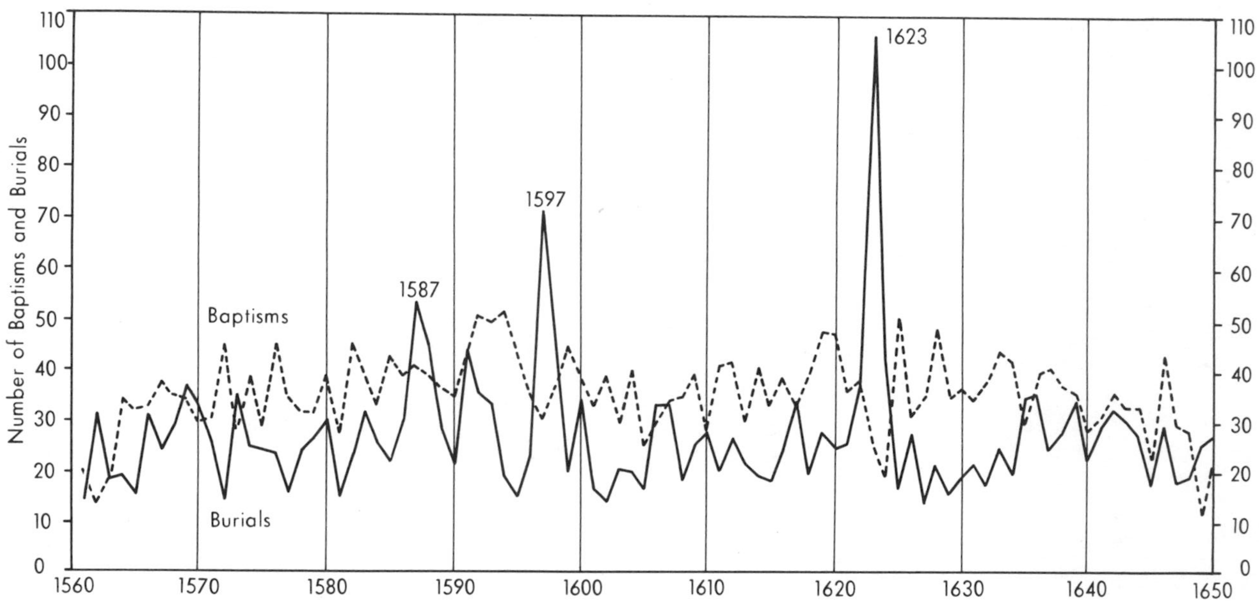

Fig. 3. Baptisms and burials, Brough-under-Stainmore, 1560–1650.

year.[5] The emphasis given to disease by the earlier writers is understandable, considering the lack of direct written evidence for starvation. Plague, in particular, fascinates historians.[6] And with good reason, for a severe epidemic was certainly the most appalling ill that could befall a community. But the role of famine as a killer in its own right has been underplayed in the history of early modern England.

In this chapter I will offer a method for differentiating between disease and famine and apply this methodology to each of the three crises. Using the burials recorded in the parish registers, I have graphed the seasonal distribution of deaths for certain parishes in the two counties during periods of heightened mortality. This distribution has been compared to the known configuration of various diseases. When this is combined with other evidence, it is possible to show that the mortality often attributed to plague or typhus was quite likely instead the result of starvation. In this context, "starvation" is defined broadly enough to include fatal intestinal disorders brought on by eating unsuitable food. If a starving person eats rotting animal flesh, grass, or tree bark—and then dies from this unsuitable fare—the historian must consider his death the result of starvation.[7] Starvation also includes "pure" starvation, where the caloric intake is reduced to the point where bodily functions slowly cease and the starving person slips into death.[8] Starvation is not, however, defined so loosely that it encompasses deficiency diseases or reduced resistance to infectious diseases. At this historical distance, medical conclusions (or retrospective diagnoses) are inevitably conjectural because they are in part based on modern experience with the various diseases known to have existed in the sixteenth and seventeenth centuries. For reasons that are still obscure, diseases change over time, increasing or decreasing in virulence.[9] But I have assumed that the broad outline of incidence, symptoms, and duration of various epidemic diseases has remained basically the same, from that time to this.

Before turning to the parish registers, it may be helpful to give a short description of the plague—the disease most often blamed for the demographic crises in Cumberland and Westmorland.[10] All plague is caused by the same microorganism, *Pasteurella pestis*, or, as it is sometimes known, *Yersinia pestis*. There are three discernibly different forms the disease can take: bubonic, pneumonic, and septicemic. In the bubonic form of the disease, the bacteria enter the human body when a person is bitten by an infected flea which has lost its usual host, a rat, and has been forced to transfer to a less desirable host, man. After infection, the incubation of the disease takes between two and six days. Then the characteristic sign of the disease appears—the bubo—which is a hèmorrhagic swelling of a lymph gland, most commonly in the groin but sometimes in the armpits or on the neck of the sufferer. Before the introduction of sulfa drugs and antibiotics, about 60 percent of those stricken died. In the second form, pneumonic plague, the bacteria invade the human system through the inhalation of droplets coughed or sneezed by someone with the bacteria in his respiratory tract. Initially, this was a person with bubonic plague, who then developed pneumonia. Unlike bubonic plague, which is a disease of animals that man catches accidentally, the pneumonic plague spreads from man to man without animal intermediaries, although it initially stems from a bubonic plague victim. This form of the disease was virtually always fatal. Plague's third form, septicemic, is an unusually virulent instance of either of the other two. It acts so quickly that it destroys the afflicted person before other symptoms, such as the bubo, or in pneumonic plague, the coughing of blood, appear. Before the discovery of streptomycin it was invariably fatal. For the historians' purposes it can be disregarded as a separate entity, because it was always accompanied by one of the other forms of the disease.

In the sixteenth and seventeenth centuries bubonic plague was predominantly an urban disease—a pestilence of cities and towns that only occasionally visited rural areas.[11] It has been described as "a disease of places . . . affording food and shelter to large colonies of rats."[12] Such places are towns and cities, not the villages and hamlets of the countryside. The rat that carried the plague flea was the black house rat, *Rattus rattus*, a relatively timid, weak, and unmigratory creature that lived in the thatch roofs or clay walls of the poor man's cottage and ate, by preference, his grain. In a climate such as Britain's, the house rat cannot survive outside a human dwelling for any length of time. It migrates only short distances, such as would be possible while searching for food in a town, and is also passively transported in bulky merchandise, for example, sacks of grain or bundles of wool, cloth, or hides. *R. rattus* was also the common ship rat and was carried from port to port. Thus the distribution of black rats tended to follow the main lines of trade between cities, fairs, and seaports.[13] It was unlikely that an infected rat would reach a rural area that had little contact with the city. If an infected rat hidden in some goods were accidentally brought into a sparsely settled area, the chances are that the infection would be limited to the house receiving the merchandise. Only the rats living in that dwelling would become infected and in turn infect their fleas. On the death of the rats, the fleas would then attack the human occupants. One of these people might carry a flea to a neighbor's house, where it would become dislodged and attack a person or a rat there. The cycle could then begin again. Such a method of transmission by humans, though, was uncommon.[14] If there was an outbreak of plague in a village, it usually was limited to one family and perhaps a frequent visitor to their house. There would be a few deaths and then the disease would die out.[15] This is not to say that plague never devastated a village; occasionally it did, but only very rarely.[16] The timidity and weakness of the rat usually kept it confined to its original location. Certainly it must have been far different in the cities, where the houses adjoined each other, and rat colonies lived in the common walls between two dwellings. There would have been little to prevent the disease moving from house to house down the length of the street. Eric Woehlkens' classic study of the plague in sixteenth-century Germany shows, however, that the width of a city street was often an effective barrier to the spread of the disease.[17] It is important to recall that contemporaries were aware of the differing incidence of the disease in the cities and the country. Those that could, promptly fled to the country on the first sign of an outbreak.

Bubonic plague in England was also characteristically a warm-weather disease; it almost always became dormant during the winter. The plague flea, *Xenopsylla cheopis*, is very sensitive to extremes of temperature and humidity. The ideal climate for its development is between 68 and 78 degrees Fahrenheit, with some humidity. The flea's eggs do not hatch below 55 degrees Fahrenheit, and temperatures below 45 degrees kill them. The adult fleas can withstand cold weather longer, but they become weak and sluggish.[18] Theoretically, of course, outdoor climatic conditions need not have affected the flea; even in winter the kitchen of an English house could offer a perfect artificial climate. But virtually all plague epidemics in England and on the European continent in the sixteenth and seventeenth centuries followed the same actual pattern: the first cases appeared in late spring or early summer, then mortality curved upward to a peak in late summer or early autumn, followed by a decline, with plague deaths stopping altogether about the first of December. Sometimes the disease then disappeared until it was reintroduced from outside. At other times it remained dormant while the fleas hibernated during the winter, and reappeared in epidemic form again the following spring.[19]

The bubonic plague thus followed a discernible pattern that should help the historian to identify it: first, it infrequently occurred in rural areas and would almost certainly not be widespread throughout a large, sparsely populated region; second, the disease almost always died out during the winter months in a temperate climate.[20] Reports of plague during the winter or plague in rural areas must be treated with suspicion and accepted only if supported by other convincing evidence.

Because pneumonic plague needs neither insect nor rodent intermediaries, its diffusion is not necessarily limited by these same factors. Unlike bubonic plague, it is usually a winter disease, dying out or changing into the bubonic form with the coming of warm weather. But like bubonic, its diffusion is difficult in an area of dispersed population. Close and prolonged contact with an infected person is required for an uninfected person to contract the disease. According to the epidemiologist L. Fabian Hirst, pneumonic plague's "epidemic spread is promoted by overcrowding and bad ventilation."[21] These are conditions of cities, not the countryside, and wide diffusion throughout a rural area is unlikely.

Fortunately for man, pneumonic plague has been a historical rarity. Of the hundreds of great plague epidemics, only two have been primarily pneumonic: the Manchurian plague of 1910–11 and, more important, the initial stages of the Black Death. The Manchurian epidemic raged among the Chinese marmot hunters, who, during the severe Manchurian winter, were crowded together for days on end in almost airtight underground inns.[22] There was little spread of the disease to other sectors of the Manchurian population. In other words, the conditions favoring the spread of pneumonic plague were a highly unusual combination of severe overcrowding and vitually no ventilation. The Black Death was an odd mixture of bubonic and pneumonic plague; certainly the high incidence of the pneumonic form both increased the terrible death toll and hastened the disease's diffusion across Europe. The relative importance of pneumonic plague at the outset of the Black Death has been recognized as an anomaly. "Where the fourteenth-century plague is said to differ from later experience is that . . . it seemed to change as the season of the year changed from pneumonic to bubonic, and then from bubonic to pneumonic, without discontinuity."[23] It is hard to tell why the disease was different in the 1340's than in later epidemics. Here it is only important to stress that epidemics of pneumonic plague were very unlikely, although never an impossibility.

Conditions in Cumberland and Westmorland were not suited to widespread diffusion of plague, should the disease gain a foothold there. From what we know of the habits of the rat, only the grain-growing lowlands of the Eden Valley and the Solway Plain were capable of sustaining a large rat population. The cold, barren highlands would have presented a most uncongenial habitat. Only in the lowlands, too, was housing suitable for the rat's burrow. Here houses were of clay, but in the highlands they were usually of impenetrable stone, often roofed with slate.[24] Highland communities were small and widely dispersed, and rats would not have been capable of moving from one hamlet to another. As we have seen, the

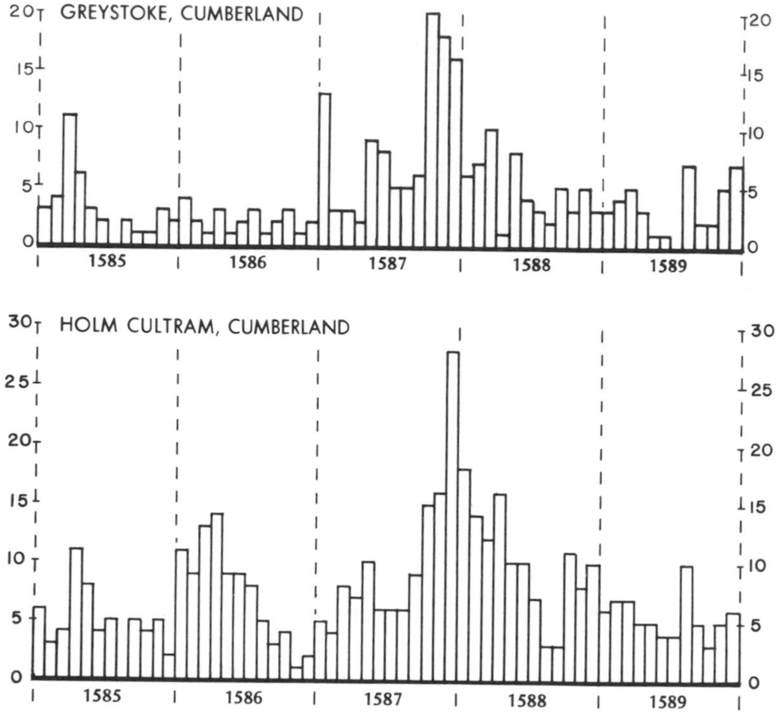

Fig. 4. Burials, 1585–89, in Greystoke and Holm Cultram.

towns and cities—Kendal, Carlisle, Penrith, Cockermouth, and Appleby—were small, but all were large enough to be ravaged by plague. It would have been very difficult for the disease to spread to the surrounding villages and hamlets, however.

The first population crisis to be examined occurred in 1587–88. The graphs of burials, Figures 4–6, show high mortality during the winter months, particularly December 1587 and January 1588, although burials were unusually numerous from late fall of 1587 to the spring of the next year.[25] This crisis, then, came during the winter: December, January, and February. This is not characteristic of plague, in which maximum mortality occurs in the summer. Nor is there any mention in the registers of plague—but registers seldom note the cause of death, and it usually has to be inferred from other evidence. An epidemiologist would suspect another disease—ty-

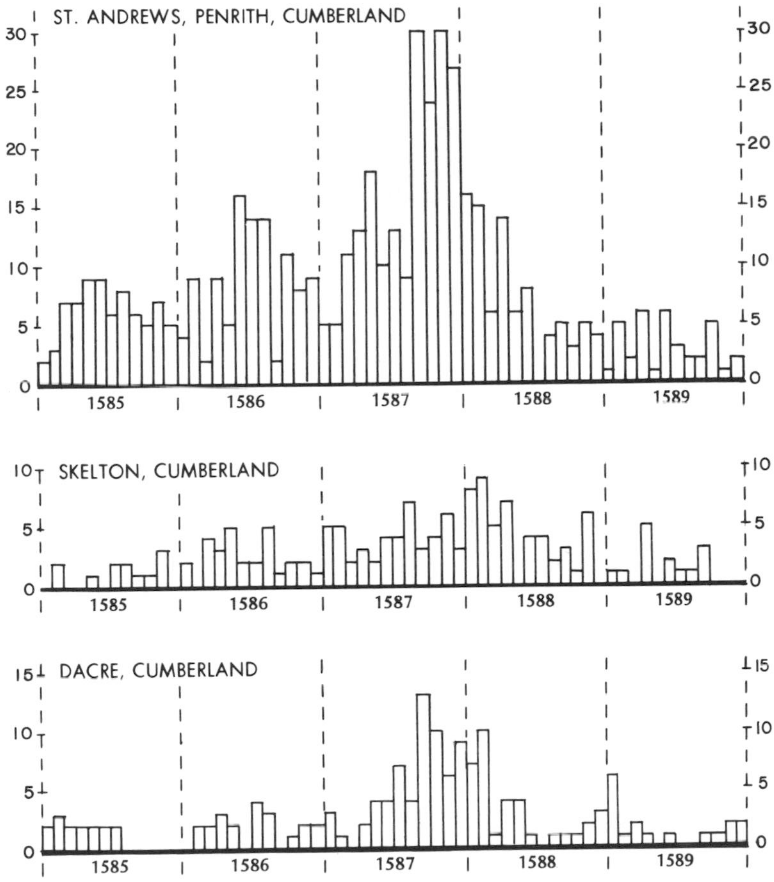

Fig. 5. Burials, 1585–89, in St. Andrews, Penrith; Skelton; and Dacre.

phus, which is carried by human body lice.[26] Epidemic outbreaks of typhus usually begin in winter, when the cold discourages bathing and changing clothes, and disappear with the coming of warm weather. In addition to its winter incidence, typhus very rarely kills children; although they sicken from the disease, their mortality rate is very low.

The registers of Cumberland and Westmorland do not show age at death, but they often indicate a person's status, which can be a rough guide to age. For example, a typical listing in the burials

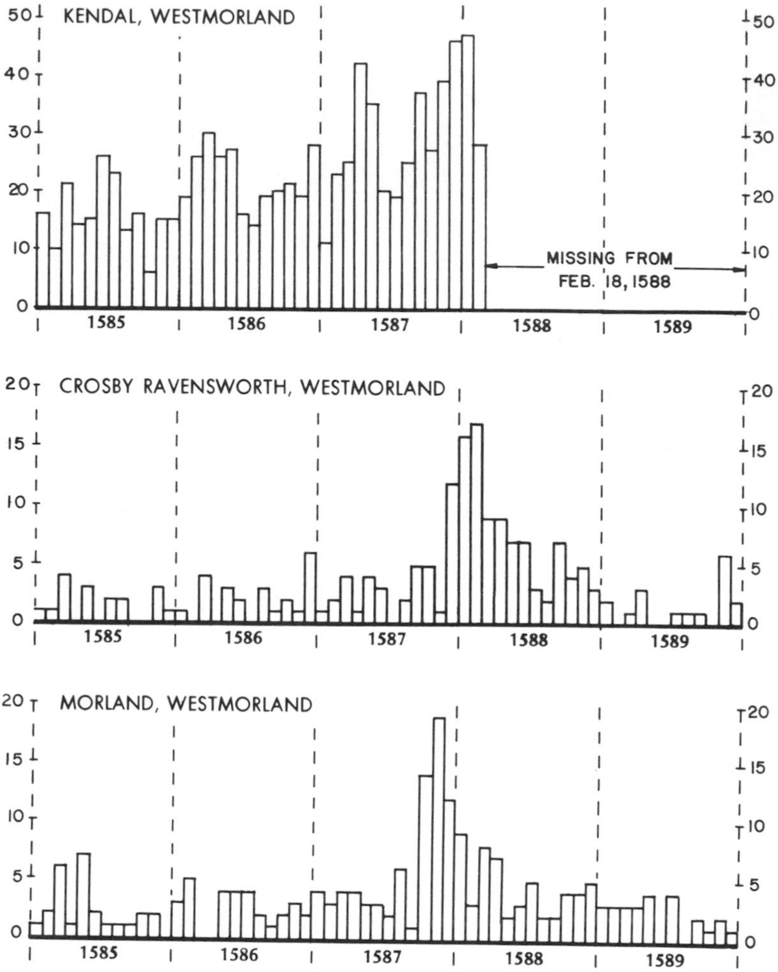

Fig. 6. Burials, 1585–89, in Kendal, Crosby Ravensworth, and Morland.

might be: "Isabell d.[aughter] of Thos. Lowes." Isabell's age at death is a matter of conjecture. She might have been two or 22. There is no way of telling at what age she would have been listed as an independent woman and not as Thomas Lowes's daughter. Certainly when she married, she would then be shown as, say, "Isabell w. of Roberte Dente." Presumably, if she left her father's house for any other reason, or he died and the tenement passed to her brother, she would then be shown simply as "Isabell Lowes'" in the burial register. Obviously, to treat all persons listed as sons and daughters as "children" and all others as "adults" is a rather crude method of determining age, yet if striking changes appear in the numbers of each group in our burial records, they offer a clue to the causes of the mortality under study.[27] In the parish of Dacre in 1587–88, such a change took place. The number of "adults"—as defined by our rough method—increased greatly compared to the previous years, while the number of "children" remained much the same (figures are missing for 1585):

	1582	1583	1584	1586	1587	1588	1589
Children	6	8	11	10	10	16	8
Adults	9	10	13	12	53	21	9

This distribution strongly suggests that the primary cuase of death, in Dacre at least, was typhus. In the adjacent parish of Penrith, adult burials during the two years prior to 1587 slightly exceeded those for children. Then, in 1587, the adult figures leaped to two and one-half times the figures for children. The great preponderance of adult deaths came in winter, as we would expect from typhus. In the parish of Morland, in Westmorland, the same preponderance of adult burials is discernible as in these Cumberland parishes. All this evidence points to typhus.

Could the epidemic have been pneumonic plague? As we have already indicated, this would have been most unlikely, but the possibility cannot be ruled out simply because pneumonic epidemics were unknown in the sixteenth and seventeenth centuries. The winter incidence would agree with the expected pneumonic pattern. Plague had been present in Durham the year before; perhaps a traveler had contracted the disease, developed pneumonia, and became a carrier of pneumonic plague on his return to the western counties. But the stability in the death rate among children argues against any such theory. Children are as susceptible as adults to all forms of plague. The number of children dying would have increased, had pneumonic plague been present.

One of the perplexing aspects of this epidemic was its widespread incidence through the two counties at the same time. In Cumberland, the parishes of Holm Cultram in the northwest, Deane in the west, and Greystoke, Watermillock, Penrith, and Dacre in the south were afflicted. In Westmorland, the parishes of Kendal in the southwest, Kirkby Lonsdale in the southeast, Brough in the east, and Morland in the center suffered. On the other hand, some parishes—such as St. Bees, Shap, and Crosthwaite—seem to have been little affected.[28] In the Wapentake of Morley, in the West Riding, Drake found mortality drastically increased, together with a marked fall in both baptisms and marriages.[29] The cause of the mortality in the West Riding may have been different, of course, but the similarity in timing suggests that it may have been part of the same crisis. Since it is unusual to have an outbreak of typhus in so widespread a rural area at the same time, perhaps famine was hiding behind what apparently was typhus in Cumberland and Westmorland.* Some of the entries in the registers hint that this was the case; there seems to have been an unusual number of deaths among poor people and beggars. The graphs of burials, too, indicate that the winter typhus epidemic may have been preceded by famine during the summer and autumn in those parishes with continued high mortality, such as Greystoke, Penrith, and Holm Cultram. Unfortunately there are no local price series for either county at this time, but food prices were very high in south-central England during the year following the harvest of 1586. Following the harvest of 1587, prices eased.[30] Reports from Northumberland indicate a similar situation in that northern county. Grain prices remained high, and misery was general until August 1587, at which time prices fell.[31] Perhaps in Cumberland and Westmorland, food shortage continued, but we do not know.

In 1586, as grain prices rose, wool prices fell to their lowest point since 1564, 24 percent below the average price for the previous 19 years. Demand for sheepskins and woolfells declined, too, and prices were lower than they had been since 1570. The next year, 1587, saw a slight recovery, but wool prices remained 21 percent

*The connection between typhus and famine was very close; one of the names of typhus was "famine fever."

below the average.[32] Here again, these are national composite figures, which may or may not faithfully reflect local price movements for Cumberland and Westmorland wools. The chances are, however, that demand for the low-quality northern wool would have declined more than these figures indicate. These price movements suggest a collapse in wool demand, at the same time that prices for grain rose in 1586. The following year, grain prices returned to normal, but wool prices remained at a level that may have drastically reduced the purchasing power of the northern farmer.

There is one further bit of evidence that suggests famine. In Chapter 1, we discussed the fall in "conceptions" that occurred during famine years in seventeenth-century France. As we noted there, the term "conception" is really recorded christenings adjusted back to the probable time of conception, that is, minus nine months. In 1587, some of the baptismal registers in Cumberland and Westmorland show such a decrease; in others the drop is too small to be significant. In the parish of Dacre, conceptions in the six years prior to 1587 averaged 28; in 1587 they fell to ten. In 1588 they rose again to 41. In Penrith, conceptions averaged 69 during the previous six years, but dropped to 47 in 1587 before rising to 81 the following year. In Holm Cultram, the five years before 1587 saw an average of 74 conceptions; in that year the number was 49. In 1588 conceptions doubled to 102. It is, of course, possible that the decline in births was not caused by amenorrhea triggered by malnutrition but simply reflected the disease deaths of pregnant women. However, in each case we have cited, the number of births the following year exceeded the average for the year before the crisis. Such an increase would be unlikely if women of childbearing age were dying of disease in such numbers as to affect the number of births.

It is hard to press the argument for starvation too far, particularly since child mortality did not increase proportionately to adult mortality. If starvation had been the sole cause of death, children would have figured prominently in the burials, because children are economically and physiologically the most susceptible to starvation. In addition, some parishes did not experience heightened mortality, while others did. This hit-and-miss pattern suggests epidemic disease, rather than starvation. On the other hand, a decline in conceptions shows that malnutrition was present in some parishes, including one where mortality remained normal. In St. Bees, conceptions averaged 35 per year for the six years preceding 1587, but fell to 17 that year. This pattern of falling conceptions but no rise in the number of burials suggests that food shortage caused amenorrhea but never reached the point of starvation—and therefore left traces on the baptismal register but not on the burial register. In sum, the excess mortality of 1587–88 appears to have been caused by typhus, with some assistance from famine.

CHAPTER EIGHT

The Crises of 1597-1598 and 1623

THE SECOND of our trio of catastrophes took place in 1597–98. It is, in fact, two separate but related crises. The first of these was characterized by high mortality from late 1596 through all of 1597 and extending in some parishes into 1598. Unlike the earlier crisis of 1587–88, it disregarded the seasons entirely (see Figures 7–9). Burials were not so high in winter as to suggest typhus nor so high in summer as to suggest plague, until the summer of 1598, when plague ravaged Penrith, Carlisle, and Kendal. The graphs for both Kendal and Penrith show that by this time the earlier mortality was beginning to subside. In the registers of the former, unfortunately, there is a gap during those months when the plague evidently was as its worst, in the fall of 1598. This visitation of the plague was the second crisis of this short period. There seems no doubt that the cause of the wave of deaths in these three towns in 1598 was plague; the Penrith registers show that it followed the usual summer-fall pattern and died out with the onset of cold weather (Figure 7). Although registers no longer exist for Carlisle, city records show a concentration of deaths in the summer of 1598, when apparently 91 persons died of the disease.[1] In addition to this expected summer incidence, plague devastated only cities and towns, although there were a few cases in rural parishes.[2] Contemporaries identified the epidemic as plague and instituted the usual Elizabethan programs of sanitation, isolation, and poor relief.[3] If we accept the traditional diagnosis of plague as correct for 1598, our

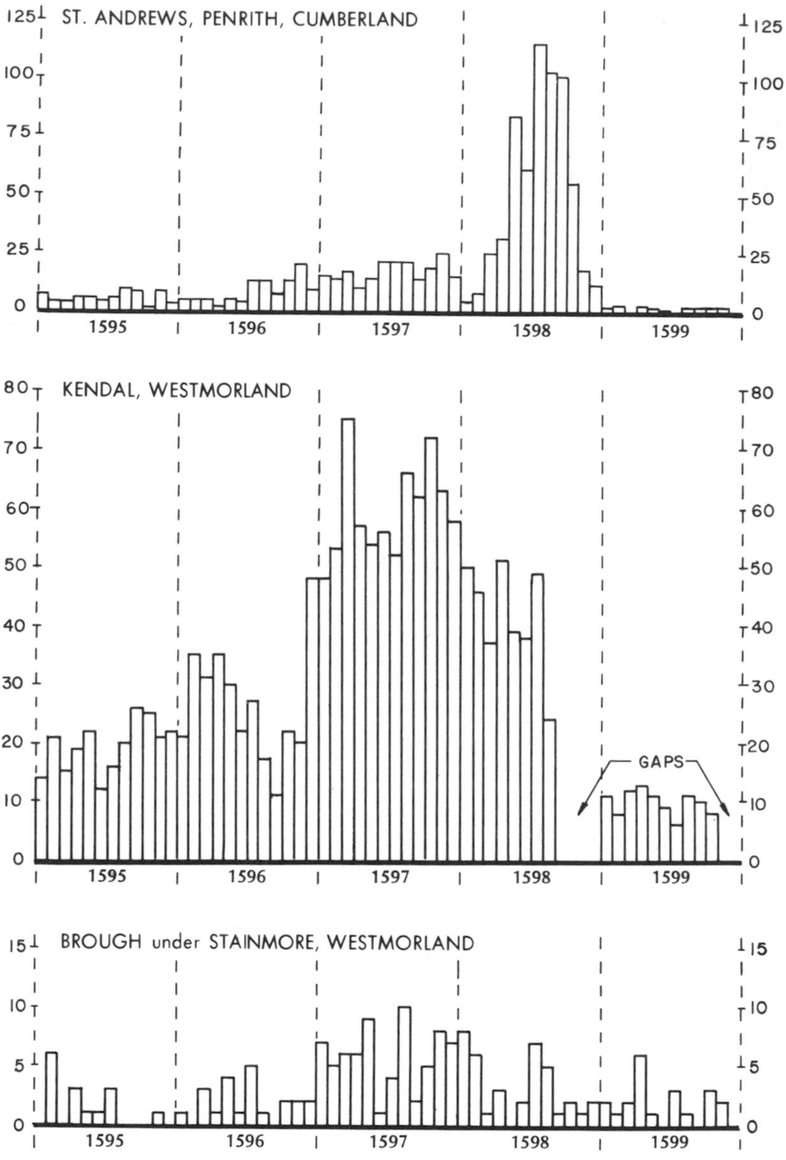

Fig. 7. Burials, 1595–99, in St. Andrews, Penrith; Kendal; and Brough-under-Stainmore.

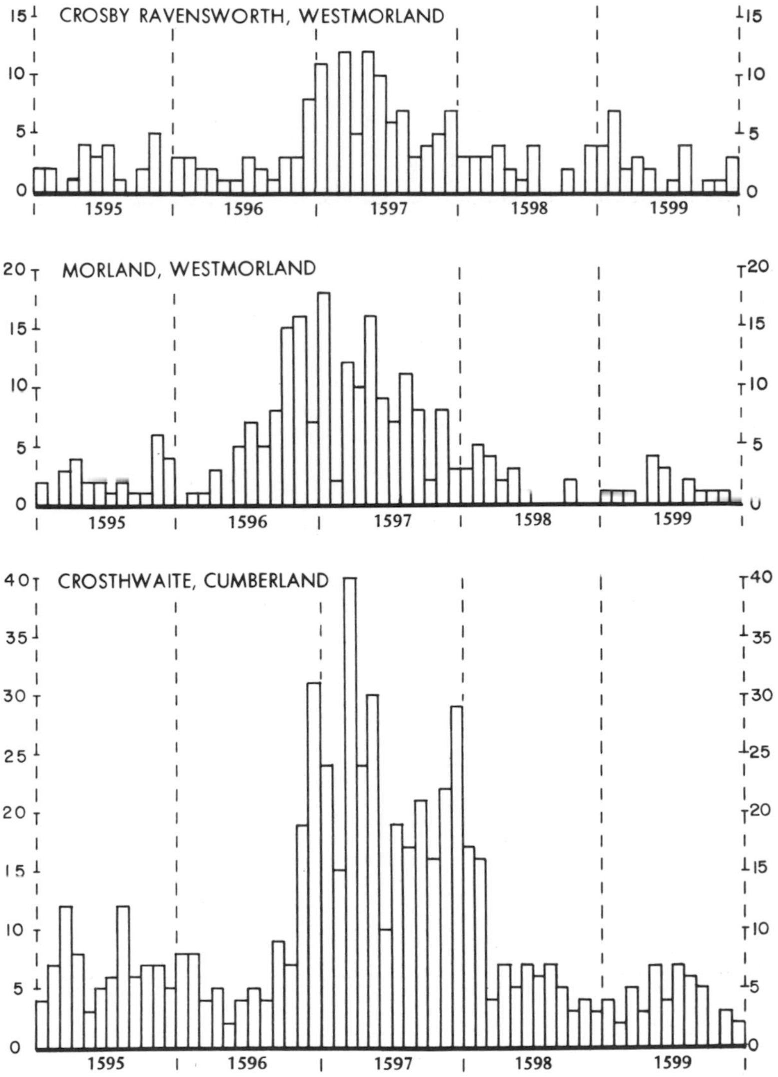

Fig. 8. Burials, 1595–99, in Crosby Ravensworth, Morland, and Crosthwaite.

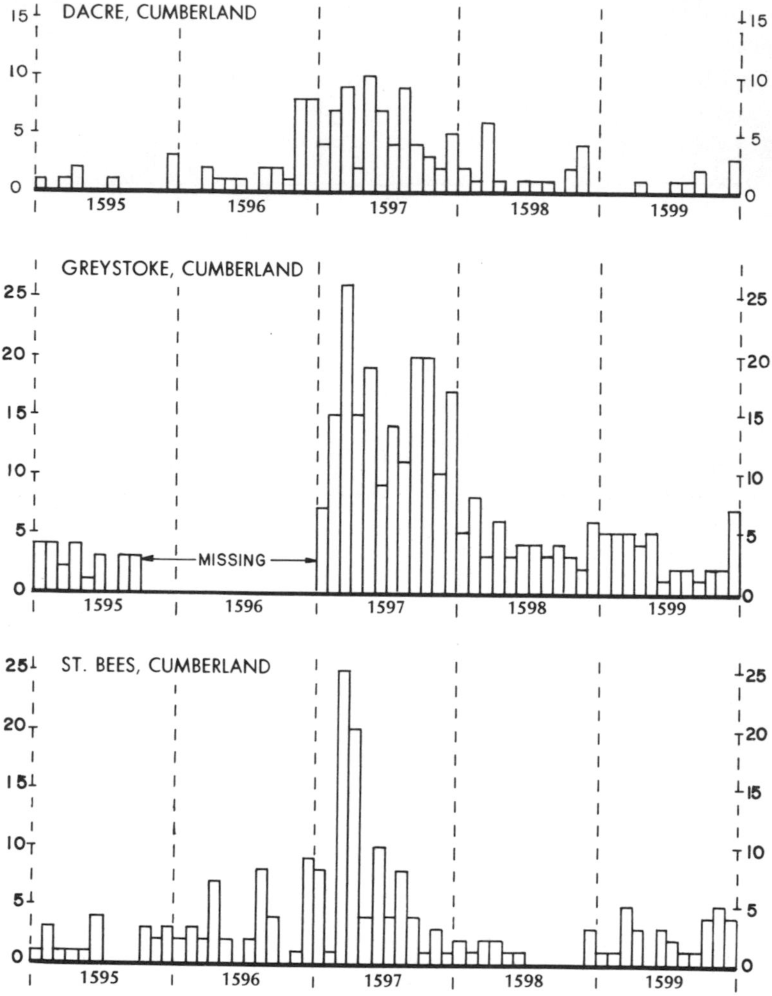

Fig. 9. Burials, 1595–99, in Dacre, Greystoke, and St. Bees.

problem then is to identify the earlier and much more widespread mortality of 1597.

Economic historians are agreed that the years 1594–97 were terrible ones for England, with four successive bad harvests.[4] In 1594, according to W. G. Hoskins, grain prices rose to 30 percent above normal, in 1595 to 36 percent above normal, in 1596 to a record 83 percent above normal, and in 1597 to 64 percent above normal.[5] In 1598 harvests were average to good; prices fell and the four lean years were over. During the years of dearth, 1594–97, not only were all the grains—wheat, barley, oats, and rye—extremely dear, but the price of peas and beans reached unprecedented levels as well. The cost of those two vegetables greatly concerned the poor, who stretched their grain by mixing peas and beans in their bread in times of grain shortage. The price statistics that we have for other items in the diet—particularly milk, cheese, and butter—indicate a somewhat mixed pattern. Cheese was evidently more expensive in 1596 and 1597 than at any previous time. Butter was relatively dear in both years, and milk prices were either average or slightly above. Price evidence of this type is too spotty to be used conclusively, but it indicates that the high cost of grains, peas, and beans was not offset by reductions in the prices of other foodstuffs consumed by the poor.[6] Despite the lack of local price series for Westmorland and Cumberland, we may assume that these statistics, gathered primarily from the south of England, also applied to the north. Such an assumption is supported by other evidence. A citizen of Newcastle wrote, in 1597, of "sundry starving and dying in our streets and in the fields of lack of bread."[7] Newcastle's corporate records confirm the distress: in September and October of 1597, 25 "poore folkes who died for want in the streets" were buried at the town's expense.[8] A dismal picture—yet Newcastle seems to have been better off than other areas in the north, thanks to the importation of foreign grain. But for these grain shipments, thousands would have died of starvation, the Dean of Durham wrote to Robert Cecil.[9] Despite the presence of plague in Newcastle, men came from as far as Carlisle, sixty miles to the west, to buy grain.[10] All along the border, the complaint was of misery caused by the great dearth of food and the raids of the Scots. In the Barony of Gilsland, one of the Queen's holdings in Cumberland, the land sergeant reported in November 1597 that the Barony was in complete decay, owing in part to the "great dearth and famyn wherwith the country hath been punished extreamelie their three hard yeares bypast."[11] The Warden of the West March, Lord Scrope, wrote of the difficulty of collecting rents due the Queen from her tenants in the Barony of Burgh, also in Cumberland. Many were unable to pay. The goods of some had been seized, but others were so poor that they owned nothing worth distraining. Scrope added coldly that these unfortunates would either be kept in prison or turned out of their tenements until they paid.[12] On the east coast the Governor of Berwick reported several deaths a week from the scarcity and the foul quality of the few provisions that were available.[13] Indeed, the dearth of 1597 was general throughout England, as we shall see in the next chapter.

In view of the evidence, the mortality was apparently caused by starvation, not by epidemic disease. If starvation was the culprit, most of the deaths should have coincided roughly with the harvest year, following a harvest failure. It is important to remember that harvest years do not correspond to calendar years, but run approximately from the end of one September to the end of the next September. The mortality following the disastrous harvest of 1596 would then have fallen mostly in 1597, allowing a short lag as the poor took the desperate measure of selling their few possessions to avert starvation. The prolonged high mortality of 1597 agrees reasonably well with what should have been expected, except that excessive deaths continued after the harvest of 1597 into the winter of 1598. As we have seen, the harvest of 1597 too was a failure—and starvation probably continued without a break.

Here we have a problem though: why did the mortality taper off in the spring of 1598? Assuming a correspondence between deaths and high prices, is there any reason to suppose that prices broke in spring? It seems more reasonable that they would have remained high until the coming harvest, or at least until May or June, when the abundance of the harvest could be predicted. If the forecast was for a good yield, farmers who had stores of grain would be anxious to sell their stocks before prices tumbled in the fall. These sales would depress grain prices in the summer. Peter Bowden has observed that wheat prices usually fell during the summer, whatever the forecast, and suggests that demand declined more sharply than the existing supply of wheat. In other words, by summer people had run out of money; either they ate less bread or they switched from wheat to inferior grains. In either case, many families had exhausted all surplus from the preceding harvest, "and starvation stared many starkly in the face."[14]

Extending this argument, demand might well decline before summer in a dearth of several years such as 1594–97. All surpluses would have disappeared long before the summer of 1598. Deaths would have depleted the consuming population. Perhaps we are thrown back on a Malthusian explanation: by the spring of 1598 there were simply few enough mouths left so that the limited supply of grain was sufficient and had fallen to a price within reach of the survivors. It is also possible that imports of grain from Ireland or directly from the Baltic may have supplemented the grain brought over the mountains from Newcastle; unfortunately, however, no records of any such imports exist.[15] The Vicar of Tamworth in Staffordshire may have described a situation as true in Cumberland and Westmorland as in his own county, however, when he wrote on March 29, 1598, that "the darth of corn [is] somewhat abated by reason of Deathe and Danske Rye."[16]

Does all this point conclusively to starvation, however? The historical demographer Peter Laslett has said there are three requirements necessary to prove that people actually died of starvation: first, that there was a "sudden, sharp" increase in mortality; second, that there was a decline in "conceptions and perhaps in marriages"; and third, that the stated "cause of death" was starvation or diseases caused by malnutrition.[17] As for the first, I think he demands a too-uniform society. All the poor did not necessarily run out of food or the ability to purchase it at the same time. The mortality might have risen gradually, as more and more families exhausted their limited resources and were pushed to the starvation point or fell prey to deficiency diseases. As Laslett himself says, the pattern Pierre Goubert found in the Beauvaisis[18]—an almost exclusively grain-growing region with cottage industry unusually sensitive to a decline in demand—would not necessarily be paralleled in the north of England. Although perhaps as poor as the Beauvaisis, Cumberland and Westmorland had a more diversified economy, with cattle and sheep raising as well as arable farming.

Laslett's second point on the decline of conceptions (as discussed above, the term refers to time of christening minus nine months) is borne out in the registers of some of the parishes with high mortality in 1597. In Dacre, conceptions for the years 1591–95 averaged 23. In 1596 they fell to 14 and in 1597 to 12. In Crosthwaite, the years 1591–95 saw an average of 93 conceptions, but 1596 had only 62 and 1597 only 51. Although there are gaps in the Greystoke baptismal register, the four years 1591–94 contain an average of 53 conceptions, whereas only 35 are recorded in 1597. In Penrith the average during 1591–95 was 70, falling then to 54 in 1596 and 29 in 1597. In all the parishes shown above, the conceptions rose again in 1598 to the level of the early 1590's, with the exception of Penrith, where they rose only to 42. This was a plague year for the town, and the epidemic held conceptions at a low level for the second straight year.

Unfortunately, Laslett's third requirement—that the stated cause of death be given as starvation or related disease—is usually impossible to fulfill. As I noted before, and as he recognizes, the stated cause of death is rarely given in any of the registers except in cases of plague. So we must rely on inference if we are to say that starvation contributed to the death figures.

I should like to suggest another method for determining whether or not people died of famine:

1. There must be a dramatic increase in mortality, rising either rapidly or gradually. It is difficult to give a precise range, but burials twice normal would alert a researcher that some type of demographic crisis was present.* In the parishes of Cumberland and Westmorland, burials in 1597 and 1623 were on the order of four times normal. In 1587–88, there was great variation between parishes, from less than two to four times normal. In Penrith in 1598—a plague year—burials reached 13 times normal. Put simply, there

*"Normal" is here defined as an average of burials for a number of non-crisis base years. The base years will vary from parish to parish because of gaps in the registers.

has to be evidence of a demographic crisis before the causes of the crisis can be examined.

2. This increase should be detectable in several neighboring parishes at approximately the same time. There are two reasons for this stipulation. First, economic distress probably would have been more widespread than an epidemic, especially in sparsely populated rural areas, where disease has difficulty spreading to all the hamlets or villages in a region. Obviously, exceptions are possible, such as small pockets of economic depression or widely dispersed epidemics. Second, finding the increase in burials in more than one adjoining parish acts as a test of the parish clerk. Quantitative evidence collected from only one parish is somewhat suspect because the registering clerk, for some reason, may record more burials at one time than another. What appears as an increase in mortality really might have been an increase in registration. It is unlikely, however, that several neighboring parish registrars all became especially zealous during the same few months. It might be mentioned here that a coincident fall of marriages and baptisms would have meant a divergence in registrations—and it seems most unlikely that any parish clerk would become enthusiastic about recording burials at the same time that he became lax about recording other vital events. My personal impression, gained from analyzing hundreds of registers, is that the parish clerks on the whole were very reliable, although inevitably they occasionally omitted a burial or baptism. This inevitable underregistration, it should be noted, would minimize the dimensions of any crisis of mortality, making it appear less deadly than it was in fact.

3. Epidemic diseases should be considered and eliminated as probable causes.

4. A correlation should exist between prices and the mortality curve. This can be extremely difficult where local price series do not exist and the correlation must then be interpolated from national price statistics—a risky business. As a contributor to starvation, food prices are relative, of course. A depression in the clothing industry would have the same effect as high food prices, since unemployment

and low returns from raw wool sales would reduce income, eventually to the point where even the cheapest food could not be bought. Conversely, relatively high food prices might easily be afforded by the same persons when cloth demand was high.

5. Some contemporary accounts should refer to dearth, misery or death from want, either in the registers or in other material.

6. The dead should include a high proportion of infants and children, who are physiologically the most vulnerable to starvation, and also of economically marginal persons, such as wanderers, beggars, widows, and—again—children.

7. There should be fewer conceptions than usual, as food shortage induced amenorrhea. A fall in conceptions is more likely to indicate famine than epidemic disease, but this decline is not conclusive proof of the presence of famine. Very often conceptions did not fall in epidemics of plague. For example, conceptions actually rose slightly in the Crosthwaite plague of 1646, and the plagues of 1603 and 1625 in southern England were not accompanied by a decline in conceptions.* At other times, however, a plague epidemic brought about a precipitous fall in conceptions.[19] (The use of the term "conceptions" is somewhat misleading when applied to plague; probably the effect on baptisms was due to spontaneous abortions, flight from the infected community, voluntary abstinence, and so forth, but plague probably did not prevent ovulation in any manner similar to malnutrition.) Perhaps the effect of plague and other epidemic diseases varied with the severity of the epidemic. Too little research has as yet been done to establish any pattern, except it seems that conceptions *always* decline during periods of famine and *sometimes* during epidemics.

8. There should be a total absence of negative evidence unless such evidence can be proved to be spurious. Examples of negative evidence would be any reports of good harvests or of general prosperity.

In the discussion of the mortality of 1597, I believe I have satisfied all the criteria except numbers 3, 6, and 8. Regarding 3—the

* See Figures 15 and 16, pp. 129, 136.

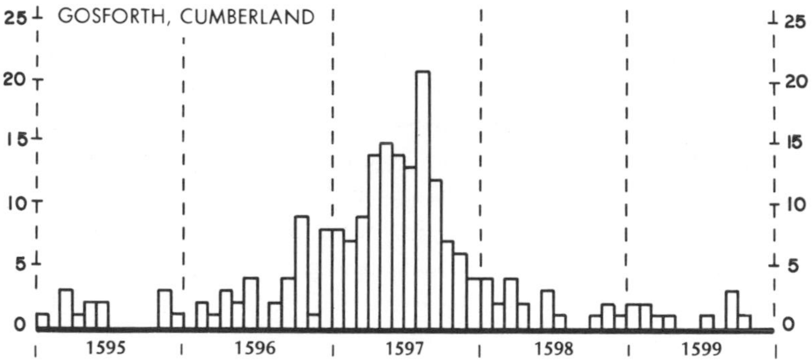

Fig. 10. Burials, 1595–99, in Gosforth.

presence of epidemic disease—I have ruled out bubonic plague and typhus. Even in the parish of Gosforth (Figure 10), where the mortality reached dreadful proportions in the summer of 1597, I doubt that plague was present. The high mortality began in the winter of 1596 and extended on through the early spring; this was not the plague pattern. The dead came from scattered small hamlets throughout this rural parish; as we shall see with the plague in Crosthwaite in 1646, the disease was usually concentrated in one or two communities. No other instances of plague were reported in Cumberland until late 1597, when a few cases were reported in eastern Cumberland, before the onset of the cold weather; it is difficult to see how the disease could have reached Gosforth a year earlier. Finally, the registers do not mention plague as the cause of death. However, Gosforth remains something of a mystery because the mortality was so extreme, considerably higher than one would expect even from the most devastating famine. Epidemic disease of some sort—and plague remains a possibility—may have added its killing power to the famine. Aside from Gosforth, however, there is nothing to suggest either plague or typhus being responsible for the mortality of 1597.

But could other diseases have caused the deaths? Pneumonic plague can be eliminated, since high mortality continued through the summer of 1597. If pneumonic plague had been the cause of death in the winter and spring of that year, it would have (as in the

Black Death) changed its aspect to bubonic in the early summer. But bubonic plague only appeared in the late fall of 1597. Influenza has been blamed for high mortality in 1557 and was probably also the true identity of the "sweating sickness" of the early sixteenth century.[20] But influenza has two characteristics that make it an improbable choice: its low mortality and its quick epidemic course through a community. Of course, a population weakened by malnutrition might have been unusually susceptible to pulmonary complications, such as pneumonia, that could have increased the death toll, but mortality of the extent seen in 1597 is very unlikely. In addition, an epidemic of influenza runs its course in approximately seven weeks. If extra time is allowed for pneumonia, this still does not coincide with the prolonged high mortality of 1597.[21] Smallpox, the dread killer of the eighteenth century, only became epidemically important in England after 1600. In the north, it appears in the records from 1650, and seems to have been centered in cities and towns.[22] The odds are certainly remote that it could have struck all these rural parishes in 1597. In addition, a widespread epidemic would probably have caused some comment in the registers or in other material. Smallpox is an ugly affliction; as Charles Creighton said, "there is hardly anything more distinctive or more loathsome."[23] But there is no mention of any such disease. Another possibility is dysentery, but it raged in late summer, killed primarily the young, and did not cause a drop in conceptions.[24] Such a pattern does not agree with our findings. The diseases I have mentioned are generally considered by medical historians to have been the great epidemic killers of the sixteenth and seventeenth centuries—and none of them satisfactorily fits the evidence from the registers.

There are some indications that a large proportion of the dead were economically marginal, thereby satisfying my sixth criterion. Unfortunately, only occasionally did parish clerks describe in any way those who died, and a quantitative analysis of such descriptions would be statistically meaningless. But the reader gains the impression that wandering paupers, widows, and children figure more frequently in the 1597 registers than at other times. The unusually informative Greystoke registers, for example, record the deaths in

October of Margaret Edmondson "a young wench fatherless and motherless" and her brother William. A large number of entries record the death of a "pore widow." Children, often fatherless and motherless like the Edmondsons mentioned above, are very frequently listed. Such entries add at least some substance to an argument favoring starvation as a cause of death.

The last criterion I have included is the absence of contradictory evidence, that is, evidence of good times or other circumstances, besides famine, that would explain the heightened death level. There is no contradictory evidence. It is true that incursions by the Scots were annoying and destructive during the 1590's, but the raiders seldom entered the parishes studied. Undoubtedly, the raiding and general lawlessness worsened the dearth, but they did not contribute directly to the mortality. No mention is made in the registers of death at the hands of Scottish raiders, yet that is the very type of information the clerk would be inclined to include. Besides, the Scots raided throughout the last half of the sixteenth century, and deaths caused by them would be more or less constant and, therefore, not a satisfactory explanation of the surmortality of 1597. Until other evidence comes to light, I think we must tentatively accept starvation as the cause of the excessive number of deaths in 1597.

Although in most parishes the mortality level returned to normal, or below, by 1599, the parish of Kirkby Lonsdale in the southeast of Westmorland experienced a crisis that year. The numbers of people dying rose in 1598, climbing to extraordinary heights in March and April of 1599. This is too early in the year for plague. Possibly there was a local outbreak of typhus. More work needs to be done to explain the cause of this mortality. Kirkby Lonsdale lies at the extreme edge of the two-county region; it may be that the cause of this crisis will be found in a study of nearby Lancashire parishes.

The crisis of 1623—the last in this depressing recital of death—is confirmed in each of the 27 registers inspected. In general, the burial curve rose in winter or early spring of 1623 and continued at a high level into 1624 (see Figures 11–14). The seasonal distribution does not suggest the presence of plague, except perhaps in the

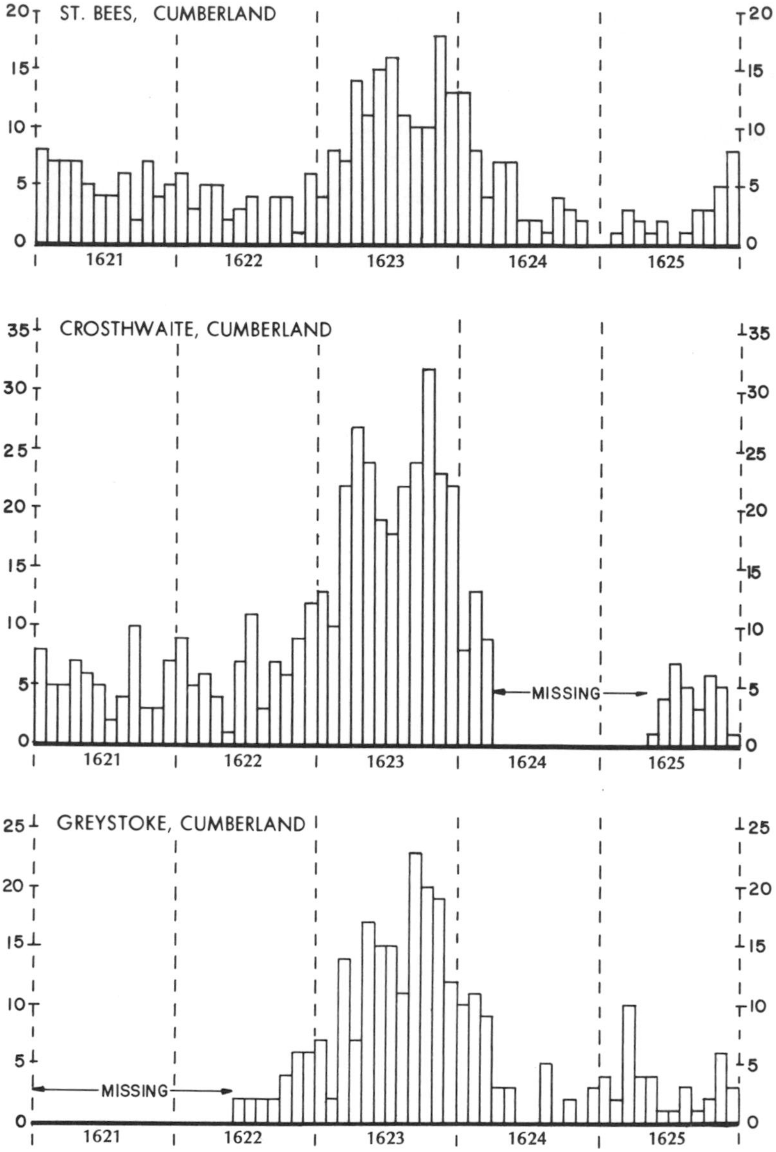

Fig. 11. Burials, 1621–25, in St. Bees, Crosthwaite, and Greystoke.

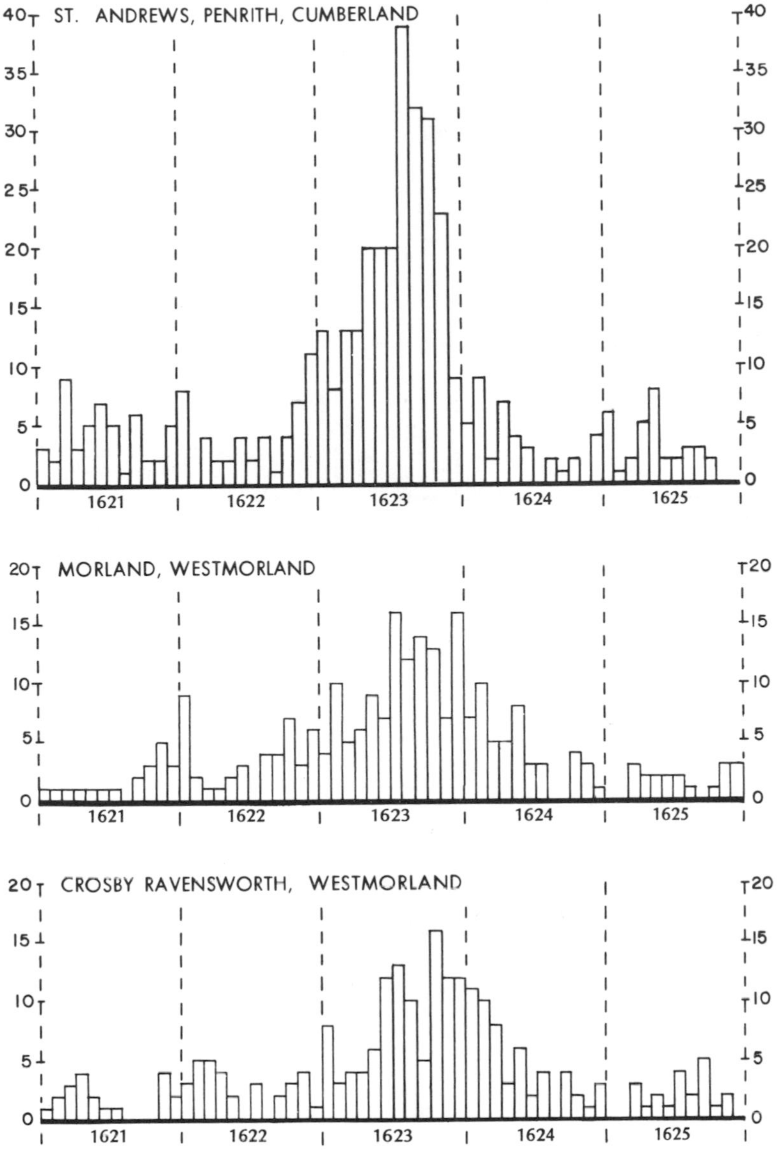

Fig. 12. Burials, 1621–25, in St. Andrews, Penrith; Morland; and Crosby Ravensworth.

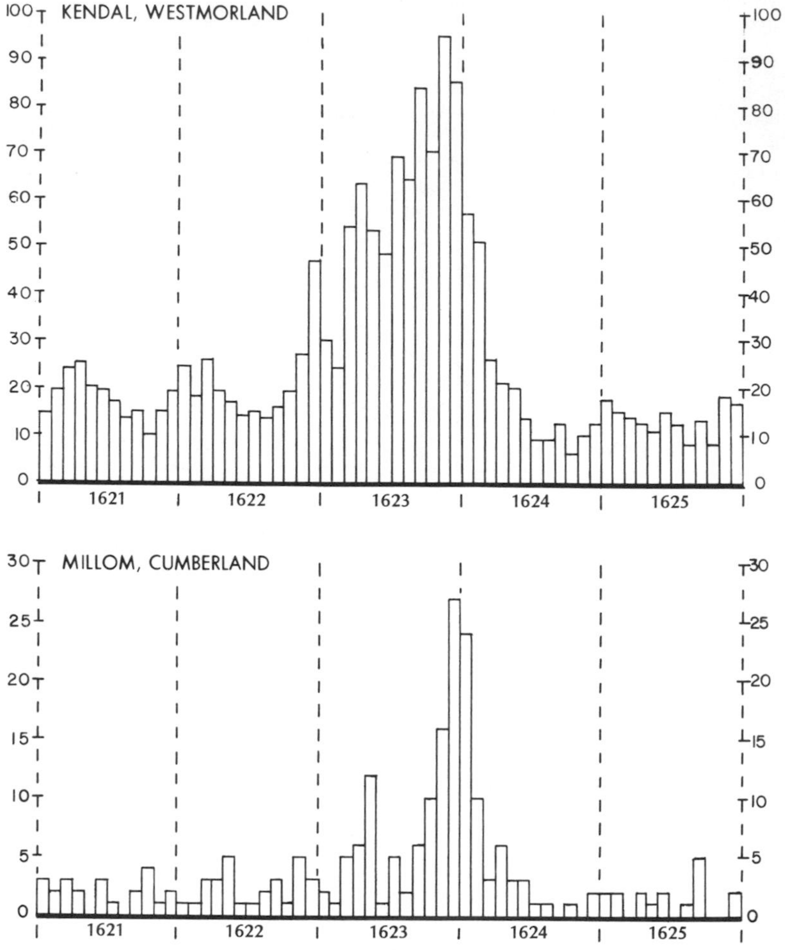

Fig. 13. Burials, 1621–25, in Kendal and Millom.

parish of Penrith. In 1598, when plague ravaged the town, it was identified in the registers; had the disease been present in 1623, it would have been quickly recognized. But the Penrith registers make no mention of plague. Kendal too had identified the disease in 1598, and again there is no reference to it in 1623. Nor are there any reports of plague in other local records or in the State Papers. The

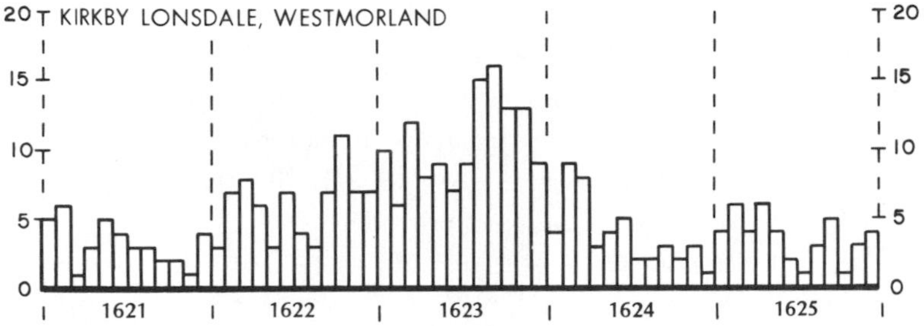

Fig. 14. Burials, 1621–25, in Kirkby Lonsdale.

importance of this should be emphasized. If plague was in an area, much normal activity came to a halt. Justices of the peace stayed home—and wrote the Council justifying their inaction by reference to the disease. Indeed, the State Papers tend to exaggerate rather than minimize the extent of a plague outbreak. Mere rumors of the disease are reported as fact in letters to Westminster. In 1597 and 1598, the parish registers, other local records, and State Papers are full of news of plague in the north. In contrast, none of these mentions plague during 1623 and 1624 until November of the latter year, when it was reported in Dunfermline, Scotland. The seasonal distribution of the burials and the deaths of many children argue against an epidemic of typhus. Smallpox, influenza, and dysentery can be ruled out, for the same reasons given in the discussion of the crisis of 1597. Apparently epidemic disease was not the cause of the majority of the deaths.[25]

A close correlation between prices and mortality is impossible for 1623, as for the other years, because of a lack of local price statistics. Nationally, however, 1622 was a year of dearth, and grain prices reached levels higher than at any other time between 1597 and 1630.[26] The north of England may have suffered more than the south, although reports from the borders are scarce. In Scotland, as we shall see in the next chapter, the shortage was appalling. In June 1623 (that is, toward the end of the harvest year of 1622) the Scottish Privy Council wrote that if some form of relief was not found for the poor during that summer, then many would migrate south to England or "will sterve through hunger."[27] The harvest of 1623 should have eased prices somewhat. However, the English Privy Council reported on December 23, 1623, that "both in the North partes and in the Westerne partes of this realme the prizes of corne does yet remaine high and are likely to increase as the yeare growes on."[28] Perhaps the harvest of 1623 varied with the locality, and dearth continued into 1624 in the north.

The evidence pointing to starvation in 1623 is extremely strong in one respect: the registers of Greystoke explicitly give starvation as the cause of certain of the deaths in that year. In January, the register records the burial of "a poore fellowe destitute of succour." In March, the interments of "a poore hungersterven beger child" and "a poore hungerstarved begger boye" were recorded. In May, "James Irwen, a poore beger striplinge . . . died . . . in great miserie." In the same month, "a poore man destitute of meanies to live" died. These examples do not exhaust the cases of starvation; the registers reflect a long year of misery for the inhabitants of the parish. Some, but by no means all, of those dying were from outside the parish. The roads must have thronged with unfortunates, many of them children, seeking a bit of food. Unfortunately, Greystoke had none to give.

These same registers show that a large number of the dead were children, widows, and the elderly—those least able to sustain themselves in times of shortage. Although the registers from other parishes do not contain the specific detail of the Greystoke register, there is no reason to suppose that their mortality arose from a different cause. In all the parishes, the seasonal distribution of the burials is very similar to that of Greystoke. Also very similar was the decline in conceptions in various other parishes. Using the precrisis years 1619–22 and the postcrisis years 1625–27 as a base, we find that conceptions in Crosthwaite fell from an annual average of 100 to 35 in 1623, in Penrith from 61 to 26, in Crosby Ravensworth from 36 to 14, and in Brough-under-Stainmore from 41 to 15. There are gaps in the Greystoke baptismal register that prevent an identical comparison, but an average based on the years 1625–28 gives 38 conceptions. In 1623, the number was 15. In St. Bees, on a base of

1620–22 and 1624–27, the average was 50 conceptions, compared with 21 in 1623. In all these instances, conceptions declined by more than half. We are forced to conclude that famine gripped the area firmly in 1623, as it had in 1597. Indeed, it appears from the burial figures that 1623 was more terrible, despite the possibility that food prices were absolutely lower than in 1597. The area was also squeezed by a depression in the clothing industry and a collapse of raw wool demand.[29] The loss of income coupled with high food prices appears to have been even more catastrophic than the series of harvest failures of the 1590's.

In the short period from 1587 to 1623, there were two years of famine, 1597 and 1623; one year of plague, 1598; and one year of typhus probably aggravated by famine, 1587. Never again was there a similar demographic crisis in the two counties. As would be expected, epidemics broke out periodically. Plague ravaged Carlisle in 1645,[30] spread to Keswick in 1646,[31] Cockermouth in 1647,[32] and St. Bees in 1650.[33] This seems to have been the same epidemic, although it took four years to cross Cumberland. An interesting comparison can be made between the epidemic in Keswick and the earlier mortalities of 1597 and 1623. In 1597, 267 burials were recorded for the parish of Crosthwaite, which included the town of Keswick. There were 256 burials in 1623. In both these years, the dead came from hamlets scattered throughout the large, rural parish. The geographic distribution of the burials in 1646, when 180 died, was totally different. The number of burials increased dramatically in May and continued high through September—the usual plague season. Of the 93 persons dying between May 14, the beginning of the epidemic, and July 28, 80 came from Keswick, 11 from "Eskenbec," and the homes of the other two were not shown. After July 28, unfortunately only the names of the dead were given, not their place of residence. Eskenbec does not appear on the Ordnance Survey Map and was apparently also unknown to the transcriber of the registers, who placed a question mark after the name. It may have been a part of Keswick or a separate small community. The striking concentration of all the dead who can be geo-

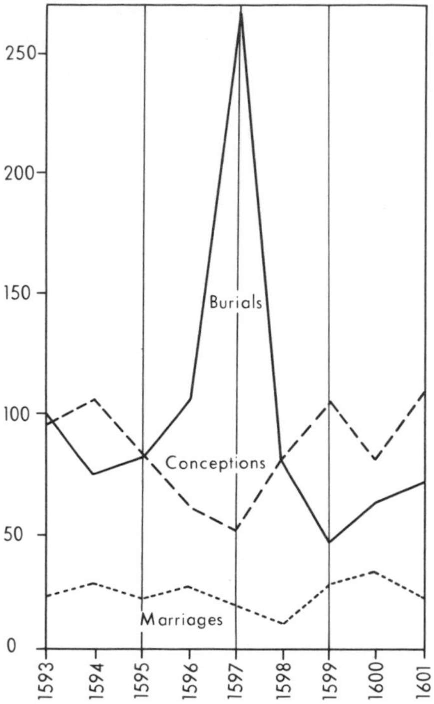

Fig. 15. Conceptions, burials, and marriages in Crosthwaite. Above, 1593–1601; opposite, top, 1619–27; opposite, bottom, 1641–51.

graphically placed in no more than two communities indicates that the disease did not spread into all the rural parts of the parish. Most of the parish was spared in 1646, in contrast to 1597 and 1623.

It is also interesting to compare the conceptions, burials, and marriages in Crosthwaite for the three demographic crises of 1597, 1623, and 1646. As before, conceptions are baptisms adjusted by nine months. Conceptions dipped in 1596 and 1597, and again in 1622 and 1623, the years of famine. In the plague year of 1646, however, conceptions remained at a normal level, even though burials rose dramatically. (See Figure 15.) Three years after the plague of 1646, burials again exceeded conceptions, by a slight degree. This year, 1649, was one of a series of bad years, when harvests failed and grain prices soared.[34] There were even reports of starva-

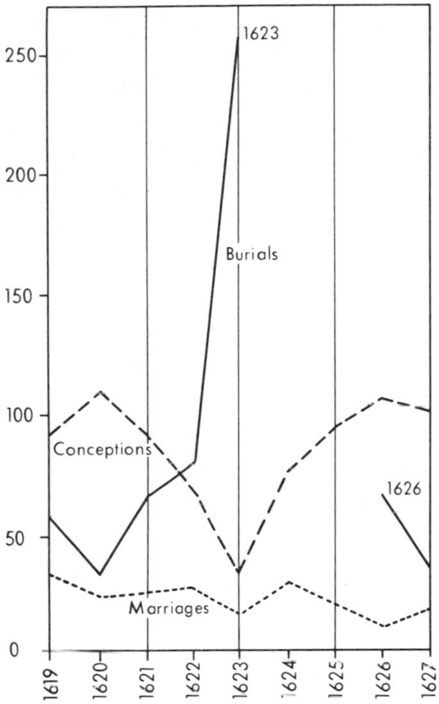

1623
Burials
Conceptions
1626
Marriages
250
200
150
100
50
0
1619
1620
1621
1622
1623
1624
1625
1626
1627

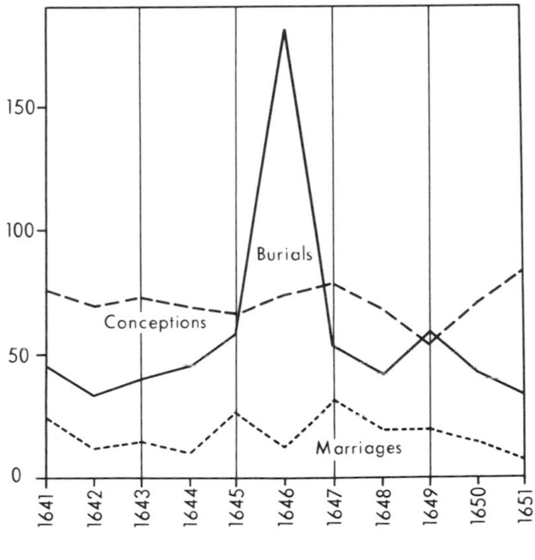

Burials
Conceptions
Marriages
150
100
50
0
1641
1642
1643
1644
1645
1646
1647
1648
1649
1650
1651

tion (see discussion on p. 155). In this year, conceptions dipped, hinting at the onset of amenorrhea, caused by severe food shortage.

Typhus appeared in Carlisle in 1781, killing 49 persons in the city and three others who tended convalescent patients who had gone to nearby villages.[35] John Heysham, a Carlisle physician who witnessed the epidemic, blamed the outbreak on overcrowding, bad ventilation, and lack of cleanliness. The fever raged primarily among the poor, who lived in "narrow, close, confined lanes, and in small crowded apartments."[36] By that time, it should be noted, Carlisle had become an industrial town of 6,300 people; with many "little dirty confined place[s]."[37] Except for the three villagers who contracted the disease, no person outside the city died. The disease showed no power to spread through the surrounding countryside.

Smallpox, the great scourge of the eighteenth century, afflicted various communities at various times, such as Penrith in 1656, but never caused as great or as widespread a mortality as any of the three great crises. In eighteenth-century Whitehaven, then the largest city in the region, smallpox smouldered endemically, killing a few children each year. Every few years, an epidemic would break out and spread quickly through the available pool of unexposed children. In 1758, such an epidemic killed 98, of whom all but two were ten years of age or younger. In 1772, 81 died, and four years later, 79 died. In these last two epidemics, only children under ten were stricken, except for one American sailor, aged fifty, who apparently had never contracted the disease in his native Rhode Island.[38] These epidemics, with the possible exception of that of 1758, had little effect on the neighboring rural parish of St. Bees and no traceable ramifications elsewhere in the county. Put simply, the epidemics of smallpox did not spread into the Cumberland countryside.

These examples of later epidemics are given to underline one point: the same diseases that could have caused the catastrophes of 1587, 1597, and 1623 were all present in the region later, but did not cause any comparable mortality. Neither typhus nor smallpox spread from the city to the country but remained localized. In 1597, on the other hand, 30 parishes out of 31 for which we have the burial figures suffered heightened mortality. The same pattern emerged in 1623, when 27 parishes out of 27 suffered. Twenty out of 24 parishes experienced the crisis in 1587. The geographical distribution of all three earlier crises, when compared with the very limited extent of later epidemics, strongly suggests that epidemic disease—unless it was some odd combination of three or four maladies all falling at roughly the same time—was not a major ingredient in the death figures for 1597 and 1623, and was only a partial factor in the mortality of 1587.

One last theory should be considered here: admitting a severe dearth, could malnutrition have so lowered the resistance of the poor that a disease exhibited a virulence that under ordinary circumstances it lacked? This relation between food shortage and famine was expressed by contemporaries as "first dearth, then plague."[39] This subject is complex and controversial, but recent studies indicate that this is an unlikely explanation.[40] In the Warsaw ghetto, where thousands of Jews were methodically starved to death between 1940 and 1943, "among both children and adults epidemics were very rare and, when they occurred, ran a benign course."[41] Typhus was endemic, but was probably more a product of the terrible overcrowding than of the starvation.[42] Tuberculosis was also very common but was not a major cause of death. In other famines of World War II, in Greece in 1942 and in Holland in 1945, there were no unusual epidemics.[43] Of course, we cannot fully test the saying "first dearth, then plague," because there was no plague in any of these modern famines, but if parallels to other diseases exist, it is probably false.[44]

It is perhaps surprising that in 1597 and 1623 there was no discernible difference in mortality between highland and lowland regions, or between towns and the countryside, or between the purely agricultural regions and the cloth-manufacturing parishes of Westmorland. Mortality for the towns of Penrith and Kendal may be exaggerated somewhat because some of the dead may have been poor from the countryside, who sought charity in the towns and died there.

Who starved, in each of these crises? Probably the hardest hit were the numerous smallholders who had enclosed a parcel of pasture or forest land and bolstered the precarious living drawn from the holding with whatever occasional farm employment they could find. In pastoral areas this employment was never plentiful and in bad years laborers would have been quickly let go, after rains destroyed the crops or depleted the flocks, because there was less work to be done and perhaps no food to share. Many of the subtenants would have been in a similar condition; their subtenancies were too small to provide for their families without outside work. The subtenants—that shadowy group—may also have been pressed by their landlords, who saw their own incomes fall. If these landlords were themselves customary tenants, they might decide to work the land themselves in a bad year, rather than let it out. At least this would assure them of more grain, at a time when grain might be impossible to buy. This is, of course, conjecture; we know too little of the impact of famine on these marginal people.

CHAPTER NINE

The Famines of 1597 and 1623 in England and Europe

At this juncture, let us momentarily shift our attention away from the northwest and place the two crises of 1597 and 1623 within a larger context to see to what extent they afflicted the other northern counties, the rest of England, and indeed other parts of Europe.

The years 1595–97 were years of starvation over much of northern Europe. In France, burials were not usually registered at that time, but Pierre Goubert is confident that the abrupt fall in baptisms and marriages in 1597 signaled "a great crisis in subsistence" that year.[1] Sweden suffered a terrible famine in 1596. A contemporary described its effects as follows:[2]

> People ground and chopped many unsuitable things into bread; such as mash, chaff, bark, buds, nettles, leaves, hay, straw, peatmoss, nutshells, pea-stalks, etc. This made people so weak and their bodies so swollen that innumerable people died. Many widows, too, were found dead on the ground with red hummock grass, seeds which grew in the fields, and other kinds of grass in their mouths. People were found dead in the houses, under barns, in the ovens of bath houses and wherever they had been able to squeeze in, so that, God knows, there was enough to do getting them to the graveyard, though the dogs ate many of the corpses. Children starved to death at their mothers' breast, for they had nothing to give them suck. . . . At times these and other afflictions came and also the bloody flux which put people in such a plight that countless died of it.

The bloody flux—that is, bloody dysentery—mentioned toward the end of the quotation was probably a symptom of terminal starvation, rather than an outbreak of bacterial dysentery. (See Chapter 1, p. 8.)

Across the borders, Scotland knew a year of great dearth in 1595 and the distress continued into 1598, aggravated by outbreaks of plague in central and southern Scotland in 1597.[3] Famine was reported from as far south as Hungary, where it was said that Tartar women ate their own children.[4] In Spain, the impact of the dearth was complicated by a widespread epidemic of plague, but prices in 1598 reached their highest point in the sixteenth century and there was undoubtedly widespread malnourishment, if not actual starvation.[5] On the other hand, Italy seems to have been largely famine-free in the 1590's, according to a recent chronological study of crises in that peninsula.[6] Possibly the Mediterranean climate, where drought was more of a danger to the crops than excessive rainfall, explains why Italy was spared.

How serious was the dearth in England, aside from the counties of Cumberland and Westmorland? Certainly other parts of the north suffered badly. In the preceding chapter, we mentioned the reports of starvation in Newcastle and Berwick and the bishop of Durham's letter to Cecil claiming that grain imports had saved thousands from starvation. The mortality was high in the West Riding of Yorkshire in 1597 although not as elevated as that of 1587–88 had been.[7] In much of Durham and Northumberland, the picture is confused; 1597 was a plague year as well as a time of food shortage, and separating the effects of the two is exceedingly difficult.

To the south, individual parish studies show that mortality rose less than in the north. In a recent analysis of plague and famine in Staffordshire, David Palliser argues that famine was present in some, but not all, parishes in that county. The parishes of Wednesbury and Brewood, for instance, had twice the usual number of burials in 1597. Palliser finds the evidence for starvation in the parish of Tamworth very convincing; both the distribution of deaths during the year and the remarks left by the clerk in the register attest to its presence.[8] It was the Tamworth register that contained evidence of the terminal dysentery associated with starvation that was discussed in Chapter 1 (p. 8). In the southwest, the parish of Colyton, Devon, also may have suffered famine in 1596–97, when the number of burials roughly doubled.[9] Additional local studies will undoubtedly turn up other pockets of starvation in England in 1596–97, but I think those parishes that saw their burials double will remain the exception, at least south of the Trent.

The best picture of the impact of the dearth of 1597 is found in the transcriptions of baptisms, burials, and marriages collected by the Cambridge Group for the History of Population and Social Structure.[10] Their sample is composed of 382 parishes scattered across England. It is somewhat biased toward the south—which would tend to underestimate the impact of the dearth—and is made up mainly of rural parishes. Figure 16 shows the number of baptisms, burials, and marriages for the years 1581 through 1640. At the top of the graph are the price index figures for all grains for the same sixty years.[11] Grain prices are usually given for harvest years—that is the year in which the autumn harvest falls—but here I have adjusted them forward one year, so that the price year coincides with the calendar year in which the effects of the harvest would have been felt. For example, the impact of the harvest failure of 1596 would have fallen primarily in 1597—and therefore carries the date 1597 on the graph.

The graph reveals a striking correspondence between grain prices and the level of baptisms, burials, and marriages. Almost invariably, burials rose and both baptisms and marriages tumbled downward in years of high prices. In 1587, when prices were high following the bad harvest of 1586, burials rose and baptisms fell, although burials did not exceed baptisms. The same process occurred in 1591, when prices again moved up. In 1597, burials soared past the falling baptisms, to actually reduce the expanding English population. A small part of the increased mortality that year can perhaps be dismissed as plague mortality rather than mortality arising from the dearth, but the drastic fall in baptisms—beginning in 1596 and lasting through 1598—leaves no doubt that the period was one of crisis for England. In our previous analyses of individual parishes, we have tried to avoid the term "mortality crisis" unless burials doubled, compared to a base of noncrisis years. Burial totals, especially in small par-

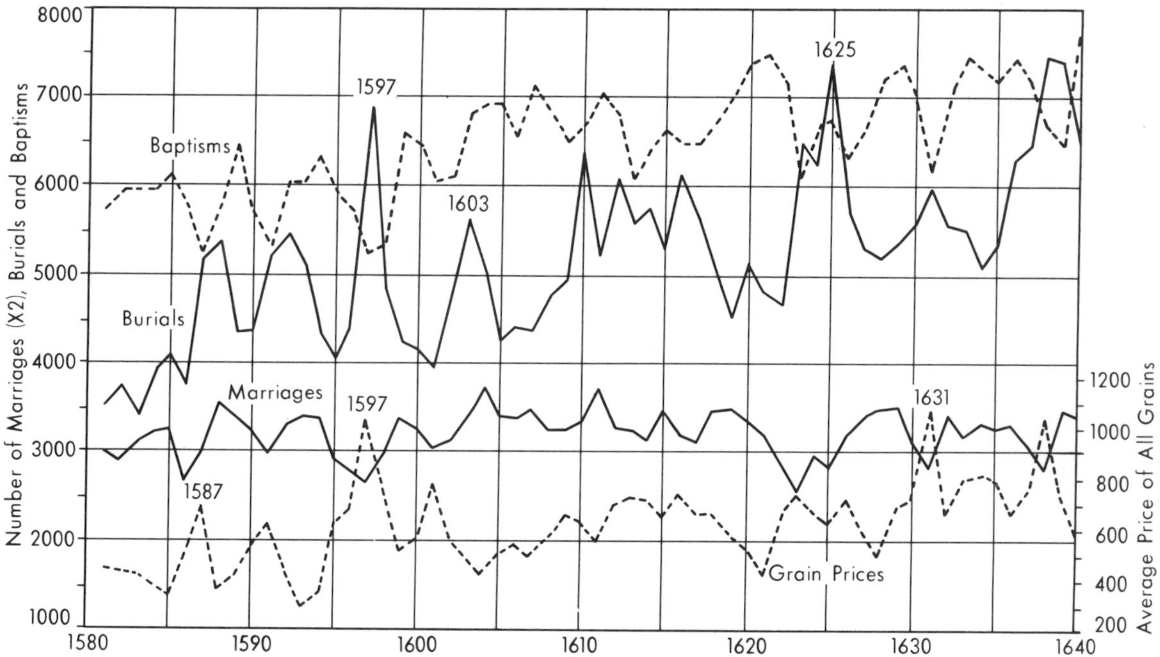

Fig. 16. Grain prices, baptisms, burials, and marriages in England, 1581–1640. Figures on marriages, baptisms, and burials from 382 parishes were collected by the Cambridge Group. Grain price index numbers are from Peter Bowden, "Statistical Appendix," in Joan Thirsk, ed., *The Agrarian History of England and Wales*. IV, *1500–1640* (Cambridge, 1967), pp. 819–21. Grain prices are adjusted one year forward, to coincide with the year of effect; 100 equals average price, 1450–99.

ishes, tend to fluctuate considerably. To avoid calling random fluctuations in the figures "crises," we need a high cutoff—such as doubling of the figures. Is this limitation suitable, however, for an aggregate figure drawn from 382 parishes? Certainly the figures are large enough to offset the effects of any random parish variation. In the aggregate figures, burials did not double; the average for the years 1592–96 and 1598–1602 was 4,557; in 1597, the number of burials was 6,919, an increase of 52 percent. Nor did baptisms fall by half; with use of the same base years, the decline was 13.5 percent. But combining the two underscores the enormous effect the harvest failure of 1596 had on English population in 1597. Should we call this famine? Perhaps. Our words—and our systems of measurement—are not sufficiently precise to allow the use of the same yardstick for individual parishes and large groupings of parishes. It is abundantly clear, however, that the grain harvest was the heart of the English economy—to borrow Hoskins' analogy[12]—and that its malfunctions were felt, with disastrous results, throughout the kingdom.

Despite this graphic proof of the importance of the harvest failure of 1596, there is no doubt that the famine of 1597 was much worse in the northwestern corner of England than it was in the Cambridge Group's sample of parishes. In Cumberland and Westmorland, burials rose two, three, or four times the normal figure. And the crisis was felt in every parish whose records we have seen.

There is some evidence that London, then a city of some 200,000 people,[13] suffered from the dearth. A noticeable rise in recorded burials took place there in 1597. In the following brief analysis, I have chosen two groups of parishes, one located in the center of the City and the other made up of suburban parishes lying outside the City walls. These two parish groupings should reflect the differences in wealth that were found within greater London. David Glass shows, in his study of the tax assessment of 1695, that the wealthier citizens of the metropolis were predominantly concentrated in the central, City parishes, while the inhabitants of the outlying parishes tended to be, on the average, poorer.[14] The same pattern can be found in London before the great fire. In 1638 the

Crown asked the clergy of each parish to compile a list of householders and estimate the "moderate" rental value of each house. The return is incomplete for many parishes, but it shows clearly enough the broad distribution of wealth within the city. In general, the 1638 returns agree with Glass's findings for 1695: the wealthier citizens in the main inhabited the central parishes and were rather scarce in the outlying ones.[15] Within the central parishes, however, considerable differences in wealth existed. The better-off citizens tended to live in large houses facing on the major streets—Cornhill, Fenchurch Street, Tower Street, and so forth. Back of these substantial houses fronting on the thoroughfares, however, lay a welter of narrow lanes, courts, and alleys, where the poor crowded together. To cite one example, the houses along Cornhill, in the parish of St. Michael, Cornhill, were valued at an average of £20 per annum in 1638. In Harp Alley, in the same parish, one dwelling had six rooms let to a total of 64 persons. The estimated yearly rental for this rookery was £5-10*s*., or less than 2*s*. per occupant.[16] In the parishes outside the walls, many houses were valued at less than £2 per year, and often entire lanes were valued singly, suggesting that a large number of small tenements—all owned by one person—were clustered together.[17] The point I wish to emphasize is that poverty was pervasive throughout the city, although the outlying parishes had a larger proportion of poor and may not have had the charitable resources that a central parish, with more well-off citizens, could draw upon.

The burials for the two sample groups of parishes are set out in Figure 17.[18] The dearth year, 1597, stands out almost equally in both groups, suggesting that the wealth of the inner parishes did not totally protect the poorer inhabitants living there from the effects of the food shortage. In the seven inner-city parishes, burials in 1597 did not quite reach double the number of those in 1600, the year of lowest mortality during the 12-year period. In the outlying two parishes, burials in 1597 were slightly more than twice those in 1594, 1600, and 1601—all years of low mortality. It is, of course, premature to blame the excess mortality of 1597 on starvation or famine-related disease. An exhaustive study of London records may reveal

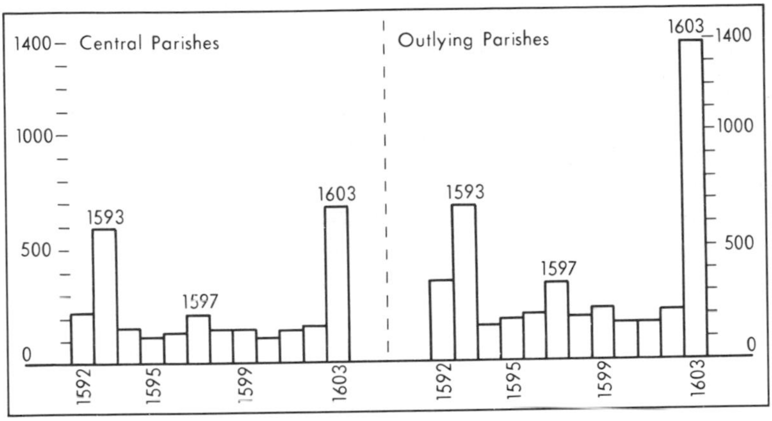

Fig. 17. Burials, 1592–1603, in London. Central parishes: St. Michael, Cornhill; St. Peter's, Cornhill; Allhallows, Bread Street; St. Dionis, Backchurch; St. Mary le Bow, Cheapside; St. Mary Aldermary; St. Mary Somerset. Outlying parishes: St. James, Clerkenwell, and St. Martin in the Fields.

that another cause was operating quite independently of the food shortage. But the figures suggest that the dearth took a toll of Londoners in 1597.

A comparison of the relative effects of plague and famine in London and the northwest reveals a sharp contrast between the two areas. In London, the enormous losses from the plagues of 1592–93 and 1603 completely dwarf the mortality of 1597. In the northwest, the picture was altogether different: plague, when it struck Carlisle or Penrith, was deadly enough, but in the countryside, where the vast majority of the people lived, it had little effect. Starvation, on the other hand, was a great killer. London, of course, had resources to ameliorate food shortage that were unknown in the northwest. The city was wealthy and could buy grain for distribution to the poor. In the seven months ending May 26, 1597, a total of 111,075 quarters* of grain were imported through the port of London.[19] We do not know what percentage of these imports was consumed by the inhabitants of the city and what proportion was transshipped to other localities, but the imports must have greatly eased the dis-

*A quarter is equal to 8 bushels.

tress caused by the dearth. Judging from the increase in burials in 1597, however, the resources of the city were not completely able to offset the effects of the shortage.

The wealthier citizens of Bristol also purchased grain for distribution to the poor during the shortage. In 1594, an alderman of the city bought £1,200 worth of wheat and rye for the city storehouse. Each day a portion of this was brought to the market, evidently in an effort to maintain a constant supply. In 1596, another merchant bought 3,000 quarters of Baltic rye to supply the city. In 1597, at the height of the dearth, all men of substance were asked to give one meal to the poor each day. The same year, a merchant gave one hundred marks* weekly for poor relief. These details indicate what measures prosperous citizens of a city could take to alleviate shortage—and prevent civil disturbance.[20]

In certain provincial cities, however, dearth brought increased mortality and considerable distress, despite efforts by the town corporations to provide for the poor. Recorded burials in three parishes in Salisbury rose from an average of 219 per year for the period 1588–94 to 389 in 1597, and conceptions fell from a yearly average of 221 to 150. In addition to the problems of feeding its own indigent, Salisbury acted as a magnet for the poor of the surrounding rural areas, and large numbers of paupers—predominantly women from nearby villages—flooded into the city in search of relief.[21]

If the rural poor sought relief in Salisbury—and no doubt in many other cities across England—does this mean that the cities, with their wealth and charities, met the problem of dearth with more success than rural areas? This seems very likely, but it is difficult to determine conclusively. Starving people did not necessarily know where to go to get aid. Indeed, they may have fled to the city, only to be turned away at the gates and left to starve outside the city walls. Or they may have gained entrance and then died, swelling the burial figures for the city parishes to make it appear as if the city had a terrible subsistence crisis, when in fact the crisis may have been entirely rural. For instance, we do not know if the 25 "poore

*A mark is worth two-thirds of a pound, or 13*s*. 4*d*. One hundred marks is the equivalent of £66-13-4.

folkes who died for want in the streets" of Newcastle in 1597 were inhabitants or strangers seeking food in the city (see p. 113). Much research remains to be done on the relative effect of famine on the countryside, the cities, and, if possible, the usually poor suburbs that grew up outside the city walls.

Whatever role starvation played in the cities and rural areas of England, the high prices of foodstuffs and the empty bellies of the poor provoked comment by contemporaries and caused unease in the government, which feared the turbulent uprisings that could come in the wake of food shortage. As early as 1595, the Oxford preacher, George Abbot, wrote:[22]

> The dearth which doth now raigne in many parts of this land . . . maketh the poore to pinch for hunger, and the children to cry in the street, not knowing where to have bread. And if the Lord do not stay his hand, the dearth may be yet much more.

But the Lord did not stay His hand, and in December of 1596, Abbot continued:[23]

> I see that all is not well. He is blind who now beholdeth not, that God is angry with us. . . . Behold what a famine he hath brought into our land, and making it to perservere, yet hitherto doth increase it. One yeare there hath been hunger; the second year there was a dearth, and a third which is this yeare, there is great cleannesse of teeth. . . . We may say that the course of nature is very much inverted; our yeares are turned upside downe; our sommers are no sommers; our harvests are no harvests; our feed-times are no feed-times . . . and the nights are like the dayes: we know not which are the better.

Other writers reflected Abbot's concern. Henry Arthington wrote that "the hand of God is heavy upon us, in most places in this Realme of England, appearing plainly in this great penury." Like Abbot, Arthington saw God's displeasure behind the famine. Reflecting on the reasons for the great number of hungry people, he wrote that "some impute the same to the dearth of graine, and the occasion thereof to unseasonable weather . . . yet we must search further . . . all windes and ill weather procede directly from the justice of God."[24]

More prosaic commentators did not seek God's hand behind the dearth, but they too described the situation as desperate. The bailiffs of Colchester wrote Sir Robert Cecil that "without some . . . provisions numbers must perish."[25] At Shrewsbury it was reported that "the people there for want are lyke to perysh."[26] These few examples could be duplicated many times; news of scarcity came to the Privy Council from every side.[27] In February 1597, the Council itself noted that the "complaint of scarcitie is so generall as we do hardly finde any countie so well stoared as to be able to releeve their neighbors."[28]

Fears of disorder grew as the dearth continued. Nor were the fears baseless. As early as November 1595, bands of from sixty to one hundred men seized grain several times in Wiltshire.[29] Early in 1596 the students of Christ Church, Oxford, rioted over the size of their bread ration.[30] A few weeks later, certain "evil disposed persons" stopped grain shipments in Kent.[31] The most serious of the disturbances took place late in 1596 in Oxfordshire with an uprising of two or three hundred men.[32] In April 1597, the Lord Mayor of London reported "great discontentment and murmuring of the people . . . specially of the poorer sort."[33] Unrest continued in Kent and Sussex that year, and the Council complained that certain "dysordered and lewde dysposed persons" in those counties did not submit patiently to the dearth but instead caused "tumult and sedicion."[34] In Norfolk, riotous assemblies were reported in three different localities. In each case, the correspondence to the Council states that scarcity was the cause of the unlawful gatherings.[35]

Faced with shortage and unrest on every side, the Crown responded with a barrage of directives to all parts of the kingdom, regulating and directing every aspect of the grain trade and, at the same time, exhorting the rich to charity and the poor to patience. Tudor policy regarding the administration of the grain trade was consolidated in the *Book of Orders*, which had been issued first in the dearth of 1587 and was reissued in 1594. The *Orders* endeavored to keep the grain trade local and out of the hands of forestallers, regrators, and ingrossers—the contemporary terms for speculators. Behind all its provisions is the overriding concern that the poor be allowed to buy grain freely on the open local market unhampered by competition from speculators, merchants, brewers, and others who tended to drive up grain prices.[36] As the dearth increased, the Council repeatedly demanded that the orders be obeyed, and that the forestallers, ingrossers, and regrators be controlled.[37] In the Council's mind, the chief cause of the scarcity was neither the weather nor the hand of God but human laxity and greed. Writing in September of 1596, the Council noted that "though it hath pleased God at this tyme to visitt this land with verie extraordinary scarcetie and dearth, yet nether the want nor the complaint of the poore people would be so great as it is" if the laws were obeyed.[38] In this letter, as in others,[39] the justices of the peace were admonished for being "authors and maynteyners" of the abuses and for profiting from the food shortage, rather than helping to lessen it. The Council's displeasure was ill-concealed in another letter, which acidly commented, "yet we will see the negligence . . . of the Justices . . . reformed."[40] Although there is no record of action against justices, the Council ordered ingrossers to appear before it and referred others to the Assizes for action. The following year, the Council again appealed to the justices to suppress the speculators.[41]

> Although Allmightie God hath mercyfully and favorably withdrawne His heavy hande, wherewith wee were deservedly punyshed by an universall scarcety thorrowe the unseasonable wether, and hath now yeelded us with His blessed hande a chaunge thereof in this latter ende of sommer, to the greate comforte of all sorts of people, yet there are seene and fownde a number of wycked people in condicions more lyke to wolves or cormerants then to naturall men, that doe moste covetusly seeke to holde up the late great pryces of corne and all other victuells by ingrossinge the same into theire private hands berganynge beforehand for corne, and in some parte for grayne growinge . . . and for butter and cheese before yt be brought to ordynarie markettes for to be bought for the poorer sorte. Against which fowle, corrupt fraude and malycious greedynes there are bothe manie good lawes and sondry orders of late yeres given to all Justices.

But despite the Council's pleas and threats, enforcement evidently remained lax, for in 1598, after the end of the dearth, the government again placed the major blame for the scarcity on speculators and again ordered that the existing laws against speculation be obeyed.[42]

The *Book of Orders* also outlined a program for the control of maltsters, brewers, and taverns, in the hope of reducing the amount of ale brewed and also of lessening its alcoholic content, because in time of shortage the maltster competed with the poor for the reduced supply of barley. From 1595 through 1597, the Council tried to breathe some life into these regulations. Letters were sent to Norwich, Gloucester, Southampton, and London, limiting brewing and malting and also prohibiting the making of expensive, strong ale. In 1596, certain offending brewers were called before the Council to answer for brewing ale that would sell above the authorized price.[43]

One of the characteristics of the Tudor grain trade was its local orientation: the justices of each county were empowered to stop all shipments of food outside the county boundaries. Although this was intended to protect the poor in buying on the local market—by preventing purchases by speculators and merchants from other areas—it was obviously inconvenient in times of great shortage because one county could not import foodstuffs from another to relieve its own distress. London, too, could not buy necessary food in the country. Recognizing the dilemma between the local protection of the poor and the need to share somehow the existing food supplies, the Council lamented that "wee have founde exceeding great difficulty to reconcile the wantes of the citty [London] and countrie, the one requiring great supply, the other not so able in these as in other tymes to affoarde such stoare."[44] In an effort to ease the London shortage, the Council issued numerous warrants authorizing Londoners to obtain food in the country and also authorized those rural areas of great shortage to buy in other counties.[45]

Naturally, the export abroad of foodstuffs was prohibited, and imports were encouraged. In fact, imports were more than "encouraged," for the Council ordered Her Majesty's Admirals at Dover and Flushing to stop all foreign grain ships passing through the Channel and bring them to England.[46] The Council justified such action by noting that other princes had seized grain for their subjects in time of famine. On arrival in England, the cargoes were ordered sold on the open market, at or below prevailing market prices, to help relieve the poor. Despite the Council's wishes, the cargo from an Emden ship detained at Dartmouth managed to find its way into the hands of some wealthy men. With the connivance of the city's mayor, they seem to have paid very low prices for the grain, and made a tidy profit on its resale to the poor—all to the Council's extreme annoyance.[47]

Acting on instructions from the Council, the Archibishops of Canterbury and York told the clergy to encourage the rich to moderate their diet and increase their charity and hospitality to the poor.[48] The Lord Mayor of London was ordered to restrain excessive feasting in the city, "where there ys more excesse of fare used then in anie other parte of the realme."[49] Gentlemen in London were told to leave for their country homes; those that did not were to be reported to the Council for further action. Nor did the Council overlook appeals to the poor from the pulpit. In the depths of the scarcity, the Council ordered the Archbishops to have the clergy teach the people "to endure this scarsety with patyence, and to beware howe they give eare to any perswasyons or practyses of discontented and ydle braynes to move them . . . from the humble dutyes of good subjects."[50]

Finally, with the coming of the harvest of 1598, prices returned to normal and the long dearth was over.[51] The four years of shortage had brought extreme hardship to most—perhaps all—of England. Famine stalked the north and some parts of the south in 1597. This year was the sorry end to a century of population growth, rising prices, and falling real wages.[52] The England of Elizabeth had experienced considerable economic expansion and—if Eric Kerridge is correct—even embarked on an agricultural revolution.[53] But England, economically expanded as it was, still could not feed all its people when a series of four bad harvests reduced food supplies and drove prices to record heights.

Compared to 1597, the crisis of 1623 was more regional in its impact. It appears that famine was limited in England to the north, although there was real distress in many localities in the south, particularly where depression in the clothing industry brought unemployment. In a preliminary discussion of the crisis of 1623 in Cumberland and Westmorland, I argued that the loss of life that year seemed to have been as much the result of loss of income from cloth making as from absolute high food prices.[54] Without local price data from the north, it was impossible to say with any assurance what the relative contribution of depression in the clothing industry and high food prices may have been, but much of the poverty of southern England suggested that failure of the cloth markets was a major cause of the crisis. The Westmorland cloth industry was then in decline—and the depression of the 1620's was probably severely felt. Both Lancashire and the West Riding were also cloth manufacturing regions and both suffered badly in 1623. All this evidence suggested that the crisis of 1623 was in no little part a result of the clothing depression. Since then I have become acquainted with the course of the crisis of 1623 in Scotland, thanks to the kindness of Michael W. Flinn,[55] and I have also investigated the impact of the crisis east of the Pennines. In neither of these areas was the manufacture of cloth important, but the year—particularly in Scotland—was a terrible one. Seen from the vantage point of Scotland and the north, rather than the south, the crisis seems to have been caused by a series of bad harvests, following on the heels of one another, not unlike the series of bad harvests of the 1590's that culminated in the famine of 1597. The major difference between the two famines was that the latter one of 1623 was localized in the north and does not seem to have touched the south with much force. Apparently the harvest of 1622 was much more deficient in the north than in the south, and even after the harvest of 1623, prices remained high in the north and across the borders in Scotland.

The Cambridge Group's sample of 382 parishes shows fewer baptisms than burials in 1623, but this comes more from the decline of baptisms than from an increase in burials. See Figure 16 (p. 136). One of the most arresting aspects of this graph is the extreme sensitivity shown by baptisms and marriages to changing price levels for the entire sixty-year period. In 1623, following the bad harvest of

1622, baptisms dipped and marriages plunged to their lowest point between 1580 and 1640, even though the mortality level did not rise dramatically. Across England, then, the year was one of food shortage and hardship, but the demographic consequences were in the main felt in fewer births and delayed marriages.

The north of England and Scotland, however, experienced widespread and terrible loss of life from starvation. Recently a group of researchers working under the direction of Colin D. Rogers analyzed the crisis of 1623 in Lancashire.[56] Burials almost tripled in that county, reaching a total of 7,970, compared with an average of 2,766 for the years 1611 through 1622 and 1624 through 1630.[57] The group came to the conclusion that famine—and perhaps associated "famine fevers"—was responsible for the excess mortality, which was estimated to have swept away 5 percent of the county's population.[58]

In Lancashire, 51 out of 54 parishes analyzed by the Rogers group had greater than normal mortality in 1623. A sampling of parishes in Durham and Yorkshire reveals somewhat less distress in those counties. Burials in 21 out of 27 Durham parishes were more numerous than normal; in the North Riding, 20 out of 24 parishes; in the East Riding, 27 out of 31, and in the West Riding, 54 out of 59. In all, 173 out of 195 parishes within these three counties offer some evidence of heightened mortality in this year of dearth.[59] In Cumberland and Westmorland, all the available registers reflect increased mortality, often two, three, or four times normal. In the other northern counties—and in particular east of the Pennines—famine does not seem to have been as severe or as extensive as it was in the extreme northwest. In Durham, for instance, in only eight of the 27 parishes sampled did the number of burials double. In the West Riding, mortality rose twofold in 12 out of 59 parishes in the sample. Eight of 31 East Riding parishes experienced this doubling, as did four of 20 in the North Riding.[60] Only Lancashire seems to have approached the extremities of Cumberland and Westmorland; in that county, the numbers of burials doubled—or more than doubled—in 41 out of 54 parishes.

This is not to deny the terrible reality of famine in many parishes of Durham and Yorkshire. In Brancepeth, a large parish to the west of the city of Durham, burials rose to 60, compared to an average of fewer than 29 for the years 1618 through 1628. In Darlington, burials were 127 in 1623, as against an average of 60 for the same base years 1618 through 1628. On the coast east of Durham city, 45 people were buried in the parish of Easington, more than double the average of 22 for 1618 through 1628.

In the East Riding, famine devastated the small parish of Bainton, near the center of the Riding. Burials there rose more than three times, to 36, compared to an average of 10.5 for the same base years. The parish clerk noted in the margin of the register for 1623, "Hoc anno multi fame periere," which strengthens the argument that starvation was the cause of death in the north of England that year. Great Driffield, a parish not far from Bainton, recorded 33 burials in 1623 and a further 67 in 1624. The terrible mortality of 1623–24 is thrown into bold relief in this parish, where burials for the years 1618 through 1622 and 1625 through 1629 averaged just over 12.

Perhaps the effect of the famine on the populous clothing parishes of the West Riding can best be gained from a graph of burials and baptisms for the chapelries of Elland and Heptonstall and the church of Halifax, all located in the parish of Halifax.[61] See Figure 18. In this example, the total impact of the dearth on the population of the parish is arresting. Burials did not quite double—compared to the base years 1618 through 1628—but the fall in baptisms helped reverse momentarily the population growth of the previous years. From 1618 through 1621, baptisms comfortably exceeded burials by 784, an average of almost two hundred per year. Then the correction began, and the next three years saw baptisms fall short of burials by 785, to wipe out the natural increase of the previous four years. The final four years of the period saw the resurgence of baptisms and a fall in burials; in those years 749 more baptisms than burials returned the demographic situation to what it had been before. The initial decline in baptisms in 1622—before the terrible increase in burials—suggests that food shortage had begun to inhibit conceptions before it had much effect on mortality.

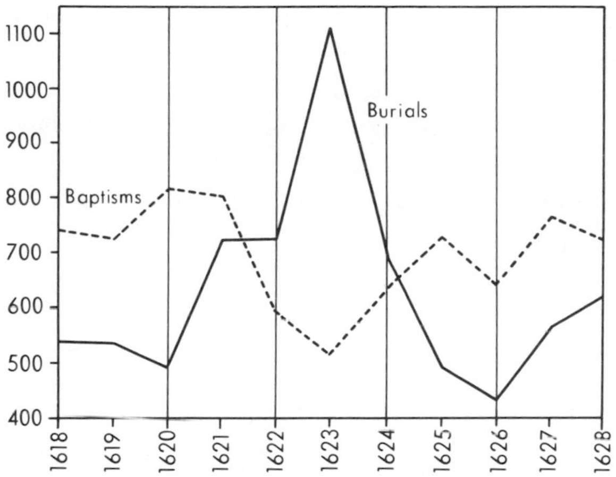

Fig. 18. Baptisms and burials, 1618–28, in Halifax, West Riding, Yorkshire.

Our sample of 195 parishes drawn from Lancashire, Yorkshire, and Durham is too limited to permit us to draw a map of the north, showing those areas that were severely afflicted and those areas that were spared. Analyzing parish registers is tedious and laborious, and —to add to the difficulty—the surviving registers are not collected in one place, but are scattered in various county record offices or remain in their respective parish churches. Until more county studies have been done, such as the study of Lancashire by the Rogers group, it will not be possible to establish conclusively all the possible geographical differences in the famine of 1623. However, our sampling, limited as it is, does permit us to raise certain questions about the distribution of famine in the north that year.

As we have already indicated, the famine seems to have affected all of Cumberland and Westmorland, the lowlands as well as the highlands, the coastal as well as the inland parishes. In Lancashire, however, a geographical pattern is clearly visible. If one were to draw an imaginary line between Manchester in the south and the southern tip of the Furness peninsula in the northwest, the parishes east and north of the line experienced severe famine while those parishes to the south and west—on the coastal plain—suffered little or not at all. In general, the parishes with the highest mortality were upland ones, lying between 600 and 1,000 feet above sea level where the annual rainfall was above 40 inches.[62]

Were these upland fell parishes of Lancashire overpopulated in the same way as the fell parishes of Cumberland, where landless encroachers had carved tiny holdings from the pasture? In the Forest of Rossendale, a large Crown property in the southeast uplands of Lancashire, a very similar process of encroachment had taken place. A commission to inquire into illegal encroachment on Forest lands in 1616 uncovered 311 illegal encroachments in the parish of Haslingden. None of the encroachments was larger than three-quarters of a customary Lancashire acre of 1.6 statute acres. Later that same year another commission found another 59 encroachments in Haslingden. Here the parcels of land were even smaller; all 59 parcels covered less than four customary acres.[63] In Rossendale, as in the forests of Cumberland, the encroachers were landless squatters and also tenants of nearby manors who sublet the tiny parcels to landless men.

At the same time that this creeping encroachment was proceeding, the established customary holdings in Rossendale were being broken up, as tenants provided land for all their sons. In the Middle Ages, there had been 23 customary holdings. By 1507, these 23 had been broken into 72. By 1537, there were 101 holdings, in 1608, 200, and by 1662, a total of 314.[64] The unfolding picture for Rossendale was much the same as that found in Cumberland and Westmorland: numerous tiny encroachments on the pastures and the inexorable fracturing of the customary holdings.[65] Crown properties, obviously, are not necessarily typical—and the amount of encroachment and fragmentation of established holdings in Rossendale may have been unusual.

In northern Lancashire, one parish stands out from the others because it seems to have managed to avoid the famine of 1623, although the surrounding parishes were badly hit. Thornton in Lonsdale, which lies both in Lancashire and in the West Riding of Yorkshire had 16 burials in 1623, compared to an average for the years 1618 through 1628 of 12. Two of the persons buried that year were strangers, one from near Carlisle in Cumberland, the other from nearby Westmorland. Probably these were wanderers, seeking food outside their own counties. If these two are subtracted from the burials for 1623, the mortality is very little above normal. What particular circumstances saved this parish from the starvation that was so pervasive in the region? We can only conjecture—but maybe the local lord had prevented squatters from settling on the common and had also acted to prevent the customary tenants from fragmenting their holdings. And thus, perhaps, the overpopulation that seems to have been so common in the northwest was averted—and the famine of 1623 avoided.

In certain parishes of the North Riding, similar anomalies are apparent. The parish of Danby, in the Cleveland Hills, was one of the few parishes in the north where mortality in both 1623 and 1624 was below normal. By contrast, many lowland parishes in the Vale of York—for example, Thirsk, Pickhill, Kirklington, Felixkirk, and Easingwold—had a substantially higher than normal level of burials. The pattern in the North Riding was thus somewhat different from that found in Lancashire, where the uplands suffered more than the lowlands.

These examples are sufficient, I hope, to show that famine was a regional or national problem, when the harvest failed and food supplies were short. But it also had its purely local side—and varied from parish to parish according to the systems of inheritance, the settlement policies of the lord, and perhaps also the availability of local charity to ameliorate the effects of high prices.

In the preceding chapter, I argued that it seems very unlikely that disease would strike all the parishes of Cumberland and Westmorland, whose registers we have inspected, at the same time. But not all the parishes in the north were affected; certain ones, such as Danby and Thornton in Lonsdale, sit as untouched islands in a sea of mortality. Could this be an indication that the cause of death was not starvation but rather some unusually widespread epidemic disease? Before we answer that question, let us turn to the evidence from Scotland.

Across the borders, the few surviving parish registers indicate that famine struck Scotland even more savagely than northern England.[66] In Dumfries, the average number of burials for the three years 1619–21 had been 91; in contrast, 488 people were buried in the first ten months in 1623, after which the register stops. The two other surviving burial registers for Scotland—Dunfermline and Kelso (Roxburghshire)—both reflect the same terrible loss of life. Not all the people dying in Dumfries were inhabitants of the town; some 101 were described in the registers as nonresident paupers, evidently the destitute from the surrounding rural areas that came to the town seeking charity. Even subtracting these, however, it seems that 10 to 15 percent of the population of the burgh died of starvation or related diseases that year. Clearly, the mortality was associated with food shortage in the minds of contemporaries, one of whom wrote that "many died in the streets and on highway sydes, for verie want of food, famished." Another wrote that the poor "dyed through famine in the fields and hie wayes." The Scottish evidence confirms the close relationship between food shortage and mortality, although diseases such as typhus may also have contributed to the death toll.

Let us briefly summarize the argument for starvation in 1623. Clearly the north of England suffered a crisis of mortality that year, a crisis observable to some degree in the great majority of the rural parishes whose registers have been inspected. Two of the burial registers refer specifically to starvation or famine and none mentions any other cause of death. In Scotland, where the same crisis took place, starvation was reported by contemporaries. Plague could not have been present in the north; it was not mentioned in the state papers or local records, either in England or in Scotland, until late in 1624. No other known disease would have produced the high mortality of that year in all these rural parishes. Of course typhus may have swelled the burials here and there, but the large numbers of children dying in Cumberland and Westmorland suggest it played at most a minor role. The parishes of the highlands and the northwest that managed to avoid the famine can, I think, be explained by unusually favorable local conditions that served to ward off starvation. As one moves toward the south, out of the famine area, the picture changes and the number of parishes exhibiting the symptoms of crisis falls.

All across the north, the most severe mortality occurred in the last months of 1623 and the first months of 1624. In other words, all across this extensive area people were dying at the same time. A recent study of population crises in the 1730's and 1740's in Scandinavia found two distinctly different patterns of mortality. Disease mortality moved in a wave motion, spreading out from the city through the countryside rather slowly as the infection spread from one community to another. Famine mortality, on the other hand, was observable over very large rural areas at the same time.[67] This second pattern is the one found in the north of England in 1623, and it reinforces the conclusion that starvation rather than epidemic disease was the major cause of death. In Scotland, the peak mortality came slightly earlier, in the third quarter of 1623, but this timing is much closer than the Scandinavian epidemics, which often took years to cover an area as large as northern England and Scotland. The study also found that disease originated in the cities of Scandinavia and then spread to the rural hinterland.[68] But the rise in mortality did not take place sooner in the cities than in the countryside. Nor did the cities suffer as severely as did the surrounding rural areas. For example, 15 parishes in the city of York had a 25.8 percent increase in burials in 1623, based on the average number of burials between 1618 and 1628.[69] By comparison, the 27 rural parishes from the East Riding included in our sample of northern parishes experienced an increase of 64 percent, using the same base years.[70] The decidedly greater rural mortality tends to confirm the diagnosis of starvation; epidemic disease would have been more severe in York—then a densely populated city of between 11,500 and 12,000 people[71]—than in the more sparsely settled surrounding countryside.

In short, it seems clear that famine ranged across the north in 1623, with its center in the northwestern counties of Cumberland and Westmorland and in northern Lancashire. We spoke of burials doubling in certain parishes on the eastern side of the Pennines, such as Brancepeth and Easington, both in county Durham, or rising to more than three times normal in Bainton, in the East Riding. In Cumberland and Westmorland, however, the mortality was on the order of three to four times normal in the majority of the parishes. In Cumberland, the parish of Lamplugh saw burials rise to 272 percent of normal, in Dalston to 401 percent normal, in Bridekirk to 418 percent, in Penrith to 409 percent, and, in the coastal parish of Millom, to 282 percent normal. In Westmorland, mortality in Lowther was 331 percent of normal; in Newbiggen, 387 percent normal; in Brough-under-Stainmore, 319 percent, and in Newton Reigny, 550 percent. In all of these instances, "normal" is defined as the average number of burials for the years 1618 through 1628, the same base used in describing the mortality in the other northern counties. In 1623, all the north suffered—but not all to the same degree.[72]

CHAPTER TEN

Signs of Change

AFTER 1623, Cumberland and Westmorland had no more years of widespread, heavy mortality comparable to 1597 and 1623, when every parish whose registers have been inspected suffered. From time to time harvests failed and grain prices soared, particularly in 1630, 1647–49, 1661, and the 1690's, but the local burial registers contain no evidence of crises similar to the earlier ones. The first of these bad years, 1630, came hard on the heels of the crisis of 1623. Perhaps the numbers of marginal poor were still too few to be swept away in another famine like that of 1623. Perhaps the north was spared the unfavorable weather that had contributed to harvest failure in the south. In September 1630, the Privy Council noted that dearth was facing the country and mentioned that there had been an "extraordinary drouth" the past summer.[1] In the north, rainfall was usually more plentiful than in the south and the drought may not have been felt there. For three years running, in 1647, 1648, and 1649, harvests failed. A Newcastle correspondent reported in April 1649 that many poor people had left Cumberland to seek food in Newcastle. Some of these apparently starved.[2] Certain parish registers in Cumberland reveal increased mortality. In Dacre, burials reached 27 in 1649, compared to an average of slightly fewer than 14 for the years 1644 through 1652. Crosthwaite's burials number 60 in 1649, slightly above the average of 49 for the six years ending in 1652. Exact comparisons with the earlier crises are difficult; the parish registers were not kept with much care during the interregnum. But I think a different pattern of mortality was emerging as early as 1649 and was clearly evident in later periods of dearth: mortality began to be limited in both intensity and extent. The numbers dying were not two or three times normal and the crisis was not observable in all parishes. One or two parishes might have had heightened mortality; in others, the numbers dying were in the normal range. The region as a whole was overcoming famine.

It was suggested in Chapter 2 that rural population in the diocese of Carlisle had declined in the early seventeenth century from a high point reached some time around 1603. There is evidence that communities along the west coast of Cumberland gained population during the mid-seventeenth century, perhaps in part offsetting the rural depopulation of the inland parishes. Much of the Cumberland coast lay in the diocese of Chester and therefore did not figure in our earlier analysis of population trends, which was largely limited to the diocese of Carlisle. One of these coastal communities, Whitehaven, had a mere six households in 1566.[3] By 1633, little growth had taken place and the hamlet had only nine or ten families.[4] But by 1685, 268 families—1,089 persons—lived there.[5] As we shall see in the next chapter, it was then a coal-mining and shipping town of considerable importance. The parishes of Harrington, Moresby, Egremont, and Cleator, located on the coast not far from Whitehaven, appear to have shared in this new economic activity. All experienced a doubling of population between 1563 and 1688. An exception to this pattern of growth along the coast was Workington. In 1566 it had been the largest port on the west coast, with thirty households.[6] In the sixteenth century, coal was mined at the nearby village of Clifton and carted to Workington, but disputes between the freeholders who worked the mines and the Curwen family, which controlled the right of way to the port, prevented any expansion of output.[7] Consequently the number of households in the parish increased only modestly, from 140 in 1563 to 189 in 1688.

Some idea of the growth of other towns can be gathered by comparing the 1563 household counts with those of the later seventeenth century. Within its walls, Carlisle had 320 households in 1597.[8] A count taken in 1685 showed 309 houses, of which 133 contained more than one family, giving a total of at least 442 families.[9] If the 1597 and 1685 figures are comparable, Carlisle's population increased by slightly more than one-third, considerably less than the growth taking place in the coal-mining areas along the west coast. In Penrith parish, the households numbered 140 in 1563 and 270 in 1688. The hearth tax returns of 1673–74 give a different figure, 316 households in the parish, of which 268 were in the town of Penrith.[10] Whichever figure is accurate, Penrith seems to have doubled its population in just over a century.

Kendal, the most populous town in Westmorland, had 338 households in 1606.[11] By 1671–73, there were 454 households within Kendal, an increase of about one-third.[12] A census of Kendal taken about 1695 gives the town a population of 2,190,[13] about what would be expected of 454 households. The borough of Appleby had 141 households in 1671–73,[14] apparently a small increase over 1563.

This pattern of increase suggests that the towns in the two counties were growing more rapidly than the surrounding countryside. Our comparisons, of course, are between 1563 and the late seventeenth century; we know nothing of shorter-term fluctuations. But the coastal communities, Penrith, and Kendal all grew more rapidly than their respective counties. Carlisle did not; its growth was to come in the eighteenth century when the town became a center for textile manufacturing.

The rural population decline that was indicated by our population analysis in Chapter 2 was paralleled by a decrease in the number of customary tenants on various manors within the two counties. Table 3 shows the change at various dates when tenant lists were made.[15] The picture is unfortunately ambiguous; certain manors lost customary tenants, others did not, in the period 1574 to 1650. Any trend in those years is unclear, but certainly after 1650 the numbers of customary tenants began to fall.

All of the above manors are in Westmorland. Tenant lists drawn from the Barony of Gilsland in eastern Cumberland show the same

TABLE 3. *Number of Customary Tenants*

Community	1574	1650	1675	1688	1743
Grasmere (Richmond Fee)	45	41	35	40	33
Loughrigg	26	20	21	21	23
Ambleside	56	45	43	39	40
Undermillbeck	105	110	81	68	75
Applethwaite	64	65	61	52	55
Crosthwaite-cum-Lyth	57	76	63	64	58
Troutbeck	56	57	48	52	57
Casterton	50	42	n.a.	41	33
TOTAL	459	456		377	374

uncertain pattern. The customary tenantry on the manor of Askerton fell from 51 in 1626 to 40 in 1699. But the number of tenants increased in Irthington, from 50 in 1612 to 60 in 1699.[16] Regrettably, there is no evidence about the tenants-at-will who had carved out pieces of the forests or the pasturelands of the two counties. Their numbers may have declined radically during the seventeenth century.

Although the numbers of tenants fell in the late seventeenth century and through the eighteenth century, contemporaries were struck by the continued smallness of the holdings and the poverty of the tenants. One observer, writing in 1766, noted that many Cumberland farmers "work like slaves; they cannot afford to keep a man servant but husband, wife, sons and daughters all . . . work in the fields . . . they very seldom taste meat or wheat bread."[17] The agricultural surveyors, John Bailey and George Culley, wrote in 1794:[18]

> There are probably few counties, *where property in land* is divided into such small parcels as in Cumberland; and those small properties so universally occupied by the owners; by far the greatest part of which are held under the lords of the manors, by a species of vassalage, called *customary tenure*; subject to the payment of fines and heriots, on alienation, death of the lord or death of tenant. [Italics in the original.]

In Westmorland, the same conditions prevailed. "A large proportion of the county . . . is possessed by a yeomanry, who occupy small estates of their own."[19] They "live poorly and labour hard."[20]

The Westmorland surveyor, a Mr. Pringle, added that fifty years before the 1794 survey the tenants seldom ate meat but subsisted on bread and butter.[21] The surveyors found little evidence of any agricultural improvement among the small farmers. In Cumberland:[22]

> One great obstacle to improvement, seems to arise from a laudable anxiety in the customary tenants to have their little patrimony descend to their children. These small properties . . . can only be handed down, from father to son, by the utmost thrift, hard labour and penurious living; and every little saving being hoarded up for the payment of the eventful fine.

Finally, Nicolson and Burn describe Westmorland in 1777 as perhaps the most populous county in the realm, relative to the value of the agricultural land.[23]

These descriptions, taken from the end of the next century, probably apply as well to the end of the seventeenth. By 1700, neither county had advanced far toward the elimination of the smallholder, impoverished by the smallness of his farm and the exactions of his landlord. It is true that some consolidation of holdings had taken place and certain tenants worked larger parcels than their ancestors, but this, by itself, can hardly account for the elimination of famine from the two counties.

Nor is it likely that improved farming techniques much affected the returns of the smallholder. In the seventeenth century there were some striking improvements, but these were probably limited to those large landowners with both technical knowledge and the capital to undertake the necessary changes. One such landowner, Sir John Lowther of Lowther, Westmorland, left a book of "observations and remembrances," which detail some of the improvements undertaken on his demesne lands.[24] At considerable expense, he constructed irrigation systems, cleared weeds and stones, limed and manured his fields, and had "greate increase" of grain. In particular, three fields, which before improvement had scarcely returned their seed, now "bore exceeding Corne for manie years." The Lowther estate account book bears him out; his grain yields were greatly improved over the Lowther yields at the turn of the century, which we have already noted. Sir John's seed-yield ratios were as shown in

TABLE 4. *Seed-Yield Ratios, Lowther*

Year	Wheat	Peas	Bigg	Oats
1657/58	13:1	3:1	6.5:1	4.9:1
1658/59	4.5:1		8:1	6.5:1
1660/61			6.1:1	5.7:1
1662			6:1	7:1
1663	8:1	3:1	7.3:1	8.6:1
1663/64	7:1	7:1	9.2:1	5.1:1
1664		1.3:1	8:1	7.3:1
1666/67	13:1	3.5:1	7:1	4:1
1668/69		4:1	4:1	4.5:1
1668/69 (another field)		1.5:1	5.5:1	4.7:1

Table 4.[25] The average for all these years was as follows: wheat, 9.7:1, peas, 4.2:1; bigg, 7:1, and oats, 5.8:1. These yields compare favorably with any shown in B. H. Slicher van Bath's appendixes of seed-yield ratios for the seventeenth century.[26] It is clear that grains and legumes could grow extremely well on some of the better lands of Westmorland, given the proper knowledge and the necessary capital for improvement.

Despite his evident success, Sir John wrote that "in corne I never found much profitt," remarking that his satisfaction had been in seeing the land made fruitful and the poor employed. Probably his remark was prompted by the agricultural price changes that had set in about 1630. He had succeeded his father in 1637, and his memoranda were probably written at one time, near the date of the last entry in 1673. They represent a retrospect of 36 years and the level of grain prices prevailing during that period. During this time England —and indeed all of Europe—had witnessed a reversal of the price trends of the preceding century. After 1630, grain prices remained stable for some years or actually declined, ending the previous long, rapid increase.[27] Livestock prices remained strong, at least relative to grain prices.[28] If the arable lands at Lowther, with their greatly increased yields, no longer produced a profit, it also indicates that Westmorland had been brought into the larger English grain market, something that was by no means certain in the first years of the century.

One of the improvements instituted by Sir John—perhaps the most interesting—reflected this change in relative livestock/grain prices. In 1653, he had converted one of his arable fields, the Millfield, from tillage to pasture and had "floated" it. By means of ditches and pipes, water was conveyed to all parts of the pasture and it was flooded. This technique, which Sir John noted he had learned in the south, gave him an enormous harvest of hay and increased the yearly value of the land from 4*s*. to 40*s*. He noted that this was "Ye Cheapest and profitablest husbandry [that] can be used."[29]

As we have already suggested, it is unlikely that the smallholder improved his lands in any similar fashion. He was too poor and probably too ignorant. He may have imitated the Lowthers by raising a few peas and perhaps laying down some lime,[30] but the expense of flooding his pastures would have been beyond his limited resources. New crops evidently were not introduced until the middle of the eighteenth century—the turnip in 1756, clover about 1750.[31] Oats remained the staple grain throughout the two counties. The probate inventories of the later seventeenth century, however, imply a degree of agricultural diversity that had been lacking before. More small farmers kept a pig or two and some geese or hens. Peas and beans appear more frequently in the inventories. Both cheese and cheese presses are listed, contrasting with their total absence at the beginning of the century. More common, too, are the inventories that list linen, hemp, and spinning wheels. Perhaps most striking is the number of carts that now appear on the inventories.[32] As we shall see, the growth of mining in the Pennines, the Cumbrians, and along the Cumberland coast brought about an expansion of transport—to get the ore out—and undoubtedly many a smallholder became a part-time carter.

The trend in agricultural prices, too, may have benefited the smallholder. In the late sixteenth and early seventeenth centuries he was forced to grow his own grain, either because he had no money to purchase it in times of dearth, or because importation was limited by the lack of land and water communications. As we have seen, the customary tenant took in parcels of the marginal common pasture to increase, however slightly, his grain production. These accretions had not been enough to ward off famine in years of harvest failure, but with the stabilization (and later slump) in grain prices, he would have been able to return to livestock farming—for which his lands were better suited—and buy his grain on the market. The prices for his livestock remained strong, so his position relative to the grain-producing farmer improved. H. J. Habakkuk has suggested that the English "peasant" was relatively prosperous during the long price increase prior to 1640; after that date—and it is only approximate—his position deteriorated because of the fall in agricultural prices.[33] But perhaps in counties such as Cumberland and Westmorland the reverse process took place. What Habakkuk describes may have been true of those farmers who were able to take advantage of the grain price increases before 1640 and were hurt by their fall after that date. The farmers of the northwest, however, may have been materially hurt by the upward surge of grain prices and, only after the price stabilization of 1640, were able to benefit from the enhanced price of livestock because they could then buy their grain cheaply and easily on the market.

One of Sir John Lowther's comments offers some support to this theory. In several places in the remembrance book, he refers to enclosures that he had undertaken, often in the face of tenant opposition. In one instance he enclosed a portion of the common pasture "because it was a rott ground, and spoyled all our flock." In other words, this particular pasture was chronically wet and he walled or hedged it off to prevent his sheep entering and picking up the liver fluke. He offered the enclosed land to his tenants for use as arable, but they declined; either the rent was too high or they had no need of arable land. In connection with possible tenant opposition to this enclosure, Sir John wrote that "Inclosures are noe new things though now it seemeth strange." Enclosures were certainly not "strange" a generation or two before, when hundreds of tenants, licensed by their lords, had nibbled away at common pasture throughout the two counties. His comment implies that all such encroachments had become rare and that the common pastures were used for animals rather than converted to tillage to help offset the continual shortage of grain.

One other point should be mentioned here: although livestock prices held up in the period after 1640, wool prices did not. Following the low point of 1622, wool prices recovered in the late 1620's and remained fairly strong until the 1650's. In that decade there was a price slide—and wool prices remained soft to the end of the century.[34] This weakness no doubt hurt the sheep farmer of the northwest, who, as we indicated before, was too far from the urban meat markets to maximize his income from the sale of mutton. But there is some slight evidence that fewer sheep and more cattle were being raised in the two counties than formerly. As we will see in the next chapter, cattle exports to the south increased through the seventeenth century. Sheep movements are not known, but according to an account of the wool trade, written about 1700, Cumberland was then thirty-fourth and Westmorland fortieth—and last—in wool production among English counties. Peter Bowden has converted these figures to packs of wool per square mile, to correct for size differences between the counties. He found that Cumberland sheared .66 packs and Westmorland .63 packs of wool per square mile. The county ranking first was Dorset, with 4.10 packs per square mile. Only Yorkshire (.52), Norfolk (.49), Durham (.50), and Staffordshire (.50) ranked behind Cumberland and Westmorland.[35] It is curious that four of the lowest six were northern counties. There are no comparable earlier figures, and hence no way to tell if wool production (and sheep farming) had declined in Cumberland and Westmorland, but perhaps this had indeed happened. If the figures are reliable, however, they do indicate that sheep raising was not a crucial factor in the economy of either county by 1700, and adverse wool price movements would have had little effect.

If these shifts in the relative price levels of grain and livestock (particularly cattle) helped the Cumberland and Westmorland smallholder, why did the number of tenants continue to decline? It must be remembered that the condition of the small farmer was still very bleak a century later, at the end of the eighteenth century. The price movements and a possible emphasis on cattle raising may have helped the tenant avoid starvation, but they hardly made him wealthy. When opportunities opened in industry, trade, and shipping, certain tenants would have gravitated to those occupations.[36]

Sons who had migrated to the towns would have been reluctant to return home and assume the family holdings on the death of a father or elder brother.

The towns of Cumberland and Westmorland would have proved attractive because they offered the hope—if not the promise—of economic betterment that still largely eluded the rural smallholder. This new urban vigor, as compared with continuing rural poverty, can be traced through the hearth tax returns of the 1660's and 1670's. According to the provisions of the enabling statute (14 Car. II, c. 10), each taxable hearth was to return two shillings a year, half at Ladyday and the balance at Michaelmas.[37] The tax proved unpopular—and was promptly repealed on the accession of William and Mary, no doubt to popularize their new regime. During the 17 years the tax was in force, assessments were made twice a year, for the Ladyday and Michaelmas collections. But only during two periods, 1662–66 and 1669–74, were the lists of assessment and collection sent in to the government. At other times, the tax was either farmed or administered by commissioners, and neither the farmers nor the commissioners were obliged to report these specific details to the treasury. These lists, however, are what interest us, for they include the names of all persons with taxable hearths, the number of hearths with which each was charged, and the names and (sometimes) the number of hearths of those who were legally exempt. Exemptions fell into one of four categories. (1) The householder paying neither church nor poor rates was free of tax. (2) A householder inhabiting a house with no more than two hearths and worth 20*s*. or less per year who also owned no other property valued at more than 20*s*. a year and earned less than £10 yearly could obtain a certificate discharging him from the tax. In both the above instances, it was the householder who was exempted (or assessed), not the houseowner. (3) Hearths in charitable institutions with endowments yielding less than £100 annually were not charged. (4) Industrial hearths, such as kilns, were exempt, although apparently smiths' forges and bakers' ovens were not.[38]

As we noted in Chapter Two, the records for Cumberland are unfortunately quite fragmentary, but some useful ones survive for Westmorland. Most helpful is an assessment roll bearing the date

"22 Car. II."[39] It is a complete list of all persons assessed in the county and the number of hearths charged to each. For many communities, it also contains the names of those exempt and their hearth count. Unfortunately, for part of the county, particularly in the parish of Kendal, the names of exempted persons are not given; only lists of taxpayers appear. Discharge certificates, showing those exempted in the summer of 1673, do survive.[40] By combining these with the assessment roll it is possible to gain an idea of the relative number of those paying and those exempt in the county, assuming that there was no great change in local assessment procedures or in economic conditions between the two dates. Some difficulties of interpretation arise, however, when these are combined. As I indicated, the assessment lists for some communities include the names of those exempt. When these are totaled and compared with the total from the exemption certificates of two years later, they agree quite closely in some parishes, but there is a wide discrepancy in others. Apparently the exemption certificates include the names of paupers and those without any hearths, whereas the assessment lists only those householders with hearths who were exempt under the property and income qualifications shown in category 2 above. In any event, I have consistently used the exemption certificates because they appear more complete than the exemption lists on the assessments.

It is possible to show the numbers of people exempt as a proportion of the whole number of householders and also the proportion of people with more than one hearth. Rather arbitrarily, the first can be termed "poor" and the second group "wealthy." This is not to say that people with two hearths in their homes were wealthy—far from it—but it does assume that they were on the average better off than their fellows with only one hearth. Writing twenty years ago, W. G. Hoskins showed the clear connection between rising incomes and more comfortable, larger houses.[41] Recently, Margaret Spufford related the worth of some one hundred Cambridgeshire villagers, as given in their probate inventories, with the number of hearths in their houses. She found the number of hearths a man had was a reliable guide to his economic status.[42]

A certain economic pattern emerges for Westmorland, on the

basis of the hearth tax material. First, the city of Kendal had a high percentage of poor—those exempt—and also of wealthy—those paying tax on more than one hearth. This was also the case in the town of Appleby and the village of Kirkby Stephen. Rural communities, on the other hand, had very few multiple-hearth houses, or a very low proportion of wealthy. Rural parishes varied considerably in the percentage exempt, but in the northern parishes it was as high or higher than in Kendal. In short, the wealth of Westmorland —excluding the great gentry families, of course—was concentrated in the towns and larger villages. The poor were everywhere, and rural poverty was as pervasive as urban poverty.

Some comparisons are possible between Westmorland and other English counties whose hearth tax records have been published. Hoskins wrote that the four northernmost counties did not participate in the great "rebuilding" of rural housing that took place between 1570 and 1640. In the north, he states, rebuilding began about 1690 and assumed real importance only in the early eighteenth century.[43] The hearth tax evidence supports his contention, as far as Westmorland is concerned. In Surrey, a county benefiting from its proximity to the London market, the number of hearths per rural household was substantially greater. Even exempt householders often had two or more hearths.[44] Not one in fifty of those exempt in Westmorland had two hearths and none more than two. Dorset also averaged more hearths per dwelling.[45] A count of 35 rural constablewicks in Staffordshire shows that 35 percent of those liable for tax had multiple hearths—a figure well above that for rural Westmorland. Only 27 percent of the Staffordshire rural householders were exempt from the tax.[46] Just two out of 32 parishes in Westmorland had lower figures. Spufford presented the hearth tax evidence for rural Cambridgeshire somewhat differently than I have given the Westmorland data here, but clearly all areas in Cambridgeshire—even the most depressed—had more multiple-hearth dwellings than did rural Westmorland.[47]

Although rural housing remained rudimentary by southern standards, urban conditions in Kendal were quite similar to other towns, in both the north and the south. In Newcastle-upon-Tyne, 41 percent of the 2,510 households were exempt from tax, compared to 47 percent of Kendal's 454 households.[48] Sixty-four percent of those charged in Newcastle were assessed for more than one hearth, as against 73 percent in Kendal. The towns of Stafford, Newcastle-under-Lyme, and Dorchester appear to have been much the same, with a high ratio of multiple hearths and also large numbers of householders exempt.[49] These samplings are too few to permit a firm generalization, but they suggest that, first, rural Westmorland remained sunk in poverty, compared with the rural south of England, and, second, by 1670 Kendal and the other towns of Westmorland were beginning to show some of the signs of wealth that characterized other cities in England. The economic differential between the towns and the countryside in Westmorland would have acted like a magnet, pulling in the rural poor who sought relief from the poverty of the countryside. The large numbers of urban poor show that many did not find it.

The Cumberland returns, although they are too fragmentary to permit quantification, give the impression that the same process was taking place in that county. In Carlisle, the assessment for 1673–74 shows that half the houses had more than one hearth. (The total number of households is suspiciously small; perhaps all those exempt were not shown.) Approximately one-third of the householders were exempt.[50] Outside the walls, the percentage exempt rose and the percentage of multiple hearths fell. Such as it was, wealth was evidently concentrated within the city proper and did not extend to the immediate suburbs. Penrith also had a large proportion of multiple hearths,[51] as did Cockermouth.[52] Although the folio listing the Whitehaven householders is mutilated, there is no doubt that here too there was a high percentage of multiple hearths.[53] In contrast, the rural community of Upper Hesket had 12 taxpayers, of whom five had two hearths, and 52 exempt households.[54] Great Salkeld had three multiple-hearth households out of 27 paying tax; 61 householders were exempt.[55] In ten other rural communities adjoining Penrith to the northwest, two-thirds of the 411 householders shown on the assessment were exempt from tax.[56] The percentage exempt, at least in this sampling, substantially exceeds that found in the towns. Rural Cumberland, like rural Westmorland, remained poor.

The continuing poverty of the two counties—although both had overcome the problem of famine—is underscored by various tax assessments made in the latter half of the seventeenth century. In the proposed tax to replace wardship of 1660, Cumberland was assessed at the lowest rate, in terms of acres to the pound sterling. Northumberland was the second lowest English county and Westmorland the third lowest. In the assessment of 1672, Cumberland still brought up the rear, but Westmorland had replaced Northumberland as the second poorest. This assessment also was calculated in acres to the pound, thus permitting comparisons between counties of different sizes. The assessment of 1693 again placed Cumberland at the bottom, in terms of tax assessed per acre, with Westmorland next lowest. These assessments are not infallible guides to the relative wealth of English counties—the northern counties may have been somewhat underassessed—but they tend to confirm the general rural poverty of the two counties, even when compared with other upland counties in England and Wales.[57]

To briefly summarize, one can find certain signs of change in the two counties by the second half of the seventeenth century. In general, towns were growing more than the surrounding rural countryside. The number of tenants slowly declined, as they trickled into the towns, attracted by the wealth and employment possibilities there. Agriculture was still backward and holdings remained small, but the desperate effort to increase tillage seems to have come to an end. The rural areas had returned to a more profitable emphasis on animal husbandry than had been possible at the beginning of the century, and there were signs of agricultural diversification into dairying and the raising of industrial crops. Although no radical change in agricultural patterns had taken place, the conditions that had led to crisis earlier were at least stabilized, as rural population ceased to push against the limited arable resources of the region.

CHAPTER ELEVEN

Trade, Industry, and the End of Isolation

DURING THE seventeenth century, Cumberland and Westmorland broke out of their isolated position on the north-western borders to become the center of a trade network tying together England, western Scotland, and eastern and northern Ireland. We have already described the hesitant beginnings of trade with Scotland and Ireland in the early years of the century, but it was then too undeveloped to offer a satisfactory alternative to agricultural employment. As the century progressed, however, commercial and industrial growth was rapid, and the number of men employed in the new enterprises increased accordingly.

The mainstay of the new economic vigor was coal. The mines at Workington, as we have seen, were troubled by disagreements, and production did not increase after the first quarter of the century. The deposits at Whitehaven, however, were mined systematically from the early 1630's. In October 1630, Sir John Lowther of Lowther, Westmorland, purchased the manor of St. Bees, which included the village of Whitehaven and the adjacent coal deposits.[1] His second son, Christopher Lowther, who was eventually to inherit St. Bees, was a merchant in Dublin in 1632, and he soon recognized the possibility of selling coal and salt in Ireland. At that time, Christopher Lowther and his trading partners (including his uncle, Robert Lowther of London) were engaged in a small trade between Whitehaven, the Irish ports of Belfast and Dublin, and France. French wine, vinegar, and prunes were shipped to

Whitehaven and bay salt (from La Rochelle) to Dublin. Northern woolens, including Kendal cottons, were shipped to Belfast, Dublin, and France. The French, Lowther wrote, were willing to pay "reasonable good prices" for Kendal cottons. Yorkshire woolens and other northern cloths were disposed of in Ireland. Lead from mines in Cumberland also found a market in France. Butter and tallow bought in Belfast was sold by Lowther in Dublin.[2] Lowther's acquaintance with the Dublin market convinced him that coal and salt from Cumberland should be added to the trade. In 1632 he wrote his uncle Robert Lowther in London that coal offered the best prospects, if suitable shipping could be obtained.

> See coles I thinck would be our best trade, for as much stock as they would require [i.e. the Whitehaven mines could supply Dublin's needs] if we had flemish bottoms to carry them, but o[ur] owne country barks soe little they carey nothing at a tyme and yet will have dear by reason they are commonly about 7 or 8 men to one of 30 tons which eateth upp the p[ro]fitt.[3]

At about the same time, Lowther estimated that seven-eighths of the salt used in Ireland came from France, with the remainder coming from England or from Irish salt panners.[4] No doubt he hoped to capture a share of this market, using the abundant cheap coal at Whitehaven as fuel for panning. Salt was panned at Whitehaven and sold in Dublin as early as 1633,[5] and the same year Lowther ordered iron sheets for additional pans "such as are used at Newcastle salt works."[6] His account books are incomplete, and unfortunately it is impossible to estimate what proportion of the Irish market was supplied from Whitehaven. Increasing amounts of coal were shipped to Dublin in the late 1630's and apparently the problem of low-cost shipping was solved.[7] Very likely Lowther had a vessel built on the Flemish model at Whitehaven.[8] Sometime in the 1630's a quay was constructed at Whitehaven to provide protection for ships in the exposed harbor.[9] At the time of his death in 1644, Lowther had laid the foundations for the later coal trade from Whitehaven to Dublin.

Lowther did not give up his trade in other wares, although he foresaw the profits that could be made in coal and salt. Shortly before his death he was shipping iron ore to Belfast and other northern Irish ports, where new forges and hearths were going into production.[10]

Like most seventeenth-century merchants, he was no specialist but dealt in a variety of products. His correspondence suggests that he imported Irish cattle to Whitehaven on the return voyages of the coal and salt carriers.[11] Not all Lowther's ventures ended well; in 1636 he was a partner in a ship trading to Hamburg that was lost with all hands, costing him, his father Sir John, and other partners in the venture £2,353.[12] The inventory of Christopher Lowther's estate at his death indicates both the variety of goods in which he dealt and the network of commercial contacts he had developed. The inventory lists, besides 436 tons of coal, two salt pans, and 400 bushels of salt at Whitehaven, various types of woolen cloth, sailcloth, pitch, deals (planks probably used for ship siding), numerous barrels of herring (all spoiled, according to the inventory), 21 millstones, seven gallons of aqua vita, and 112 pounds of tobacco. The tobacco was probably brought to Whitehaven from Ireland for sale in England, rather than from Virginia to Whitehaven for transshipment to Ireland, as was the case later in the century. Lowther's debtors resided in Cumberland and Westmorland, as expected, and also Dumfries (Scotland), Castletown (Isle of Man), Preston (Lancashire), Carrickfergus, Carlingford, and County Kilkenny (all Ireland).[13]

Christopher Lowther—who died a baronet—had been given the manor of St. Bees by his father before the latter's death in 1637. At Sir Christopher's death, in 1644, the manor passed to his infant son, Sir John. For some years during Sir John's childhood, there was apparently little effort to expand the coal and salt trade begun by Sir Christopher. The salt pans were leased to two of his former business associates,[14] but whether the coal shipments to Ireland from Whitehaven continued or not is unclear. Port books for the period from November 1, 1648, to March 25, 1649,[15] show that 260 chaldrons of coal, or 520 tons, were exported from the west coast ports of Cumberland, but do not indicate whether the shipments originated in Whitehaven or Workington. In the next three months, 184 tons were shipped, all to Scotland, northern Ireland, and the Isle of Man. Fourteen tons of iron were exported, presumably to northern Ireland, and 800 pounds of salt were sent to Scotland. The destination of the exports indicates that the coal trade to Dublin had temporarily lapsed following the death of Sir Christopher Lowther.

Imports through the west coast ports for eight months ending July 1, 1649, include twenty tons (approximately eighty quarters) of malt, barley, and rye from northern Ireland. Harvests were bad in 1647 and 1648 in England, and perhaps these grain shipments alleviated the shortage locally, but there is no way to tell what portion, if any, went to the poor. In the same period, 61½ lasts of herring came in (a last equaled 12 barrels, each with 1,200 fish).[16] This considerable amount shows the importance of the fishing industry in the Irish Sea in the middle of the century. Much of the herring probably was transshipped south by way of the coastal trade. Other imports listed were barrels of preserved beef, 600 pounds of prunes, 400 pounds of butter, and wine, vinegar, linen, and tobacco. All these items seem to have been transshipped from Ireland. These port books for 1648–49 are the only ones that survive between the few that exist for 1610–11 and the series that start again in December 1687. The growth of trade, marked no doubt by periods of depression, cannot be traced year by year but must be inferred from these three dates. A comparison of the port books for 1648–49 with those for 1610–11 shows clearly that commercial activity had expanded significantly. Coal was shipped in greater quantities than formerly and many other items appear, suggesting that a diversified exchange had developed with Scotland and Ireland by the middle of the century.

The Lowther records supplement the limited data that can be gathered from the port books. By 1665 Sir John Lowther's mines at Whitehaven were again producing coal for the Dublin market. By 1667 production had reached at least 9,200 tons annually, and the yield may have been considerably higher, since the figures for all the mines were not given.[17] During the 1670's exports to Ireland of coal and iron ore far exceeded the levels of the late 1640's.[18] See Table 5.

Our concern here is not primarily with coal production, however, but with the employment it gave. One of Sir John's collieries, Greenbank, employed 19 men to produce between 70 and 90 tons

TABLE 5. *Coal and Iron Exports, Whitehaven*

Year	Tons of coal exported	Coal mining, est. employment	Tons of iron ore exported
1672	17,992	92	1,020
1673	17,658	90	810
1674	17,834	91	817
1675	21,228	108	674
1676	21,100	107	880
1677	19,880	101	734
1678	23,648	121	1,522
1679	20,890	106	1,226
1680	24,400	124	925
1681	23,798	121	1,205
1682	19,166	97	1,699
1683	21,544	110	1,801
1684	32,784	167	1,371
1685	27,406	140	844

of coal a week during the spring and summer of 1675. In another colliery, Three Quarters Bank, nine men mined 30 tons a week.[19] Extending these figures for a full year brings the annual coal production per man in the first colliery to 219 tons and in the second, 173, or an average of 196 tons per year per man. Assuming that this was roughly the typical man-year coal output, it is possible to estimate the number of miners needed to produce the coal shipped from Whitehaven. These figures are given in Table 5. The coal tonnage represents the exports from Whitehaven only and does not include shipments from Workington or mining for domestic use. Unfortunately, I have found no satisfactory figures for total coal production in the two counties, and we cannot say how much it increased during the seventeenth century, apart from the Lowther tonnage.[20]

In 1675–76 coal production at Greenbank was highest in July, August, and January. It fell off badly in September—to about one-half to one-third the August figure. By the 1690's, on the other hand, such seasonal variations no longer occurred.[21] This change implies that by the 1690's coal mining was a full-time occupation but that earlier it had been a useful and important by-employment, and that miners returned to their holdings at harvest time. If this was the case, our employment figures are misleading. Actual employment was much higher on a largely seasonal basis.

The men employed in mining were only a part of the expanded work force that coal made possible. Probably as important was the increased employment in shipping. A 1678 muster of seamen in Cumberland listed 179 sailors, boatsmen, and fishermen scattered along the coast from Holm Cultram south to Ravenglas. Whitehaven had at that time the most seamen, followed by Workington. Fishermen generally came from the other, lesser ports, such as Ravenglas, Flimby, and Holm Cultram.[22] This muster was made in the face of local opposition and quite likely understates the true number of sailors in the county. About the year 1690, another list of all the mariners was compiled, evidently for Sir John Lowther's own use, and it appears to be more complete. The list contains 672 names. At that time Whitehaven had 351 seamen, Workington 60, and Harrington 39. The balance was largely concentrated on the west and southwest Cumberland coast and in the parishes just inland.[23] Whitehaven was home port for 37 vessels of 3,118 tons in 1682, and another 11 ships of 662 tons sailed from Workington.[24] Both towns had grown during the century, but Whitehaven's expansion was particularly striking, from six fishermen's cottages in 1566 to 1,089 inhabitants in 1685.[25] In that year, Sir John described the recent growth of the town:

> The Port of Whitehaven from a very meane & inconsiderable place, is of late yeares advanced to a Towne of some Trade & Comerce by the Industry of the Inhabitants, who from their ancient Imploym[en]t of small Barques for the Importation of Cattle and Exportac[i]on of a small quantity of Coales thither, are become owners of 30 or 40 serviceable Vesselles, for any other sort of Trade as well as Coales, and for many other places as well as Ireland.[26]

Aside from the lists of mariners and the estimates of the number of miners employed in the coal pits, we have little information on employment. Increased iron mining suggests growing employment, however. Iron mines were operated at Millom, Eskdale, and Egremont. Between the end of March 1635 and the middle of October 1636, one mine in Egremont—Nicholson's Pit—produced 1,440 tons of ore, most of which was carted to Whitehaven at a cost of 4*d*. the ton. In less than six months in 1638, 1,240 tons of ore were mined at this pit. During that time, wages of £51-13-4 were paid to the miners, but unfortunately the accounts do not say how many men were employed. The accounts also show purchases of timber, buckets, and troughs for the mines. The Egremont mines were leased to Mr. William Pennington by the Earl of Northumberland, and the Earl's receipt book shows a constant increase in the royalties paid, from about £7 a year in the mid-1640's to about £300 a year in the 1680's. This growth in revenue, however, may not have been paralleled by a similar increase in ore mined; relations between Pennington and the Earl were not always happy and the per ton royalty paid to the Earl may have been increased. Further to the south, Pennington in the 1630's built a forge at Muncaster Head in Eskdale, which was supplied with ore from mines nearby and with wood for smelting from the Earl's forest there. Pennington's forge may have provided local employment, but the Earl's tenants in the manor of Eskdale complained that he was ruining the local timber. In a petition to the Earl, they noted that if Pennington did not stop, they would not have timber for their houses and would have to live in caves.[27]

Lead was mined on Alston Moor in the Pennines and also in the Newlands area of the Cumbrians, just to the west of Keswick. In the year ending October 1651, the three Cumbrian mines at Newlands, Rowling, and Barrow Hill produced 316 tons of ore. The output seems to have declined after that year, although mining continued to the end of the century. In 1646–47, the mine at Newlands expended from £2-5-0 to £3-3-0 in wages, but the account books do not say how many men were employed. They do mention one man by name who was paid 10*s*. for ten days work. If his rate of pay was typical, the Newlands mine employed about ten men. The Barrow Hill mine, which apparently was somewhat more productive, probably had a larger work force. The work was irregular, varying from week to week and month to month, suggesting that mining was predominately a by-employment to agriculture at this time. One of the principals of the operation was Joseph Höchstetter, no doubt a descendant of the Daniel Höchstetter who had supervised the copper mines in the same area in the sixteenth century. After it was mined, the lead was carted to Braithwaite, then to Cockermouth, and on to Workington, where it was shipped to London.[28]

In addition to the men directly employed in mining, these mining operations had further ramifications. As we have seen, the shipping industry was based first upon the coal trade with Ireland, although it later diversified into other activities. The transport of the minerals to the various ports brought employment to farmers, who became draymen and packhorse men. In turn, cart makers, harness makers, and horse breeders benefited. The quickened tempo of the economy affected, little by little, all of western Cumberland. J. U. Nef has fully described the impact that coal mining and the coal trade had on other industries, such as iron making, shipping, and salt panning.[29] It is only necessary here to note that this same process of interaction took place in Cumberland in the last half of the seventeenth century.

Toward the end of the century, commercial activity involved many goods besides minerals. The most valuable of these was tobacco, which came directly from Virginia to Whitehaven. As we mentioned earlier, in the 1640's tobacco had been shipped from America to Ireland and then transshipped to Whitehaven. But the Navigation Act of 1671 prohibited the direct importation of colonial goods to Ireland—and Whitehaven became a major supplier of tobacco to the island, as well as to Scotland and northern England. In 1688 the *Resolution* of Whitehaven returned from Virginia carrying 160,373 pounds of tobacco.[30] Part of the tobacco was warehoused at Whitehaven for eventual shipment to other destinations; the *Resolution* took on a cargo of coal and sailed for Dublin with the remainder of the tobacco. By this time at least two other ships were also sailing to Virginia: the *Freeman* of 150 tons and the *Adventure* of 140 tons. Like the *Resolution*, they also carried coals to Dublin.[31] In other words, shipping, which had been built primarily for the coal trade, was available to exploit other economic opportunities when these opened up, as Lowther had astutely observed.

Exports to Ireland included, besides coal and tobacco, iron ore, northern woolens, leather goods, iron wares, and a variety of other goods, such as tobacco pipes, books, stockings, and even 73 pounds of "head hair," which the *Charles*, of Whitehaven, carried to Dublin in the winter of 1687–88. Numerous shipments of iron ore went to Dublin, Belfast, Wexford, and Wicklow. The *Mary*, out of Dublin, delivered 60 tons of iron ore in Dingle, on the southwest Irish coast. Wicklow was a major consumer of iron ore; in the period from March 25 to June 24, 1688, the *Fortune*, the *Phoenix*, and the *Ann and Elizabeth*, all of Whitehaven, sailed to that town with cargoes of iron ore totaling 234 tons. The port books for the next quarter of the year show a shipment of iron from Whitehaven to Lancaster and carry the notation that the iron had been imported from Wicklow. In the third quarter of 1688, 928 bars of iron were imported into Whitehaven from London. These imports of iron and exports of iron ore suggest that—although Cumberland was rich in iron ore—wood was insufficient locally to smelt more than a small portion of the available ore.[32]

Goods sent to the American colonies were northern woolens, saddles, leather gloves, pots, pans, plows, cordage, linen, silk, and undifferentiated "iron manufactures."[33] What proportion of these goods were manufactured locally we cannot tell. Probably some of the northern woolens came from the old clothing parishes of Westmorland, although the few that are identified by place of origin are from Yorkshire. The leather goods—saddles and gloves—were almost certainly made in the two counties.

The imports entering the west coast ports from Ireland underwent a major shift in the 1660's. Live, lean cattle had been the major Irish export, but a series of acts, culminating in the "Great Cattle Act" of 1666, barred further Irish cattle shipments to England.[34] After the passage of the Cattle Acts, Irish goods entering Whitehaven were linen, soap, sheepskins, cattle hides, and horses.

The Whitehaven port books also reveal commercial connections with Scotland, the Isle of Man, and various English and continental ports. In 1688 iron ore, coal, and, most important, tobacco went to Scotland from Whitehaven. The Isle of Man received coal and tobacco.[35] Lancaster imported, in one three-month period, 332 tons of coal, 550 pounds of Virginia tobacco, 700 deals, which were initially shipped to Whitehaven from Sweden and Ireland, and substantial amounts of freestone from the Cumberland quarries. To the north, Carlisle received 7,550 deals in a year's time, most of which had been brought to Whitehaven from Bergen. As I have already noted, deals were used for ship siding, and these quantities (along with the frequent shipments of canvas, resin, tar, and nails) suggest considerable shipbuilding at Carlisle. The destination shown on the port books seems misleading, however, because Carlisle is too far upriver for vessels of any size. Probably the town is named simply because the customs officials were stationed there. The materials were carried in ships from Allonby and Silloth, and it seems likely that the shipbuilding was centered in those ports and at Skinburness, another small port just north of Silloth. Carlisle, or these small adjoining ports, also imported herring, tobacco, soap, and brandy, perhaps for transshipment across the border to Scotland.[36]

A coastal trade had developed also between Whitehaven and London by this time. In exchange for a variety of manufactured and luxury goods from London—for example, ships' anchors, "oyle and capers," currants, anchovies, lime juice, wine, brandy, and books—Whitehaven sent south 2,930 quarters of oats, large quantities of lead, butter, bacon, and five dozen hats.[37] The export of oats is noteworthy, for it suggests that a surplus of oats was then being grown in the two counties.

In the spring of 1688 the *Orange* of Whitehaven sailed to Danzig with a cargo of lead, northern woolens, stockings, and over 21,000 pounds of Virginia tobacco.[38] Trade was also carried on with Rotterdam and, as we saw, Bergen. The carriers were Whitehaven ships. This continental trade was in its infancy at the end of the seventeenth century; in the next, it would grow until Whitehaven became the second or third English port in the tobacco trade, shipping to all parts of Europe and as far as Madras.[39] But clearly by the end of the seventeenth century, the sea had ceased to be the barrier it had been in the sixteenth century. Rather, it had become the avenue for the distribution of coal, iron ore, leather goods, and perhaps the woolens of the two counties.

The bulk of the Scottish trade was not carried on from Whitehaven, but overland through Carlisle. The major import entering

Cumberland was Scottish cattle, which were driven across fords in the Esk and Eden rivers near Carlisle. We have already seen that this cattle trade had a beginning in the sixteenth century, but had suffered from various governmental prohibitions and the unsettled state of the borders. As the seventeenth century wore on, the trade grew in volume, until by the middle of the century, Scotland could be described as "little more than a grazing field for England."[40] Most of the cattle entering England from the Scottish highlands and the southwestern counties came through Cumberland. The cattle, once they had crossed the border, followed one of the great drove roads that led to either the southern or the eastern counties. The principal road led along the valley of the Eden, crossing out of Cumberland at Eamont Bridge just south of Penrith, and then to Brough in Westmorland. There a cattle fair was held each September, after which the beasts were driven on to Bowes in Yorkshire. An alternate route passed south from Brough to Kirkby Stephen, then followed a more southerly path to Richmond, in Yorkshire. The usual destination for the cattle was Norfolk, where they were fattened before being offered on the London market. Other drove roads connected Cumberland with the northeastern counties, one evidently leading east from Bewcastle, through the Tyne Gap to Newcastle, another passing along the foothills of the Pennines to Alston Moor and then east to Durham.[41]

The borough of Carlisle had the right to collect a toll on all cattle passing into or out of Cumberland.[42] The "Scotland" toll was the name given to the toll on incoming cattle; the "Shire" toll that on outgoing cattle. The corporation accounts show the amounts received on each toll for most years in the late sixteenth and on through the seventeenth century. Unfortunately, these revenues only partially indicate the growth of the cattle trade because, first, the tolls were farmed and only net revenues to the corporations were recorded, and, second, there was a massive and probably increasing evasion of the tolls. In 1662, the number of cattle on which toll was paid at Carlisle was 18,574. Another 7,866 came in through Whitehaven from Ireland, making a total of 26,440 cattle entering Cumberland.[43] That year the farmer paid the Carlisle corporation

£85. The revenue to the corporation had risen from £5 at the beginning of the century, climbed to a peak of £110 in 1639–40, then declined to an average of about £75 in the 1660's and 1670's. Assuming that the revenues to the city reflected fairly closely the number of cattle on which toll was paid over the years and that the evasions remained a fairly constant percentage of all cattle entering the county, we can say that the cattle trade grew 22-fold between 1600 and 1640, then declined during the interregnum, to level out at about 15 times the 1600 figure. It seems more likely, however, that evasions of the tolls increased as trade grew. Carlisle was simply not able to collect what was legally due it, and the number of cattle coming into Cumberland probably increased steadily after the Restoration. Certainly many drovers were successful in evading the tolls. In the period from September 1 through October 2, 1669—that is, in 32 days—1,336 cattle and 400 sheep passed over Alston Moor toward Durham without paying toll. The informer who reported these evasions to the farmer of the tolls at Carlisle complained that the bailiff of Alston Moor had "much threatened" him for counting the animals,[44] which indicates that local officials were in league with the drovers, no doubt being paid for their help in evading the toll collectors. Droving was at its height in the fall, and the 1,300 cattle on Alston Moor was certainly not a monthly average, but these figures hint that cattle on which toll was not paid may have exceeded those on which it was paid.

It is difficult to evaluate the impact of cattle droving on the economy of Cumberland and Westmorland. The drovers themselves, judging by their surnames, were usually either borderers or Scotsmen. The local inhabitants alongside the drove roads would have benefited, however, by supplying the drovers with food and drink and by receiving payment for right of way and overnight pasture.

More important was the relative advantage that Cumberland and Westmorland cattle now enjoyed in the national cattle market. The substantial numbers of Scottish and, prior to 1666, Irish cattle entering England indicate that the kingdom was not self-sufficient in meat production during the seventeenth century. The relative disadvantage of distance from the major London market, which had worked against the cattle producers of the two counties in the sixteenth century, now was transferred to Scotland and Ireland. Cumberland and Westmorland, instead of being at the periphery of the agricultural supply area, had moved much closer to the center. Tolls and customs duties also gave a competitive advantage to all English cattle, including those from the two counties. The Shire tolls, collected on cattle leaving Cumberland, indicate that cattle moving from Cumberland to market increased by 70 percent between 1600 and 1640. The Civil War caused a temporary drop in the trade, but by 1670 the numbers again reached the 1640 level. This conclusion is drawn from the increase in the toll revenue; if evasion increased, the numbers were higher.

By the end of the seventeenth century the barriers that had hindered economic improvement in Cumberland and Westmorland had begun to break down. Mining, shipping, and droving combined to bring the two counties into a commercial network that stretched from Scotland and Ireland to the markets of London. The largely local orientation of the economy had been replaced by a national and international orientation.

CHAPTER TWELVE

Conclusions and Further Thoughts

In the first chapter of this essay I set forth a working hypothesis—or crude model—of the economic conditions that could have led to famine. It is time to see how closely the experience of Cumberland and Westmorland agrees with the hypothesis, to point out shortcomings in the evidence, and, finally, to outline the importance of famine to early modern English society, both in the regional context of the northwest and in the larger national framework.

The increase in Cumberland's population between the date of our first figures, 1563, and that of our last, 1688, was on the order of 50 percent; Westmorland's population declined slightly over roughly the same period. The intervening ecclesiastical census of 1603 for the diocese of Carlisle suggests that rural population was somewhat greater at the beginning of the seventeenth century than later. This impression is reinforced by the limited data which indicate an increase in the number of customary tenants during the sixteenth and early seventeenth centuries, followed by a leveling-off in tenant populations and, finally, by a decline after 1650. Many of the tenants-at-will and subtenants, who are so elusive to historical scrutiny, may have left the land earlier. The rural parish registers show a decline in the surplus of baptisms over burials beginning in the years 1590 to 1610, and the total number of baptisms also began to fall during these two decades, following a continuous long rise in the sixteenth century. In short, what evidence there is suggests that rural population reached its peak around the year 1600 and then slowly declined.

As we indicated in the first chapter, there is no absolute overpopulation, but only overpopulation relative to the agricultural and industrial resources available. In Cumberland and Westmorland, such an imbalance between people and resources seems to have existed, at least when harvest failure disrupted the already fragile economy. The agricultural productivity of the two counties was certainly low at the time of the famines. In part, this deficiency arose from the low level of agricultural technology, witnessed by the poor seed-yield ratios obtained on some of the better agricultural land. In part, too, the general unproductiveness stemmed no doubt from the conversion of pastureland to tillage. Particularly in the uplands, such lands were ill-suited to grains and soon became exhausted. In brief, productivity in the agricultural sector, especially in arable agriculture, did not keep pace with population growth. At the same time, demand for the coarse local wool was weak and wool prices were subject to great fluctuation, often collapsing after a harvest failure redirected purchasing power to foodstuffs and away from cheap woolens. The degree to which depressed wool and woolen demand in periods of crisis contributed to the famines is not clear. In Westmorland, Lancashire, and the West Riding, the clothing industry was important—but in other areas of the north and across the borders in Scotland where famine was pervasive there was little or no cloth industry. Finally, the market for cattle, the other staple of the region, was hampered by the distance separating the two counties from the main consuming areas in the southeast of England.

In the crises of the end of the sixteenth and beginning of the seventeenth centuries the relative importance of each of these weaknesses is somewhat obscure. In 1597 there was no doubt a classic *crise de subsistances*. Harvests failed in 1594, 1595, 1596, and 1597, following repeated heavy summer rains, and the price of foodstuffs soared beyond the reach of the poor. Very likely farm laborers and servants were let go, as the diminished harvests required fewer hands to bring them in and because feeding servants was expensive —perhaps impossible—in times of dearth. Wool prices remained strong until 1597 and then dipped only moderately,[1] and it seems probable that there was no precipitous drop in incomes from wool sales or cloth manufacturing. But the divergence between wool prices (or cloth prices) and grain prices was crucial and the real purchasing power of those dependent on either raw wool or woolen cloth would have fallen.[2] In the best of years, the two counties were corn-poor; after a series of bad harvests there would not have been enough grain to feed the inhabitants. And—given the divergence of wool and grain prices—there would have been inadequate purchasing power to buy sufficient grain elsewhere, say in Newcastle, to alleviate the shortage. These comments apply only to the poor, of course; the better-off may have had ample reserves of grain or money to tide them over.

The crisis of 1623 also seems to have been caused by harvest failure, although falling wool prices may have also brought about a collapse of earning power in the clothing regions of the northwest. The same may have taken place in 1587.[3] But all three crises were made worse by the price differential that favored the grain-producing areas of England at the expense of the pastoral regions. In the long term, the price differential led to the conversion of pasture to arable cultivation, for which the land, or much of it, was unsuitable. Grain had to be grown locally, for it could not be bought with the proceeds from sales of wool, hides, and other products of a predominately pastoral economy. In the short run, this was disastrous, because in years of harvest failure the land simply did not produce enough grain to keep the poor alive.

By the middle of the seventeenth century, three correctives had taken place within the agricultural sector. First, it appears that rural population dependent on agriculture was declining. Second, the so-called agricultural depression led to the stagnation and eventual decline of grain prices. However, livestock prices, particularly cattle prices, remained firm. The relative price advantage enjoyed by the grain producer in the sixteenth and early seventeenth centuries now shifted to the livestock producer. Speaking broadly, land in pasture returned relatively more than arable land. The livestock producers of the two counties could now buy their grain with the proceeds of the sale of animals and animal products. Third, the new market conditions favored cattle over sheep, at least for a region as distant from the urban meat markets as Cumberland and Westmorland. Wool prices remained fairly strong from the middle 1620's to the 1650's, when a decline began that lasted to the end of the century. But by then, both Cumberland and Westmorland had successfully deemphasized wool production.

Is this theory of changing price advantage borne out by the absence of famine after 1623? The next harvest failure came in 1630 and there is little evidence of famine in that or the following year.[4] As we indicated in Chapter 10, possibly the drought that destroyed the 1630 harvest in the south was not felt in the wetter north. Also, wool prices remained high, rather than collapsing as they had following the harvest failure of 1622, and perhaps real incomes did not fall to the point they had in 1623. Or, maybe 1630 followed the famine of 1623 too closely, and the marginal population had not had time to replace itself. By 1630 the shift in relative grain/livestock prices had not yet taken place, but by the next period of harvest failure, 1647–49, perhaps the relative strength of livestock prices helped avert famine. By this time, too, industry and trade picked up and may have provided purchasing power to buy grain. The later harvest failures of 1661 and the 1690's came when agricultural prices favored the two counties, and trade and industry were firmly established.

Turning back from the seventeenth century to the sixteenth century, it seems unlikely that Cumberland and Westmorland suffered famines in the first half of the sixteenth century. As I indicated, the parish registers are too few and unreliable for analysis before (roughly) 1570, and it is impossible to test this theory. But population was absolutely lower and thus placed less strain on the grain-producing capacity of the region. Before 1552 the price of wool was higher, in relation to the price of grain, than later in the century.[5] Finally, the cloth industry of Westmorland had not yet seriously declined.

In the model sketched in Chapter 1, it was posited that a market economy permits agricultural specialization; each region grows the crops or animals best suited to it, and the larger economy benefits. The experience of the two counties suggests that such specialization works only if there are no relative price disadvantages between various agricultural products. Price inequalities disrupt the theoretical advantages of specialization, and lead to the relative impoverishment of the region specializing in crops with low relative prices. Price equilibrium is obviously a chimera; one or another region, with its agricultural strengths, is either well-off or badly-off relative to other regions with other agricultural strengths. It seems that the two counties in the first part of the sixteenth century were moderately well-adapted to the larger English market. Both their wool and woolens, although coarse, found a market. In the last half of the century the change in agricultural prices, and the decline of the woolen industry, led to a long period of depression. Then around the middle of the seventeenth century the two counties again supplied a needed commodity, cattle, to England and developed an expanding international market for their minerals.

At the end of Chapter 5, we questioned whether changes in the division of the profits of the land—the level of rents and fines the lords extracted from their tenants—had much to do with the famines or the disappearance of famine from the northwest. Both rents and fines rose during the sixteenth century, but it was only after 1603 that they reached their peak, that is to say, after two of the famines. Also, if the rents and fines had been determining, parts of Westmorland and much of Cumberland would have known famine in the bad years after 1623, but there is no evidence of such famines. In the Barony of Kendal and in other manors where the tenants paid a fee for the confirmation of their old rents and fines, further upward pressure by the lord was impossible. But in the majority of the manors within the two counties, fines remained arbitrary and the lords pushed them as high as they dared. This is not to say that the exactions of the lord had no effect on the tenant's economic level; clearly the rents and fines that the lord imposed helped keep the tenant impoverished and agriculturally backward through the end of the eighteenth century. The timing of the famines, however, does not correspond closely enough to changes in the level of fines to suggest that they were much of a factor in the famines.

Perhaps, however, we should regard the exactions of the lords in a somewhat different light. If their rents, fines, and heriots pushed the tenants down toward subsistence, harvest failure had a more devastating impact than it would have had if these pressures had been absent. If impoverishment of the tenants was more extreme in the northwest than in other parts of the north, and if impoverishment was more extreme in the north than in the south of England, this poverty—in part caused by rents and fines—could explain the differential effects of the harvest failures of 1597 and 1623. We have two levels of causation: one was the complex of background conditions that made the famines possible, once the proximate cause, the failure of the grain harvest, was felt. The level of landlord exactions was, of course, only one of the background conditions; others were overpopulation, isolation, pastoral farming in a period of long-term grain price increases, and a lack of alternative employment. The weight that we assign to each is a matter of conjecture—but all certainly contributed to the famines. Let us return, however, to the problem of timing and the question why there were no more famines after 1623, even though fines continued to creep up, where the lords could manage to increase them. I think, first of all, that fines were close to their maximum in 1623. The few instances of greater fines later in the century that were noted in Chapter 5 are probably exceptional. The most common level of fines—of twenty to thirty times the old rent—was reached in the 1620's. In addition, the other background conditions that had led to economic weakness were changing, and the lord no longer had the leverage that he had enjoyed before. Population was declining; alternative employments were becoming available within the region. With fewer men competing for holdings, the lords would have been forced to restrain their pressure for higher fines or lose their tenants. The decline in the number of customary tenants supports this view; a small trickle of tenants left the land and apparently no others presented themselves to take the vacant holdings at the terms the lords set.

Quite probably the lord's attitude toward encroachment and squatting on the common pasture played a major role in initially creating conditions favorable to famine. As we have seen, the lords did not prevent squatters from settling on the pastures, if they paid rents and entry fines. The Crown, too, was agreeable to this type of settlement in the Forest of Inglewood. This process of encroaching, of carving tiny parcels of land out of the great pastures, created a large group of impoverished tenants and subtenants, each man with a cottage and perhaps an animal or two to complement the meager wages he might earn as a farm laborer. Had the lords firmly prohibited squatting on the commons, such an army of poverty-stricken cottagers, vulnerable to famine, would never have been created. The landless men would have been forced to emigrate. Judging from the evidence, the famine of 1597 was considerably more severe in the north than in the south of England, although it was felt throughout the kingdom. Certainly the disastrous famine of 1623 was much worse in the north. It may be that the practice of squatting on the upland pastures explains part of this difference between the north and the south. Of course, not every lord would necessarily have permitted squatting. The attitudes of the Crown and the great magnates—the Percys or the Dacres—might not have been typical of the smaller lords who lived closer to the land and closer to their tenants. But too often we are limited to the evidence from the great estates because their records have survived while the records of smaller estates have been lost. Perhaps certain manors in the north entirely escaped the famines of 1597 and 1623 because their lords prevented the squatting that led to an imbalance between population and food production.

W. G. Hoskins, in his penetrating study of the midland village of Wigston, paints a quite different picture of rural life than the one I have presented here.[6] In Wigston there was an improvement in the lot of the average peasant toward the end of the sixteenth century instead of the decline found in the village communities of Cumberland and Westmorland. Hoskins also emphasizes the stability and continuity of life in Wigston,[7] as contrasted with the dislocation that must have accompanied the great famines of the north.

Two points should be made here: first, the peasants of Wigston were largely freehold, unlike the customary tenants of the two counties, and were able to reap for themselves the profits of rising grain prices. Even though the Wigston economy was largely diversified and primarily subsistence, a peasant with small grain surpluses to sell could accumulate money.[8] Second, this very subsistence economy made for strength in times of high grain prices, assuming of course that bad weather did not completely destroy the crop. The smallholder may have had to take up his belt a notch, but he did not starve.[9] The customary tenant of Cumberland and Westmorland was basically not a subsistence farmer but a market producer of livestock and animal products. This was true even in the lowlands, although less pronounced than in the highlands. And the tenant's relation with the market in years of consistently high corn prices was skewed; he had wool, hides, and meat to sell and corn to buy—and the market was unfavorable.

Hoskins' village was a pleasant place to live until the second half of the seventeenth century. Only then was it clear that "the poor" existed as a class in the village, whereas in the sixteenth century the poor had been "incidental, a matter of individuals (the old, or the orphaned, the maimed or the sick)."[10] In Cumberland and Westmorland the poor—as a class—had existed throughout the latter years of the sixteenth century. It is clear that they continued to be numerous into the seventeenth and eighteenth centuries; but their lot seems to have improved over what it had been earlier.

The differences between a Midland village and the hamlets of the northwest show how hazardous generalization about the "English peasantry" is. There was no "English peasantry" (and no one knows this better than Hoskins), but only local, or at best, regional peasantries. Even the counties of Cumberland and Westmorland reveal considerable variation in local communities—between highlands and lowlands, between clan groups and clothing parishes, or between towns and the countryside.

Certain aspects of the economic and demographic transformation of Cumberland and Westmorland remain obscure. First, our population evidence indicates a decline in population after 1603. Total baptisms reach a peak around 1600—then begin a long decline that is not arrested until the later eighteenth century. Why? Were population limitations present that had not existed before? One possibility was family limitation, either through a higher age at marriage for women or through some method of contraception. A study of female age at marriage, number of births per marriage, and the span of years from the first to the last child, might show different patterns before and after the famines. Such a study has not been done. Another obvious possibility was migration, which would have siphoned off excess population, but here too we draw a blank. Emigration to America appears to have been minimal,[11] but nothing is known (and probably little will ever be known) about migration to other parts of England or to northern Ireland. It seems reasonable to suppose that the opening of the two counties to trade with Ireland and Scotland and, through droving, to the rest of England made the outside somewhat less strange to the average native of the two counties, but this is pure supposition, unsupported by evidence.

Second, the lack of a local price series means that the historian has to assume that price movements taking place in other parts of England were faithfully mirrored within the two counties. Although reasonable similarities can be expected, local price trends may have diverged at certain times—and the divergences might suggest alternative explanations for the famines. Even more important, there is no information about incomes, that is, no idea what a tenant was earning from his holding or what a laborer received in wages. Movements in real incomes could be determined if both price and income series were available. Without them, it becomes necessary to argue from medical evidence rather than economic evidence. We are equally ignorant of the role, if any, played by either private charities or disbursements under the poor law. Parish records dealing with the local administration of the poor law begin—for a few parishes—only in the 1660's and 1670's.

As I have mentioned elsewhere in this study, the answers to some of the questions that remain can only be answered by detailed local studies. If such a study combined the skills of the demographer—in a reconstitution—with all of the literary evidence available in the records of manorial and church courts and wills and inventories, it might enable us to evaluate the true dimensions of the demographic crisis of the late sixteenth and early seventeenth centuries and its effects on the family and on the village social structure in the two counties. This larger regional study, I hope, has set the stage for further local research.

As local studies should prove useful to measure the impact of famine on the society of the northwest, further work on the larger issue of starvation in England will broaden our understanding of the role of food shortage in heightened death tolls and reduced baptisms and marriages. In this essay, I have limited myself to a consideration of the two famines of 1597 and 1623, because they were the most severe in the northwest, the region that provides the core of the research. A glance back to Figure 16 (p. 136), however, reveals that England may have suffered a subsistence crisis in 1638–39, when for two years burials again exceeded baptisms. Prices were elevated in 1638, following the deficient harvest of 1637. As far as I am aware, no studies of this crisis have been undertaken, and we cannot be sure what form it took. It would be useful, too, to know more about the relationship between disease and malnutrition or starvation. Typhus, for example, does not seem to have been an important ingredient in the mortality of the northwest, but it may have played a much larger role in the other areas. Other diseases may have also contributed to the deaths, as malnutrition lowered the resistance of humans to infectious microbes. Any clear relationship between malnutrition and reduced resistance to the great epidemic diseases is somewhat questionable, but too little research has yet been done to permit any generalizations.[12] Finally, comparative studies of regional economies might clarify the relative importance of the conditions that apparently contributed to the impoverishment of the inhabitants of the northwest. A growing population, agricultural weakness, isolation, grasping landlords, and a lack of employment alternatives—all were present in the northwest. But another region may have had all these and yet somehow avoided famines when the harvest failed. Or conversely, famine may have struck a community where only some of the above conditions were present. Such studies would help us refine our picture of famine in early modern society.

Within the regional context of the northwest, this has been a study of economic conditions and their demographic consequences. Within the larger framework of the north and, to a lesser extent, all England, it has traced the demographic impact of the two famines of 1597 and 1623. Recent scholarship has begun to uncover the social effects of the dearths, particularly the wrenching dislocations resulting from the famine of 1597. Margaret Spufford has shown that the bad years 1596 and 1597 helped eliminate the smallholders of Chippenham, Cambridgeshire. Unable to pay their rents, the Chippenham smallholders fell into debt and many of them later lost their holdings, although they evidently did not starve, as did the smallholders of the northwest.[13] In a suggestive paper, David Levine and Keith Wrightson pointed out that illegitimacy rose markedly in the village of Terling, Essex, during and after the shortages of the 1590's. This rise, they argue, may have been a result of postponed marriages arising from the inability of many of the poorer inhabitants of Terling to gain financial independence in a time of economic distress. Normally, premarital sexual relations resulted in marriage, but marriage may have become impossible for a substantial proportion of the poorer people of Terling and the children they conceived were born out of wedlock. As economic conditions improved during the seventeenth century, the percentage of illegitimate births declined.[14] It should be noted, perhaps, that neither the rise of illegitimacy in Terling nor the disappearance of the smallholder in Chippenham coincided with the famine years; the effect was spread out over the following several years. More immediate in its relation to the famine was the rise in crime, particularly theft, that Joel Samaha found in Essex, one of England's richer counties. In 1596, 111 thefts were recorded; in 1597, the number rose to 258, and then fell back in 1598 to 165.[15] Samaha concludes that "economic hardship in the 1590s drove expanding numbers of people to steal in order to live."[16] Clearly the harvest failures of 1594–97 had important and lasting ramifications for English society, even where no evidence—as in Essex—of actual starvation has turned up. The harvest was the heartbeat of the English economy—again we borrow Hoskins' analogy—and when it faltered the effects were felt throughout the body of the society.

Over a decade ago, Peter Laslett complained that although we know so much about kings and statesmen, about the growth of Parliament and the rise of the British Empire, we know very little about the life of the average man and woman in early modern England. Indeed, Laslett noted, we "do not know whether all our ancestors had enough to eat."[17] Since that time, research—much of it inspired by Laslett—has begun to uncover the conditions of life and the familial and societal ties of the ordinary person in the preindustrial period. The "world we have lost" is lost forever—but perhaps we shall begin to understand what it once was.

Reference Matter

APPENDIX A

Populations of Cumberland and Westmorland Parishes in the Sixteenth and Seventeenth Centuries

MY SOURCES for the figures in this Appendix are BL, Harl. 594, fols. 85–87, 105–6; House of Lords Record Office, Protestation Returns, 1641/42, Cumberland; *The Westmorland Protestation Returns, 1641/42*, ed. M. A. Faraday (Kendal, 1971); F. G. James, "The Population of the Diocese of Carlisle in 1676," *Transactions of the Cumberland and Westmorland Antiquarian and Archaeological Society*, n.s., 51 (1951); D. Lysons, *Magna Britannia* (London, 1816; Denton's figures), 4: xxxv–xliv; PRO, E179/195/73 but using discharges from E179/348.

The numbers in parentheses for 1563 represent my estimates rather than households counted in 1563. I computed the average percentage of change between 1563 and the Denton figure for 1688 for all adjoining parishes. Using this percentage, I then interpolated backward from the parish's 1688 household count to determine the missing 1563 figure.

Appendix A

DIOCESE OF CARLISLE, CUMBERLAND

Parish	1563 returns Households	X4.75	1641–42 Protestation Returns Adult males	X3.6	1676 returns	1688 Denton returns Households	X4.75
Addingham	111	527	219	788	403	117	556
Aikton	80	380	99	356	349	106	504
Ainstable	50	238	81	292	239	72	342
Allhallows	20	95	43	155	104	30	143
Arthuret	100	475	198	713	316	120	570
Aspatria	140	665			354	126	599
Bassenthwaite	60	285			154	106	504
Beaumont	26	124	65	234	87	28	133
Bewcastle	70	333	123	443	78	84	399
Bolton	111	527			163	126	599
Bowness	82	390	204	734	303	166	789
Brampton	66	314	146	526		126	599
Bridekirk	140	665	311	1,120	642	204	969
Bromfield	200	950	288	1,037	416	222	1,055
Burgh by Sands	100	475	97	349	218	78*	371
Caldbeck	182	865	339	1,220	670	191	907
Camerton	58	276	78	281		68	323
Carlisle, St. Cuthbert	228	1,083	726	2,614	361	484	2,299
Carlisle, St. Mary's	249	1,183			591	528	2,508
Castle Carrock	46	219	51	184	84	72	342
Castle Sowerby	100	475	250	900	242	141	670
Croglin	24	114	54	194	61	69	328
Crosby on Eden	47	223	100	360	178	122	580
Crosscanonby	31	147	76	274	98	42	200
Crosthwaite	320	1,520	373	1,343		312	1,482
Cumrew	30	142	67	241	180	51	242
Cumwhitton	56	266	97	349	210	62	295
Dacre	98	466	177	637	346	124	589
Dalston	200	950	347	1,249	615	260	1,235
Dearham	70	333	80	288	203	110	523
Denton, Upper and Nether	14	67	79	284	31	55	261
Edenhall	60	285			126	53	252
Farlam	28	133	55	198	120	52	247
Flimby	(49)	(233)				70	333
Gilcrux	35	166	58	209	173	44	209
Greystoke	200	950	707	2,545	1,189	502	2,385
Grinsdale	13	62	23	83		40	190

*The household count given in D. Lysons, *Magna Britannia* (London, 1816; 4: xxxv–xliv), for Burgh by Sands in 1688 is incorrect. I am indebted to Mr. Bruce Jones for the correct figure.

DIOCESE OF CARLISLE, CUMBERLAND *(continued)*

Parish	1563 returns		1641–42 Protestation Returns		1676 returns	1688 Denton returns	
	Households	X4.75	Adult males	X3.6		Households	X4.75
Hayton	74	352	147	529	140	74	352
Hesket in the Forest	200	950	265	954	425	247	1,173
Holm Cultram	300	1,425	646	2,326		469	2,218
Hutton in the Forest	46	219	115	414	174	57	271
Ireby	46	219	113	407	193	108	513
Irthington	82	390	154	554		128	608
Isel	80	380	147	529	224	83	394
Kirkandrews upon Eden	11	52	29	104	38	20	95
Kirkandrews	(50)	(238)	126	454	120	127	603
Kirk Bampton	40	190	122	439	201	51	242
Kirkbride	24	114	49	176	128	68	323
Kirkland	104	494	184	662	281	120	570
Kirklinton	78	371	211	760		90	428
Kirkoswald	60	285	187	673	238	124	589
Lanercost	(70)	(333)	265	954		117	556
Langwathby	(39)	(185)	59	212	117	43	204
Lazonby	107	508	63	227	258	87	413
Melmerby	33	157	89	320	152	54	257
Newton Reigny	36	171	74	266		52	247
Orton	47	223	95	342	189	68	323
Ousby	51	242	64	230	143	73	347
Penrith	140	665	411	1,480	961	270	1,283
Plumblands	36	171	78	281		82	390
Renwick	16	76	41	148	41	53	252
Rockliffe	14	67			203	66	314
Great Salkeld	40	190	79	284	201	69	328
Scaleby	41	195	71	256		68	323
Sebergham	60	285	140	504		99	470
Skelton	120	570	108	389	356	123	584
Stanwix	80	380	237	853	373	89	423
Stapleton	60	285	121	436	62	62	295
Thursby	48	228	123	443	332	107	508
Torpenhow	120	570	220	792	516	206	979
Uldale	60	285	69	248	126	104	494
Walton	(45)	(214)	70	252		69	328
Warwick	60	285	60	216	124	45	214
Westward	66	314	285	1,026	447	122	580
Wetherall	117	556	231	832	455	103	489
Wigton	220	1,045	429	1,544	652	250	1,188

Appendix A

DIOCESE OF CARLISLE, WESTMORLAND

Parish	1563 returns		1641–42 Protestation Returns		1676 returns	1670–73 hearth tax	
	Households	X4.75	Adult males	X3.6		Households	X4.75
Asby	84	399	57	205	251	56	266
Askham	80	380	71	256	223	67	318
Bampton	140	665	210	756	415	152	722
Barton	150	713	167	601		148	703
Brough (under Stainmore)	140	665	142	511	667	204	969
Brougham	44	209	52	187	145	20	95
Cliburn	20	95	38	137	98	40	190
Clifton	40	190	50	180	156	43	204
Crosby Garrett	33	157	90	324	168	33	157
Crosby Ravensworth	112	532	146	526		138	656
Dufton	44	209	91	328	165	56	266
Kirkby Stephen	300	1,425	350	1,260	1,457	394	1,872
Kirkby Thore (with Milborne and Temple Sowerby)	98	466	154	554	380	149	708
Long Marton	64	304	82	295	240	91	432
Lowther	70	333	48	173		59	280
Morland	308	1,463	248	893		262	1,245
Musgrave	30	143	40	144		31	147
Newbiggin	20	95	46	166		32	152
Ormside	47	223	56	202	140	35	166
Orton	211	1,002	345	1,242	696	238	1,131
Ravenstonedale	116	551	269	968	614	184	874
St. Lawrence, Appleby	147	698	148	533	420	175	831
St. Michael, Appleby	90	428	143	515	398	103	489
Shap	180	855	245	882		153	727
Warcop	100	475	98	353	347	111	527

Populations of Cumberland and Westmorland

DIOCESE OF CHESTER, CUMBERLAND

Parish	1563 households	1687–88 households	Parish	1563 households	1687–88 households
Arlecdon	58	86	Millom	212	180
Bootle	120	111	Moresby	32	109
Brigham	374	574	Muncaster	70	124
Cleator	32	66	Ponsonby	32	75
Corney	72	96	St. Bees	464	669
Dean	80	124	St. Bridget Beckermet	52	97
Distington	46	82	St. John Beckermet	28	86
Drigg	60	112	Waberthwaite	45	75
Egremont	80	282	Whicham	100	89
Gosforth	140	126	Whitbeck	(79)	87
Haile	30	86	Workington	140	189
Harrington	48	97			
Irton	63	103			
Lamplugh	63	142			

DIOCESE OF CHESTER, WESTMORLAND

Parish	1563 households	1670–73 hearth tax households	Parish	1563 households	1670–73 hearth tax households
Beetham	277	218	Kendal	1,750	1,348
Burton	226	165	Kirkby Lonsdale	528	440
Grasmere	272	252	Windermere	246	146
Haversham	450	418			

APPENDIX B

Parish Registers Consulted

Registers in italics are published; the rest are in manuscript or typescript.

CUMBERLAND

Bridekirk, The Registers of, Penrith, 1927
Crosthwaite, Registers of, Penrith, 1928–31
Dacre, The Registers of the Parish Church of, Kendal, 1912
Dalston, The Parish Registers of, Dalston, 1893
Dean Registers, A Transcript of the First Volume of, Cumbria Record Office PR 27/6
Gosforth, Ms. copy, Cumbria Record Office
Greystoke, The Registers of, Kendal, 1911
Holme Cultram, The Registers of, Penrith, 1948
Kirkoswald, Cumbria Record Office PR 9/1
Lamplugh, Registers of, Penrith, 1936
Lorton, Cumbria Record Office PR 28/1
Millom, The Registers of, Kendal, 1925
Muncaster, Cumbria Record Office PR 24/1
Newton Reigny, The Registers of, Penrith, 1934
St. Giles, Great Orton, The Registers of the Parish Church of, Kendal, 1915
St. Andrews, Penrith, The Parish Registers of, Penrith, 1938
St. Bees, Cumberland, The Registers of, Newcastle, 1968
Skelton, The Registers of the Parish Church of, Kendal, 1918
Threlkeld, Cumbria Record Office PR 70/1
Watermillock, The Registers of the Parish of, Kendal, 1908
Westward, Cumbria Record Office PR 56/1, 2
Whicham, The Registers of, Penrith, 1926

Parish Registers Consulted

WESTMORLAND

Brough under Stainmore, The Registers of, Kendal, 1923
Cliburn, The Registers of, Penrith, 1932
Crosby Garrett, The Parish Registers of, Penrith, 1945
Crosby Ravensworth, The Parish Registers of, Penrith, 1937
Crosthwaite-cum-Lyth, Registers of, Penrith, 1935
Dufton, Cumbria Record Office PR 69/1
Kendal, The Registers of, Kendal, 1922, and Penrith, 1952
Kirkby Lonsdale, Ms. copy, Cumbria Record Office, Kendal
Kirkby Thore, Ms. copy, Carlisle Public Library, Tullie House
Lowther, The Registers of, Penrith, 1933
Morland, The Registers of, Durham, 1957
Newbiggen, The Registers of, Penrith, 1927
Shap, The Registers of the Parish of, Kendal, 1912
Ravenstonedale Parish Registers, The, Kendal, 1893
Warcop, The Registers of, Kendal, 1914

APPENDIX C

Geographical Distribution of Mortality

PARISHES with high mortality in 1587–88 were, in Cumberland: Dacre, Dalston, Dean, Greystoke, Holm Cultram, St. Giles (Great Orton), Newton Reigny, St. Andrews (Penrith), Skelton, Threlkeld, and Watermillock. In Westmorland: Brough-under-Stainmore, Crosby Garrett, Crosby Ravensworth, Crosthwaite-cum-Lyth, Dufton, Kendal, Kirkby Lonsdale, Morland, and Ravenstonedale. St. Bees, Lamplugh, and Shap were unaffected, Crowthwaite only slightly affected. Figures for other parishes shown in Appendix B are unavailable.

Parishes with high mortality in 1597 were, in Cumberland: Bridekirk, Crosthwaite, Dacre, Dalston, Gosforth, Greystoke, Holm Cultram, Kirkoswald, Lamplugh, Muncaster, St. Andrews (Penrith), St. Bees, Skelton, Threlkeld, Watermillock, and Whicham. In Westmorland: Brough-under-Stainmore, Crosby Garrett, Crosby Ravensworth, Crosthwaite-cum-Lyth, Dufton, Kendal, Kirkby Lonsdale, Kirkby Thore, Lowther, Morland, Newbiggen, Shap, and Ravenstonedale. Newton Reigny had high mortality in 1596 rather than 1597. St. Giles (Great Orton) had high mortality in 1596; the register for 1597 is missing. Mortality in Kirkby Lonsdale continued to increase in 1598. No parishes were unaffected. Figures for other parishes listed in Appendix B are unavailable.

Parishes with high mortality in 1623 were, in Cumberland: Bridekirk, Crosthwaite, Dalston, Dean, Greystoke, Lamplugh, Lorton, Millom, Muncaster, Newton Reigny, St. Andrews (Penrith), St. Bees, Threlkeld, Watermillock, and Westward. In Westmorland: Brough-under-Stainmore, Cliburn, Crosby Garrett, Crosby Ravensworth, Crosthwaite-cum-Lyth, Dufton, Kendal, Kirkby Lonsdale, Lowther, Morland, Newbiggen, and Warcop. No parishes were unaffected. Figures for other parishes listed in Appendix B are unavailable.

APPENDIX D

Parish Mortality Figures

LANCASHIRE

C. D. Rogers and his researchers analyzed the following registers (the crisis death rate for 1623 for each is given in *The Lancashire Population Crisis of 1623* [Manchester, 1975]): Altham, Ashton-under-Lyne, Blackburn, Blackrod, Bolton, Burnley, Bury, Cartmel, Caton, Chorley, Clitheroe, Cockerham, Colne, Coniston, Dalton, Didsbury, Eccles, Eccleston, Farnworth (Widnes), Flixton, Hale, Halton, Hawkshead, Ingleton, Kirkham, Lancaster, Leigh, Manchester, Middleton, North Meols, Ormskirk, Padiham, Pennington, Penwortham, Poulton, Prescot, Preston, Prestwich, Radcliffe, Ribchester, Rochdale, Sefton, Stalmine, Standish, Tatham, Thornton-in-Lonsdale, Urswick, Walton on the Hill, Warrington, Warton, Whalley, Whittington, Wigan, Winwick.

DURHAM

The number after the parish name in the following lists of parishes indicates the percentage mortality in 1623, based on an average of the mortality of the years 1618–28. (In other words, total mortality 1618–28 is divided by 11. The average is then divided into the mortality figure for 1623.) Where no figure is given below, the mortality for 1623 can be judged from the registers, but one or more of the other years is incomplete.

The following Durham registers are in the County Record Office, County Hall, Durham DH1 5UL: Auckland, St. Andrew (179); Auckland, St. Helen (173); Bishopwearmouth, St. Andrew (166); Boldon, St. Nicholas (18); Brancepeth (210); Cockfield (89); Darlington, St. Cuthbert (212); Durham, St. Giles (145); Durham, St. Nicholas (170); Easington (209); Escomb (69); Esh; Greatham (102); Grindon (177); Hamsterley; Heighington (239); Houghton-le-Spring (193); Newton Long (145); Pittington (250); Redmarshal; Sedgefield (208); Stockton, Holy Trinity; Whitworth (176); Witton-le-Wear.

The following registers have been published by the Durham and Northumberland Parish Register Society: Bishop Middleham (109); Coniscliffe (119); Durham, St. Mary-le-Bow (180); Durham, St. Mary of the South Bailey; Middleton St. George (75); Whitburn (112).

YORKSHIRE, WEST RIDING

The following registers have been published by the Yorkshire Parish Register Society (for explanation of the mortality percentages that follow many of the parish names, see above under Durham): Addingham (196); Austerfield chapelry (180); Bingley (169); Bolton-by-Bolland; Braithwell (118); Brodsworth (172); Carlton-Juxta-Snaith; Clapham (182); Cowthorpe (245); Darrington; Dewsbury (80); Gargrave (143); Gisburne (207); Hampsthwaite (183); Heptonstall (202); Hooton Pagnell; Ilkley (218); Ingleton (135); Kildwich-in-Craven (220); Kippax (Kippax, 1624: 203); Kirkby Malham (234); Ledsham (212); Maltby (177); Otley; Pontefract (109); Rothwell (125); Saxton-in-Elmet; Sheffield (121); Snaith (152); Swillington (165); Thornton-in-Lonsdale (134); Horbury chapelry (154) Wath-upon-Dearne (158); Wragby (152).

The following registers are in the Sheffield City Libraries, Central Library, Sheffield S1 1XZ: Arksey (205); Drax (99); Melton-on-the-Hill (183); Norton (166); Royston (131); Tickhill (100); Worsbrough (121).

The following registers are at the Borthwick Institute of Historical Research, St. Anthony's Hall, York YO1 2PW: Aberford (191); Bramham (147); Tadcaster; Wistow (190).

Figures for the following registers have kindly been supplied by Professor Michael Drake, The Open University, Walton Hall, Milton Keynes, Bucks, MK7 6AB (all years here are old style; certain registers shown here have been included above, with new-style dating): Batley (163); Bingley (185); Birstal (150); Bradford (192); Dewsbury (146); Elland (182); Halifax (166); Hartshead (99); Heptonstall (208); Horbury (171); Huddersfield (197); Keighley (285); Leeds (160); Methley (88); Mirfield (173); Rothwell (142); Swillington; Thornhill; Wakefield (141).

YORKSHIRE, EAST RIDING

The following registers have been published by the Yorkshire Parish Register Society: Askham Richard (92); Atwick (227); Burton Fleming (97); Cherry Burton; Drypool (122); Patrington (116); Settrington (116); Winestead (238); Wintringham (206).

Figures for the following registers are available at the Cambridge Group: Howden (160); Hunmanby (260); Sutton & Stoneferry, Hull.

The following registers are at the East Riding County Record Office (now Humberside), County Hall, Beverley, Yorkshire: Bainton (343); Cottingham (122); Driffield, Great [Driffield, 1624: 337] (175); Driffield, Little (225); Etton [Etton, 1624: 220] (107); Flamborough (149); Lund (272); Muston (272); Ottringham (97); Owthorne (115); Reighton (309); Sancton (139); Skerne (172).

The following registers are at the Borthwick Institute of Historical Research: Catton (237); Dunnington (136); Elvington; Huggate; Norton (148); Wheldrake (164).

YORKSHIRE, NORTH RIDING

The following registers have been published by the Yorkshire Parish Register Society: Coxwold (147); Danby-in-Cleveland (70); Easingwold (156); Eston (111); Gilling; Hackness (135); Kirklington (229); Pickhill-cum-Roxby; Rokeby (235); East Rounton (127); Thirsk (174).

Figures for the following registers are at the North Yorkshire County Record Office, County Hall, Northallerton, Yorkshire: Barton, St. Cuthbert (150); Bedale (170); Felixkirk [Felixkirk, 1624: 151] (101); Hauxwell [Hauxwell, 1624: 175] (118); Kirby Ravensworth (165); Middleton Tyas (144); Stainton-in-Cleveland (57).

The following registers are at the Borthwick Institute of Historical Research: Rosall (47); Overton.

CITY OF YORK

The following registers have been printed by the Yorkshire Parish Register Society: All Saints, Pavement (122); Holy Trinity, Goodramgate (136); St. Crux (156); St. Lawrence (115); St. Mary, Bishophill, Junior (133); St. Mary, Castlegate (143); St. Olave (97).

Figures for the following registers are at the Cambridge Group: St. Martin, Coney Street (134); St. Michael-le-Belfrey (124).

The following registers are at the Borthwick Institute for Historical Research: All Saints, North Street (154); Holy Trinity, King's Court (115); Holy Trinity, Micklegate; St. Cuthbert; St. Helen, Stonegate (146); St. John, Ousebridge (130); St. Martin cum Gregory, Micklegate; St. Margaret, Walmgate (132); St. Mary, Bishophill, Senior; St. Savior (57).

Notes

The following abbreviations are used in the Notes.

APC, E	Acts of the Privy Council of England, J. Dasent, ed., London, 1890–1907
BL	British Library, London
Border Papers	*The Border Papers: Calendar of Letters and Papers Relating to the . . . Borders of England and Scotland*, J.Bain, ed., 2 vols.; Edinburgh, 1894–96
C3	Chancery Proceedings
C33	Chancery Entry Books of Decrees and Orders
Ca	Carlisle Corporation Records
Cambridge Group	Cambridge Group for the History of Population and Social Structure, 27 Trumpington St., Cambridge
Cecil Papers	*Calendar of the Manuscripts of the Most Hon. the Marquis of Salisbury* (Historical Manuscripts Commission)
CRO	Cumbria County Council Archives Department, The Record Office, The Castle, Carlisle
CSP,D	*Calendar of State Papers, Domestic*, R. Lemon and M. A. E. Green, eds.
D/HG	Howard of Greystoke papers
D/Lons/L	Lonsdale of Lowther papers
D/Lons/W	Lonsdale of Whitehaven papers
D.L. 44	Duchy of Lancaster, Special Commissions and Returns
E122	Exchequer, Customs Accounts
E134	Exchequer Depositions Taken by Commission
E164	Exchequer, Miscellaneous Books, Series 1
E179	Exchequer, Subsidy Rolls
E190	Exchequer, Port Books
E317	Exchequer, Parliamentary Surveys
E351	Exchequer, Declared Accounts
F.E.C.1	Forfeited Estates Commission, Papers
H of N	Howard of Naworth papers, University of Durham, Department of Palaeography and Diplomatic
Harl.	Harleian Manuscripts

L.R.2	Land Revenue, Miscellaneous Books
LRO	Lancashire Record Office, Sessions House, Preston
Lans.	Lansdowne Manuscripts
Lec	Leconfield papers
PC	Parish Council Records
PR	Parish Register
PRO	Public Record Office, Chancery Lane, London
Records of Kendal	*Records Relating to the Barony of Kendal*, W. Farrer and J. F. Curwen, eds., 3 vols.; Kendal, 1923–26
Req. 2	Court of Requests, Proceedings
S.C.	Special Collections
S.P.	State Papers
Sta. Cha. 8	Court of Star Chamber, Proceedings
WRW (C)	Wills, Archdeaconry of Richmond, Deanery of Copeland
WRW (K)	Wills, Archdeaconry of Richmond, Deanery of Kendal

CHAPTER ONE

1. C. H. Andrewes, "Epidemiology of Influenza," *Influenza*, World Health Organization (Geneva, 1954), pp. 9–12.

2. Pierre Goubert, *Beauvais et le Beauvaisis de 1600 à 1730* (Paris, 1960), chap. 3, particularly p. 47.

3. *Ibid.*, pp. 72–75.

4. P. V. Sukhatme, "Human Calorie and Protein Needs and How Far They Are Satisfied Today," in B. Benjamin, P.R. Cox, and J.Peel, eds., *Resources and Population* (New York, 1973), pp. 27–28.

5. *Ibid.*, pp. 25–28.

6. V. R. Young and N. S. Scrimshaw, "The Physiology of Starvation," *Scientific American*, 225, no. 4 (1971): 21–22.

7. Jack C. Drummond and Anne Wilbraham, *The Englishman's Food, A History of Five Centuries of English Diet* (London, 1958), p. 41.

8. In 1641, for example, Henry Best was selling oats at 14*s*. the quarter, barley at 22*s*. the quarter, rye at 27*s*. 6*d*. the quarter, and "best" white wheat at 35*s*. the quarter. See Joan Thirsk and J. P. Cooper, eds., *Seventeenth Century Economic Documents* (Oxford, 1972), p. 356. For other examples, see *CSP,D, 1619–23*, pp. 495, 498, 506.

9. See the discussion of this point in A. B. Appleby, "Nutrition and Disease: The Case of London, 1550–1750," *The Journal of Interdisciplinary History*, 6 (1975): 4–5.

10. Price data in this and the following paragraph are drawn from Peter Bowden, "Statistical Appendix," in Joan Thirsk, ed., *The Agrarian History of England and Wales*. IV, *1500–1640* (Cambridge, 1967), pp. 814–70.

11. Frances M. Lappé, *Diet for a Small Planet* (New York, 1971), pp. 50–53, 88–89.

12. Drummond and Wilbraham, *Englishman's Food*, pp. 29–30, 38–39, 55.

13. Quoted in *ibid.*, p. 88.

14. For the symptomology and effects of starvation, see Young and

Scrimshaw, "The Physiology of Starvation"; Ancel Keys et. al., *The Biology of Human Starvation*, 2 vols. (Minneapolis, 1950); Emil Apfelbaum, *Maladie de famine* (Warsaw, 1946), and Jean Mayer, "Management of Famine Relief," *Science*, 188 (1975): 571–77.

15. Goubert, *Beauvais et le Beauvaisis*, pp. 51, 52n.

16. Keys, *Biology of Human Starvation*, I: 587–90; Mayer, "Management of Famine Relief," p. 572.

17. *Tamworth Parish Register* (Staffordshire Parish Register Society, 1917).

18. Pierre Goubert, "Une richesse historique: les registres paroissiaux," *Annales E.S.C.*, 9 (1954): 92. See also Goubert, *Beauvais et le Beauvaisis*, p. 49.

19. See T. N. A. Jeffcoate, "Amenorrhea," *British Encyclopedia of Medical Practice*, ed. Lord Horder (3d ed., 1952), 1: 359–65; Zena Stein, Mervyn Susser, Gerhart Saenger, and Francis Marolla, *Famine and Human Development: The Dutch Hunger Winter of 1944–1945* (New York, 1975), pp. 73–76; A. N. Antonov, "Children Born During the Siege of Leningrad in 1942," *Journal of Pediatrics*, 30 (1947): 250–59. See also the historical discussion in E. LeRoy Ladurie, "L'amenorrhée de famine (XVIIe–XXe siècles)," *Annales E.S.C.*, 24 (1969): 1589–1601.

20. Goubert, *Beauvais et le Beauvaisis*, pp. 46–48.

21. For a valuable account of the impact of dearth on marriage, see David Levine and Keith Wrightson, "The Social Context of Illegitimacy in Early Modern England," forthcoming in P. Laslett, ed., *Comparative Studies in the History of Bastardy* (London).

22. In the following paragraphs, I am indebted to the excellent theoretical description of the interplay between agriculture, population, and industry in B. H. Slicher van Bath, *The Agrarian History of Western Europe, A.D. 500–1850* (London, 1963), pp. 7–25.

23. J. C. Russell, *British Medieval Population* (Albuquerque, N.M., 1948), p. 162.

24. Most of these limitations are self-evident but a few are not. For particular interest, see John Hajnal, "European Marriage Patterns in Perspective," in D. V. Glass and D. E. C. Eversley, eds., *Population in History* (London, 1965), pp. 101–43.

25. E.L. Jones, *Seasons and Prices* (London, 1964), pp. 53–59; E. LeRoy Ladurie, *Historie du climat depuis l'an mil* (Paris, 1967), pp. 282–83.

26. Jones, *Seasons and Prices*, pp. 86–92. Liver fluke was more feared than foot rot.

27. W. C. Hoskins, "Harvest Fluctuations and English History, 1480–1619," *Agricultural History Review*, 12 (1964): 32–33.

28. For agricultural improvements in England, see E. Kerridge, *The Agricultural Revolution* (New York, 1968), pp. 181–325.

29. See W. O. Ault, *Open-Field Farming in Medieval England* (London, 1972), pp. 38–39; J. Z. Titow, *English Rural Society, 1200–1350* (London,

1969), pp. 41–42, and W. G. Hoskins, *The Midland Peasant: The Economic and Social History of a Leicestershire Village* (London and New York, 1965), p. 154.

30. See the interesting discussion of famine and its disappearance in M. W. Flinn, "The Stabilisation of Mortality in Pre-industrial Western Europe," *Journal of European Economic History*, 3 (1974): 285–318.

31. See D. Sabean, "Famille et tenure paysanne: aux origines de la Guerre des Paysans en Allemagne (1525)," *Annales E.S.C.*, 27 (1972): 903–22.

32. The shrinking demand presupposes that his market, domestic or foreign, was also affected by the same crop failure. It need not have been, and prices for both wool and cloth may have remained high.

33. See Hoskins, "Harvest Fluctuations, 1480–1619," pp. 40–42.

CHAPTER TWO

1. Meteorological Office Publication No. 635, *Averages of Rainfall for Great Britain and Northern Ireland, 1916–1950* (HMSO, 1958). Rounded to the nearest inch, rainfall averages were: Penrith, 48 in.; Keswick, 58 in.; Carlisle, 32 in.; Workington, 40 in.; Appleby, 37 in.; Grasmere, 95 in.; Borrowdale, 132 in. By comparison, average rainfall in St. James Park, Westminster, was 23 in., and in Edinburgh, 28 in.

2. Meteorological Office Publication No. 735, *Averages of Temperature for Great Britain and Northern Ireland, 1931–60* (HMSO, 1963). Mean temperatures for the two stations in Cumberland and one just across the Solway Firth in Dumfries, Scotland, average the same as Edinburgh and 3.8 degrees Fahrenheit cooler than London; E. Kerridge, *The Agricultural Revolution* (New York, 1968), p. 161.

3. BL, Harl. Ms. 594, fols. 85–87, 105–6. The return for Alston is on folio 193.

4. It is necessary to combine the households paying tax (PRO, E179/195/73) with those exempted from tax (E179/348). The dates of the two are not the same but span the years 1670–73.

5. PRO, E179/90/74, E179/90/76, E179/90/77. The returns are useful for some localities but not the entire county.

6. Printed in D. Lysons, *Magna Britannia* (London, 1816), 4: xxxv–xliv.

7. A census, taken in 1695 for the West Ward and the Barony of Kendal in Westmorland (CRO, D/Lons/W/Commonplace Book beginning "An abstract," pp. 5–6), tends to confirm the number of households in the West Ward, but suggests that the household count for the Barony of Kendal was either too high in the hearth tax returns or that rural population had declined from 1670–73 to 1695. The latter seems more probable.

8. Peter Laslett, "Size and Structure of the Household in England over Three Centuries," *Population Studies*, 23 (1969): 200: "mean household size remained fairly constant at 4.75 or a little under, from the earliest point for which we have found figures, until as late as 1911." Mean household sizes for several Cumberland and Westmorland communities toward the end of

the eighteenth century can be found in Peter Laslett, "Mean Household Size in England since the Sixteenth Century," and Richard Wall, "Mean Household Size in England from Printed Sources," in Laslett and Wall, eds., *Household and Family in Past Time* (Cambridge, 1972), pp. 130–31, 175–76, 187–88.

9. Laslett, "Mean Household Size in England since the Sixteenth Century," *ibid.*, p. 131.

10. Problems of estimating household size are discussed in T. H. Hollingsworth, *Historical Demography* (London, 1969), pp. 118–20.

11. BL, Harl. Ms. 280, fol. 172. For a critique of the 1603 census, see Hollingsworth, *Historical Demography*, pp. 82–84.

12. The "age to communicate" or "age at communion" was the age at which communion was compulsory, although a person might be confirmed and take communion at an earlier age. See William Howard Frere, ed., *Visitation Articles and Injunctions* (London, 1910), 3: 259–60, 287, and Edmund Gibson, *Codex Juris Ecclesiastici Anglicani* (Oxford, 1761), 1: 376.

13. Hollingsworth, *Historical Demography*, pp. 81–87. In his comparison of the censuses of 1603 and 1688, Hollingsworth assumed that 16 was the age to communicate in both cases. If it was not, or if it varied from one date to the other, the two lists are not strictly comparable. The Denton census of 1687–88 may have been prepared for the so-called Dalrymple census of 1688 (printed in Hollingsworth, p. 83), but never included.

14. M. A. Faraday, ed., *The Westmorland Protestation Returns, 1641/42* (Kendal, 1971), vii–xii. The Protestation Returns for Cumberland are in the House of Lords Record Office (H.L.R.O., Protestation Returns, 1641/42, Cumberland), a Xerox copy is in the CRO.

15. Printed in F. G. James, "The Population of the Diocese of Carlisle in 1676," *Transactions of the Cumberland and Westmorland Antiquarian and Archaeological Society*, new ser., 52 (1952): 137–41. This is part of the so-called Compton census.

16. The multiplier of 1.67 is recommended by Michael Drake, in his *Historical Demography: Problems and Projects* (Milton Keynes, Bucks, 1974), p. 82. Unlike the earlier census of 1603, the instructions were explicit about the age to communicate, which was specified as sixteen. This does not mean that the instructions were carried out; Drake, *ibid.*, p. 82, remarks, "Some incumbents returned number of inhabitants, some, the number of families and some the number of communicants. [And they] did not always specify which."

17. The weaknesses of the returns for Carlisle are discussed in the text. See also C. W. Chalklin, ed., "The Compton Census of 1676: The Diocese of Canterbury and Rochester," *Kent Records*, 17 (1960): 173–83, and David Bond, "The Compton Census—Peterborough," *Local Population Studies*, no. 10 (1973): 71–74.

18. The parishes of Greystoke, Crosthwaite, Dacre, and Dalston were used because they are central, rural parishes. Unfortunately, their registers are incomplete, but the registers that survive intact for the entire period are

either town registers or registers from parishes on the periphery of the region. These parishes often enjoyed considerable commercial or mining activity in the later seventeenth century and do not reflect the population problems of the isolated rural central parishes. It should be mentioned also that the 1563 population figure for Greystoke seems much too small, compared with the later parish totals. Perhaps the 1563 count only included the households served by the central parish church, while later parish censuses included the people within the outlying chapelries.

19. 1502 Survey in Latin, Xerox copy in CRO; H of N, C201/7; PRO, L.R. 2/213/fols. 41v–42v; *ibid.*, fols. 53–54v; H of N, C176a/6; H of N, C217.

20. 1502 Survey in Latin, Xerox copy in CRO; Survey, 17 Eliz. I, Xerox copy in CRO: T. H. B. Graham, ed., *The Barony of Gilsland: Lord William Howard's Survey, Taken in 1603* (Kendal, 1934), pp. 120–32.

21. CRO, Mounsey-Heysham/Penrith-Inglewood Survey 1619, p. 91.

22. F. Grainger and W. G. Collingwood, *Register and Records of Holm Cultram* (Kendal, 1929), p. 173.

23. PRO, L.R. 2/212/fol. 376.

24. *Ibid.*, fols. 367–87.

25. PRO, L.R. 2/213/fols. 67–74.

26. CRO, Mounsey-Heysham/Penrith-Inglewood Survey 1619, pp. 66–89.

27. PRO, L.R. 2/258/fol. 62.

28. *Ibid.*, fols. 64–65, 71.

29. PRO, E164/37/fols. 60–69.

30. Survey of Gilsland, incorrectly dated 1558. Xerox copy in CRO.

31. Occasionally the tenants objected to squatters, but I think only when the squatters were placed on the pasture by the lord, not when the squatters took the initiative themselves. See A. B. Appleby, "Agrarian Capitalism or Seigneurial Reaction? The Northwest of England, 1500–1700," *American Historical Review*, 80 (1975): 574–94.

32. This line of argument is developed at greater length in *ibid.*

33. Kendal Corp. Ms. A3 1606 (1–10), located at the Cumbria County Record Office, County Hall, Kendal.

34. CRO, Mounsey-Heysham 1/130–32.

35. BL, Harl. Ms. 594, fols. 85–87.

36. *CSP, D Addenda, 1566–79*, p. 6.

37. *Ibid.*, p. 7.

38. See K. F. Helleiner, "The Population of Europe from the Black Death to the Eve of the Vital Revolution," in E. E. Rich and C. H. Wilson, eds., *The Cambridge Economic History of Europe*. IV, *The Economy of Expanding Europe in the Sixteenth and Seventeenth Centuries* (Cambridge, 1967), pp. 1–95.

39. See E. A. Wrigley, "A Simple Model of London's Importance in Changing English Society and Economy, 1650–1750," *Past and Present*, no. 37 (July 1967): 44–70.

CHAPTER THREE

1. Agricultural accounts of the region appear in Joan Thirsk, "The Farming Regions of England," in Joan Thirsk, ed., *The Agrarian History of England and Wales*. IV, *1500–1640* (Cambridge, 1967), pp. 16–28; and E. Kerridge, *The Agricultural Revolution* (New York, 1968), pp. 160–65, 171–73.

2. R. S. Dilley, "Common Land in Cumberland, 1500–1850" (Cambridge M.Litt. thesis, 1972), pp. 21–22. The description of field systems in this chapter owes much to Mr. Dilley's careful study. See also G. Elliott, "Field Systems of Northwest England," in A. R. H. Baker and R. A. Butlin, eds., *Studies of Field Systems in the British Isles* (Cambridge, 1973), pp. 41–92.

3. Thirsk, "Farming Regions of England," pp. 22–23.

4. CRO, P(robate) 1570, B. Wills and inventories for the Diocese of Carlisle are at the Cumbria Record Office, boxed by year and bundled alphabetically.

5. CRO, P 1614, B.

6. CRO, P 1614, B.

7. CRO, P 1614, B.

8. CRO, P 1565, G.

9. CRO, P 1614, D.

10. CRO, P 1565, K.

11. CRO, P 1614, D.

12. H of N, C713.

13. Dilley, "Common Land in Cumberland," pp. 21–22, 41, 48.

14. *Ibid.*, pp. 29–32.

15. *Ibid.*, p. 44.

16. Inventories of John Atkinson, 1613, LRO, WRW (C); Elizabeth Myers, 1581, LRO, WRW (C); Robert Saull, CRO, P 1565; John Atkinson, CRO, P 1565; William Martin, CRO, P 1600; Richard Mabson, CRO, P 1600.

17. See C. M. L. Bouch and G. P. Jones, *A Short Economic and Social History of the Lake Counties, 1500–1830* (Manchester, 1961), table on p. 101. The Lowthers also grew wheat on their demesne at Lowther (CRO, D/Lons/L/A1/1, fols. 223–36).

18. Inventory of Richard Speight, 1600, LRO, WRW (K). See also William Harrison, *The Description of England*, ed. Georges Edelen (Ithaca, N.Y., 1968), p. 135, for mention of spring-sown wheat and rye around Kendal.

19. Mr. Bruce Jones, archivist at the Cumbria Record Office, informed me that peas and beans appear in the local inventories much less often than in the inventories from the south of England. For their importance in Leicestershire see W. G. Hoskins, *The Midland Peasant: The Economic and Social History of a Leicestershire Village* (London and New York, 1965), p. 154.

20. Inventories of John Atkinson of Workington, 1597, LRO, WRW (C); John Atkinson of Millom, 1613, LRO, WRW (C); John Moore of Distington, 1592, LRO, WRW (C); William Martine of Longwathby, CRO, P 1600; Richard Speight of Heversham, 1600, LRO, WRW (K).

21. Usually in those inventories that also list hemp. The two were woven together to make a coarse cloth called "harden" cloth.

22. With rare exceptions (e.g. Richard Miller of Skelton, CRO, P 1600), poultry seems to have been limited to the well-off. The poor cottager seldom owned any geese or chickens.

23. Swine appear in not more than one in 20 of the rural inventories. As was the case with poultry, swine were usually owned by well-off yeomen (e.g. Richard Baron of St. Cuthbert's, CRO, P 1614) or gentlemen (e.g. Henry Blenkinsop of Kirkby Stephen, CRO, P 1614).

24. Dilley, "Common Land in Cumberland," pp. 132–33.

25. CRO, P 1614, D.

26. CRO, P 1614, B.

27. CRO, P 1614, B.

28. CRO, P 1565, S.

29. CRO, P 1570, C.

30. CRO, P 1565, S.

31. CRO, P 1599, S.

32. CRO, P 1600, S.

33. Alan Everitt, "Farm Labourers," in Joan Thirsk, ed., *The Agrarian History of England and Wales. IV, 1500–1640* (Cambridge, 1967), pp. 412–25.

34. Bouch and Jones, *Lake Counties*, p. 105. Other examples of probate inventories are also given there.

35. CRO, D/Lons/L/A1/1, fols. 199, 224, 225.

36. *Ibid.*, fols. 182, 222–32.

37. "Skilling" as it appears in the Lowther accounts, or "sheelings" as it is written in G. Ornsby, ed., *Selections from the Household Books of the Lord William Howard of Naworth Castle* (Surtees Society, 1878), 68: 72.

38. CRO, D/Lons/L/A1/1, *passim*.

39. *Howard Household Books*, pp. 46, 47, 95, 137, 249, 267.

40. LRO, WRW (K).

41. LRO, WRW (K).

42. LRO, WRW (K).

43. CRO, P 1614, B.

44. CRO, P 1570, A.

45. CRO, P 1570, B.

46. Alan Macfarlane, *The Family Life of Ralph Josselin: An Essay in Historical Anthropology* (Cambridge, 1970), pp. 55–56.

CHAPTER FOUR

1. *Border Papers*, 1: 24.

2. *Ibid.*, 1: 20–23, 30, 99; 2: 131. See also D. L. W. Tough, *The Last Years of a Frontier: A History of the Borders During the Reign of Elizabeth* (Oxford, 1928), pp. 173–85.

3. Quoted in G. P. Jones, "King James I and the Western Border," *Transactions of the Cumberland and Westmorland Antiquarian and Archaeological Society*, new ser., 69 (1969): 132.

4. *Border Papers*, 2: 131. For a discussion of the role of partible inheritance and land use, see Joan Thirsk, "The Common Fields," *Past and Present*, no. 29 (1964); J. Z. Titow, "Medieval England and the Open-Field System," *ibid.*, no. 32 (1965); Joan Thirsk, "The Origin of the Common Fields," *ibid.*, no. 33 (1966); Richard C. Hoffman, "Medieval Origins of the Common Fields," in William N. Parker and Eric L. Jones, eds., *European*

Peasants and Their Markets: Essays in Agrarian Economic History (Princeton, N.J., 1975); Donald N. McCloskey, "The Persistance of English Common Fields," *ibid.* See also the important article by Joan Thirsk, "Industries in the Countryside," in F. J. Fisher, ed., *Essays in the Economic and Social History of Tudor and Stuart England* (Cambridge, 1961), esp. pp. 81–84.

5. Alexander Luders et al., eds., *The Statutes of the Realm* (London, 1810–28), 4, part 1 (1819), pp. 663–67.

6. R. P. Sanderson, ed., *A Book of the Survey of the Debatable and Border Lands, 1604* (Alnwick, 1891), pp. 21–33.

7. "Rowclidge" in the survey.

8. Sanderson, *Survey of the Debatable and Border Lands*, pp. 29–30. See also J. V. Harrison, "Five Bewcastle Wills, 1587–1617," *Transactions of the Cumberland and Westmorland Antiquarian and Archeological Society*, new ser., 67 (1967): 103, 107–8.

9. The acreage shown in the survey was probably given in statute acres. The total acreage of Bewcastle was given in the survey as 32,960 (p. 34), the same as that given in William Hutchinson, *History of the County of Cumberland* (Carlisle, 1794), 1: 77, which would have been in statute acres.

10. Sanderson, *Survey of the Debatable and Border Lands*, pp. 14–16. The Grahams were then in trouble with the Crown because of a severe outbreak of banditry that followed Elizabeth's death in 1603.

11. *Records of Kendal*, 2: 14n.

12. These two clans, or "surnames," were especially feared on the West March. "Kinmont Willie," the hero of a ballad of the same name, was an Armstrong. For the reputation of the two clans, see *Border Papers*, 1: 93, 109, 120–27; 2: 150–57, 159–62, and *passim.*

13. *Ibid.*, 1: 117–18, 123.

14. Mary L. Armitt, "Fullers and Freeholders of the Parish of Grasmere," *Transactions of the Cumberland and Westmorland Antiquarian and Archaeological Society*, new ser., 8 (1908).

15. F. Grainger and W. G. Collingwood, *Register and Records of Holm Cultram* (Kendal, 1929), p. 173; and PRO, L.R. 2/212/fol. 308. Population increased despite the inheritance practices, as other families settled on the demesne and freehold lands.

16. Joan Thirsk, "The Farming Regions of England," in Joan Thirsk, ed., *The Agrarian History of England and Wales*. IV, *1500–1640* (Cambridge, 1967), p. 24.

17. *Records of Kendal*, 2: 104–5.

18. Thirsk, "The Farming Regions of England," p. 24.

19. PRO, E317/Cumberland 1, 6, 7, 8; E317/Westmorland 3, 5, 6.

20. PRO, E164/37. Part of this survey is abstracted in F.E.C. 1/N12. This quote is taken from the latter.

21. CRO, D/Lons/L/A1/fols. 35–36.

22. T. H. B. Graham, ed., *The Barony of Gilsland: Lord William Howard's Survey, Taken in 1603* (Kendal, 1934), p. 162.

23. *Ibid.*, pp. 4–15.

24. *Ibid.*, pp. 120–32.

25. R. S. Dilley, "Common Land in Cumberland, 1500–1850" (Cambridge M.Litt. thesis, 1972), p. 254.

26. BL, Lans. 61, fol. 86.

27. CRO, D/HG 19, fols. 36–37.

28. *Ibid.*, fol. 38.

29. *Ibid.*, fols. 39–40.

30. PRO, E164/37, fols. 18–29. The foliation in this document is confused.

31. *Ibid.*, fols. 35–38.

32. *Records of Kendal*, 2, page references as follows: Grasmere, pp. 12–15; Loughrigg, p. 26; Undermillbeck, pp. 80–82; Applethwaite, pp. 83–84; Crosthwaite & Lyth, pp. 102–04; Casterton, pp. 335–36; Troutbeck, pp. 54–55.

33. Land size in these surveys was determined by the testimony of local jurors, who would have given it in customary acres. A customary acre in Westmorland contained about 1.4 statute acres. In the southern part of the county, along the Lancashire border, the acre was 1.62 statute acres. See W. Marshall, *Review and Abstract of the County Reports to the Board of Agriculture* (York, 1818), 1: 233; and F. W. Garnett, *Westmorland Agriculture, 1800–1900* (Kendal, 1912), p. 2.

34. The 1578 Survey of the Earl of Northumberland's Lands, Cockermouth Castle, fol. 100v.

35. PRO, E164/37, fols. 26–29.

36. *Ibid.*, fols. 35–38.

37. PRO. L.R. 2/213/fols. 27, 47.

38. All references to tenants and lands in the manors of Wigton, Kirkland, Rosewain, Aikhead, Woodside, Dundraw, Waverton, and the Forest of Westward are found in *ibid.*, fols. 39–69. The manors appear in the survey in the order shown in this note. Spelling of the manor names has been modernized.

39. C. M. L. Bouch and G. P. Jones, *A Short Economic and Social History of the Lake Counties, 1500–1830* (Manchester, 1961), pp. 77–78; Hutchinson, *Cumberland*, 2: 397n.

40. PRO, E164/37, fol. 8; F.E.C. 1/N12, pp. 2–6.

41. M. E. James, *Change and Continuity in the Tudor North* (Borthwick Papers no. 27, York, 1965), pp. 24–25.

42. CRO, D/Lons/Denton, no foliation.

43. Peter Bowden, "Statistical Appendix," in Joan Thirsk, ed., *The Agrarian History of England and Wales.* IV, *1500–1640* (Cambridge, 1967), pp. 818–19; W. G. Hoskins, "Harvest Fluctuations and English History, 1480–1619," *Agricultural History Review*, 12 (1964): 46.

44. Hutchinson, *Cumberland*, 2: 448.

45. CRO, D/Lons/L/A1/1, fols. 223–36.

46. Bowden, "Statistical Appendix," p. 820.

47. B. H. Slicher van Bath, *The Agrarian History of Western Europe, A.D. 500–1850* (London, 1963), pp. 330–31.

48. E. Kerridge, *The Agricultural Revolution* (New York, 1968), p. 330.

49. In 1589, Parliament passed a statute prohibiting the construction of cottages with less than four acres of land, in an attempt to limit the number of paupers that occupied cottages without land and lived off the charity of their neighbors. See Joan Thirsk, "Enclosing and Engrossing," in Thirsk, *Agrarian History of England and Wales*, pp. 227–28.

CHAPTER FIVE

1. J. Nicolson and R. Burn, in *The History and Antiquities of the Counties of Westmorland and Cumberland* (London, 1777), 1: 13, said that it was a "vulgar mistake" to maintain that the two counties paid no lay subsidies in the Tudor period. However, the mistake seems to be theirs. The Exchequer 179 class of documents for the reign of Elizabeth contains only alien lay subsidies; furthermore, cases at law frequently state that the inhabitants were not burdened with subsidies prior to 1603, e.g. PRO, E134/7 Car I/M38. See also R. S. Schofield, "The Geographical Distribution of Wealth in England, 1334–1649," *Economic History Review*, 2d ser., 18 (1965): 494.

2. The two counties were consistently assessed at the bottom of all English counties in the seventeenth century. Subsidies were not assessed in the sixteenth century, and in the early seventeenth century they were not reliable guides to wealth. See the Schofield article cited immediately above, pp. 494, 503. The new Parliamentary assessments of 1657 assessed Cumberland at just over £92 and Westmorland at £63. By comparison, Devon was assessed at £2,574 and Norfolk at £3,106. See C. H. Firth and R. S. Rait, eds., *Acts and Ordinances of the Interregnum, 1642–1660* (London, 1911), 2: 1058–61.

3. E.g. F. Grainger and W. G. Collingwood, *Register and Records of Holm Cultram* (Kendal, 1929), pp. 190–99.

4. PRO, Req. 2/165/165. The phraseology was formulaic, appearing in almost identical wording in numerous other descriptions of tenant right.

5. BL, Lans. 169, fols. 107–8. The Crown manors shown in this document had 238 freeholders, most of whom were holders by burgage in Carlisle or Kendal, 37 leaseholders, 95 tenants at will, 297 copyholders, all at Holm Cultram, and 1,363 customary tenants. For a general discussion of the various forms of tenure, see Eric Kerridge, *Agrarian Problems in the Sixteenth Century and After* (London and New York, 1969), pp. 32–60, and A. W. B. Simpson, *An Introduction to the History of the Land Law* (Oxford, 1961), particularly pp. 1–23, 135–62.

6. Carlisle, Kendal, and Appleby were royal boroughs, Cockermouth and Egremont seigneurial boroughs.

7. Cf. M. E. James, *Change and Continuity in the Tudor North* (Borthwick Papers no. 27, York, 1965); and the same author's *A Tudor Magnate and the Tudor State* (Borthwick Papers no. 30; York, 1966), pp. 7–8.

8. Cf. Kerridge, *Agrarian Problems*, pp. 45–56.

9. E.g. CRO, D/HG19, Survey, lands of Leonard Dacre, fol. 23.

10. Simpson, *Land Law*, p. 158.

11. CRO, PC/21/50 and 55. The obligations and duties of the customary tenants at Threlkeld were confirmed by agreement in 1635, based on the old custom.

12. The custom varied from manor to manor about the proportion of the tenement the widow was to have. Probably most commonly she retained a third. Usually she also paid a heriot, or the best animal on the holding, for her widow's share. See Annette Bagot, "Mr. Gilpin and Manorial Customs," *Transactions of the Cumberland and Westmorland Antiquarian and Archaeological Society*, new ser., 62 (1962): 238, 243.

13. Kerridge, *Agrarian Problems*, pp. 43–45, somewhat underestimates the size of fines that were considered "reasonable." On the other hand, R. H. Tawney, *The Agrarian Problem in the Sixteenth Century* (New York, 1967, orig. publ. 1912), pp. 287–310, overstates the freedom of the lord to push up "arbitrary" fines. See the discussion in A. B. Appleby, "Agrarian Capitalism or Seigneurial Reaction? The Northwest of England, 1500–1700," *American Historical Review*, 80 (1975): 581–94.

14. PRO, F.E.C. 1/N12, pp. 2–6.

15. PRO, Req. 2/186/157. For a similar case involving a fine following a sale, see Sta. Cha. 8/97/15.

16. Quoted in Kerridge, *Agrarian Problems*, p. 147.

17. PRO, Req. 2/178/52.

18. The quotations are from PRO, Req. 2/165/165. See also Req. 2/211/5, Req. 2/233/10, Req. 2/164/127, C3/284/34, C33/95.

19. See proceedings in PRO, Req. 2/218/42, C3/284/34, E134/35–36 Eliz/M23.

20. BL, Cotton, Titus, F13, fol. 256. See also *Border Papers*, 1: 20–23, 30, 106; 2: 131.

21. *CSP, D, Addenda, 1566–1579*, pp. 347–48.

22. PRO, L.R. 2/212/fol. 481.

23. *Ibid.*, fol. 202.

24. PRO, D.L. 44/333, 342.

25. PRO, L.R. 2/212/fol. 308.

26. G. R. Batho, "The Finances of an Elizabethan Nobleman: Henry Percy, Ninth Earl of Northumberland (1564–1631)," *Economic History Review*, 2d ser., 9 (1957): 433–50. See also the brilliant essay by M. E. James, "The Concept of Order and the Northern Rising of 1569," *Past and Present*, no. 60 (1973): 49–83.

27. CRO, D/HG19, Survey, lands of Leonard Dacre, fol. 23; PRO, L.R. 2/212/fol. 122; H of N C201.5, and tenant depositions in PRO, E134/7–8 Chas. I/H1.

28. *CSP, D Addenda, 1566–1579*, p. 348.

29. H of N C176a.5,6. For an account of similar moves by landlords in Northumberland, see S. J. Watts, "Tenant-Right in Early Seventeenth-Century Northumberland," *Northern History*, 6 (1971): 72–74, 83–85.

30. Now apparently lost, but referred to in Northumberland County History Committee, *Northumberland County History* (Newcastle-upon-Tyne, 1893–1940), 8: 238.

31. PRO, Sta. Cha. 8/161/16; CRO, Mounsey-Heysham, 6/pp. 2–8; H. S. Reinmuth, Jr., "The Struggle over Corby, 1605–1626: Lord William Howard and Thomas Salkeld," *Transactions of the Cumberland and Westmorland Antiquarian and Archaeological Society*, n.s., 66 (1966): 190–200.

32. T. G. Barnes, "Fines in the High Court of Star Chamber, 1596–1641" (privately printed: copies in the PRO; the Huntington Library, San Marino, California; the Folger Library, Washington, D.C.; and the Boalt Hall Law Library, University of California, Berkeley), p. 136.

33. CRO, D/Lec/Correspondence/169/1614, letter from Wilfrid Lawson and Thomas Fotherly dated August 1614; CRO, D/Lec/Correspondence/169/1616, letter from Wilfrid Lawson dated June 3, 1616.

34. CRO, D/Lec/Correspondence/169/1616, letter from Wilfrid Lawson dated October 28, 1616.

35. PRO, S.P. 14/203/11.

36. J. F. Larkin and P. L. Hughes, eds., *Stuart Royal Proclamations. I, Royal Proclamations of King James I, 1603–1625* (Oxford, 1973), pp. 488–90; PRO, S.P. 14/187/fol. 203.

37. Any one of these offenses could bring the tenants before Star Chamber. This assembly was apparently directed only against the lesser lords, not against Prince Charles. See PRO, Sta. Cha. 8/34/4, for accounts of the affair.

38. PRO, S.P. 14/154/fols. 11–12.

39. The above quotes are from Nicolson and Burn, *History of Westmorland and Cumberland*, 1: 56–59.

40. Tawney, *Agrarian Problem*, pp. 297–98.

41. PRO, C3/302/66.

42. CRO, PC/21/54 and 55.

43. The evidence for this long and complicated dispute is in CRO, PC/26/24 and PRO, E134/8 Chas I/M16.

44. A conversion to leasehold was not necessarily disadvantageous, as long as the necessary initial payment could be raised by the tenants. The customary tenants of Alston, in eastern Cumberland, became lessees in the years 1611–16. Their leases ran for 999 years and called for a "running" fine of twenty years' old rent, payable every 21 years. This amounted to slightly less than doubling the old rent, which was far better than paying a twenty- or thirty-year fine at unforeseen intervals. A lease of that duration certainly gave the tenants security of tenure and an inheritable estate. See William Hutchinson, *History of the County of Cumberland* (Carlisle, 1794), 1: 214, 216.

45. Numerous examples are given in the depositions in PRO, E134/7 Car I/M38. See also Hutchinson, *Cumberland*, 1: 98, 132, 153, 175, 181, 208, 212, 405, 511, 577.

46. PRO, E134/8 Chas I/M16, deposition of Thomas Salkeld. The tenants at Holm Cultram had paid running fines in the sixteenth century.

47. Hutchinson, *Cumberland*, 1: 220, 179, 563; 2: 125, 153, 469.

48. PRO, E134/8 Chas I/M16, deposition of Anthony Curwen.

49. H of N C173.8.

50. PRO, E317/Cumberland 1, 7, 8; E317/Westmorland 5, 6.

51. E.g., Threlkeld in 1635 (CRO, PC/21/55), Bewcastle in 1630 (Hutchinson, *Cumberland*, 1: 79), Parton in 1672 (Hutchinson, *Cumberland*, 2: 461), Burgh by Sands in 1674 (Hutchinson, *Cumberland*, 2: 500), Grayrigg, Lambrigg, and Docker in 1695 (Nicolson and Burn, *Westmorland and Cumberland*), Preston Richard in 1679 (Hutchinson, *Cumberland*, 1: 212). Not all tenants on the manors were party to these agreements; some simply could not afford the cost and remained customary tenants under arbitrary fines.

52. Hutchinson, *Cumberland*, 1: 37–39, 133.

CHAPTER SIX

1. *Border Papers*, 2: 343; *CSP, D, 1595–97*, p. 347.

2. F. J. Furnivall, ed., *Harrison's Description of England in Shakespere's Youth* (London, 1878), 2: 146–47.

3. *Ibid.*, 2: 111.

4. Quoted in *Records of Kendal*, 3: 4. See also C. M. L. Bouch and G. P. Jones, *A Short Economic and Social History of the Lake Counties, 1500–1830* (Manchester, 1961), pp. 18–21.

5. Quoted in F. W. Garnett, *Westmorland Agriculture, 1800–1900* (Kendal, 1912), p. 32.

6. *CSP, D Addenda, 1566–1597*, pp. 6–7; William Hutchinson, *History of the County of Cumberland* (Carlisle, 1794), 2: 48.

7. Hutchinson, *Cumberland*, 1: 33n.

8. BL, Harl. 589, no. 20, fol. 142. In a breviate of customs for 1535 (PRO, E122/164/4), no Cumberland port is listed, which suggests that sea trade had not been important earlier in the century.

9. BL, Harl. 589, no. 21, fol. 145; Lans. 110, no. 37.

10. PRO, E122/216/21.

11. PRO, E190/1448/1.

12. A. R. B Haldane, *The Drove Roads of Scotland* (Edinburgh, 1952), pp. 13–16. For cattle tolls collected by the city of Carlisle, see CRO, Ca/4/141.

13. Mary L. Armitt, "Fullers and Freeholders of the Parish of Grasmere," *Transactions of the Cumberland and Westmorland Antiquarian and Archaeological Society*, new ser., 8 (1908): 195, 198. See also B. C. Jones, "Westmorland Pack-horse Men in Southampton," *ibid.*, new ser., 59 (1959): 72; and G. Elliott, "The Decline of the Woollen Trade in Cumberland, Westmorland and Northumberland in the late 16th Century," *ibid.*, new ser., 61 (1961): 112.

14. Quoted in Bouch and Jones, *Lake Counties*, p. 136.

15. Richard Brathwaite, *The English Gentleman: Containing Sundry Excellent Rules* (London, 1630), p. 125.

16. BL, Additional Mss. 34,324, fols. 14–16. This document contains much valuable information on the northern woolen industry. See also P. Bowden, *The Wool Trade in Tudor and Stuart England* (London, 1962), p. 68.

17. PRO, E134/9 Jas I/M29.
18. Except for homespun, cloth was evidently not made in Cumberland. See *CSP, D, 1619–23*, p. 383.
19. PRO, E190/1448/1.
20. BL, Additional Mss. 34,318, fol. 29.
21. J. U. Nef, *The Rise of the British Coal Industry* (London, 1932), 2, facing p. 380. Nef estimates average yearly production for Cumberland in the decade 1551–60 at 6,000 tons (1: 19), which is probably too generous. But see below, Chapter 11, note 20.
22. *Ibid.*, 1: 70–71.
23. CRO, D/Lec/29/33 (Westward).
24. CRO, D/Lec/Correspondence/169/1615.
25. CRO, D/Lec/Westward Colliery Accounts, 1603–4.
26. CRO, D/Lec/Correspondence/169/1615. Adits were drainage tunnels dug from a lower level to a point in the mineshaft where water collected. Digging them was a dangerous job, for when the adit tunneler broke through into the mine, he risked being swept back down the adit by the water rushing out. For a general picture of mining technology, see J. U. Nef, "Mining and Metallurgy in Medieval Society," in M. Postan and E. E. Rich, eds., *The Cambridge Economic History of Europe*, vol. 2 (Cambridge, 1952), reprinted in J. U. Nef, *The Conquest of the Material World* (Cleveland and New York: Meridian Books, 1967). The high level of German mining technology in the sixteenth century is portrayed in the contemporary account of G. Agricola, *De re metallica* (H. Hoover, English trans., London, 1912).
27. J. Wilson, ed., *The Victoria History of the Counties of England. Cumberland* (London, 1905), 2: 359. Peat was also the usual domestic fuel throughout the two counties.
28. G. Ornsby, ed., *Selections from the Household Books of the Lord William Howard of Naworth Castle* (Surtees Society, 1878), 68: 5, 8, 69, 119, 156, 212.
29. CRO, D/Lec/Correspondence/169/1616.
30. In 1703 two salt pans used at Whitehaven were respectively 12 and 15 inches deep and both were 9 feet 6 inches square. (CRO, D/Lons/W/Sir John Lowther's memo book, no pagination.)
31. M. B. Donald, *Elizabethan Copper: The History of the Company of Mines Royal, 1568–1605* (London, 1955), p. 103.
32. *Ibid.*, p. 36.
33. W. G. Collingwood, *Elizabethan Keswick* (Cumberland and Westmorland Antiquarian and Archaelogical Society, Tract Series, 8, Kendal, 1912), pp. 1–2.
34. *Ibid.*, p. 2.
35. Donald, *Elizabethan Copper*, p. 25.
36. *Ibid.*, pp. 107, 230–32.
37. *Ibid.*, pp. 137–38, 166–67. The name was evidently a corruption of the German name for the mine, *Gotes Gab*, or God's Gift.
38. *Ibid.*, p. 45.
39. *Ibid.*, pp. 104–6.

40. *Ibid.*, pp. 116, 120, 126.
41. *Ibid.*, p. 131.
42. *Ibid.*, pp. 143–44.
43. *Ibid.*, pp. 22, 38, 107, 114, 137.
44. *Ibid.*, pp. 120–22, 136; Collingwood, *Elizabethan Keswick*, p. 47.
45. Donald, *Elizabethan Copper*, p. 155.
46. *Ibid.*, pp. 185–87, 284.
47. *Ibid.*, p. 367; Collingwood, *Elizabethan Keswick*, pp. 61, 73, 82, 83, 91, 109–11.
48. *Ibid.*, pp. 32–34.
49. *Ibid.*, pp. 55, 79, 93.
50. *Ibid.*, pp. 9–12, 201; Donald, *Elizabethan Copper*, pp. 173, 176–77, 216–18.
51. G. Hammersley, "Technique or Economy? The Rise and Decline of the Early English Copper Industry, ca. 1550–1660," *Business History*, 15 (1973): 4. Footnote 4, p. 1, gives the extensive bibliography on the copper mines.
52. *Ibid.*, p. 4; Donald, *Elizabethan Copper*, pp. 38–39.
53. Hammersley, "Early English Copper Industry," pp. 5, 10–12.
54. *Ibid.*, pp. 14–15.
55. Donald, *Elizabethan Copper*, pp. 166–68; Collingwood, *Elizabethan Keswick*, pp. 50–51.
56. *Ibid.*, pp. 108–11.
57. Hammersley, "Early English Copper Industry," p. 2. This article has, on pp. 18–27, an interesting discussion of the reasons for the decline of copper mining.
58. See A. Everitt, "The Marketing of Agricultural Produce," in Joan Thirsk, ed., *The Agrarian History of England and Wales. IV, 1500–1640* (Cambridge, 1967), pp. 466–592, especially pp. 540–42. See also Haldane, *Drove Roads*, pp. 166, 178.

CHAPTER SEVEN

1. In Penrith, for example, average burials were 47.1 per annum for the base years 1560–85, 1599–1622, and 1625–40. Designating 47.1 as 100, the indexes of mortality were as follows: 1587, 414; 1597, 437; 1598, 1,297; 1623, 512. In Greystoke (base years 1570–86, 1599–1606, 1609–19; average 39.8 = 100): 1587, 271; 1597, 460; 1598, 128; 1623, 407. In St. Bees (base years 1570–90, 1625–40; average 35.5 = 100): 1587, 59; 1597, 251; 1598, 121; 1623, 386. In all cases, the modern calendar year is the year used. The seriousness of the mortality has been recognized by the historians whose works are listed in note 3.
2. F. J. Fisher, "Influenza and Inflation in Tudor England," *Economic History Review*, 2d ser., 18 (1965): 120–29.
3. E.g. Thomas Short, *New Observations . . . on City, Town and Country Bills of Mortality* (London, 1750), pp. 86–87, 103–4; H. Barnes, "Visitations of the Plague in Cumberland and Westmorland," *Cumberland and Westmorland Antiquarian and Archaeological Society Transactions*, orig. ser., 10 and 11 (1891), *passim*; W. G. Howson, "Plague, Poverty and Popu-

lation in Parts of North-West England, 1580–1720," *Transactions of the Historical Society of Lancashire and Cheshire*, 112 (1961): 29–55; Charles Creighton, *A History of Epidemics in Britain* (2 vols.; Cambridge, 1894), 1: 349, 358–60, 411.

4. Michael Drake, "An Elementary Exercise in Parish Register Demography," *Economic History Review*, 2d ser., 14 (1961–62): 432–36. Also see Drake's superb chapter "La crise démographique," in his *Historical Demography: Problems and Projects* (Milton Keynes, Bucks, 1974).

5. Colin D. Rogers, *The Lancashire Population Crisis of 1623* (Manchester, 1975).

6. Among the recent books on plague are Philip Ziegler, *The Black Death* (London, 1970); J. F. D. Shrewsbury, *A History of Bubonic Plague in the British Isles* (Cambridge, 1970), and Carlo M. Cipolla, *Cristifano and the Plague* (London, 1973). Other titles will be cited in the following notes.

7. Cf. J. Meuvret, "Demographic Crisis in France," in D. V. Glass and D. E. C. Eversley, eds., *Population in History* (London, 1965), p. 519: "Death from starvation pure and simple is obviously an extreme case. But hunger can lead to the same end by roundabout means. Bad food—even more dangerous than long fasting—could kill."

8. "Pure" starvation, a condition denied by some physicians, is discussed, along with its effect on the human body, in Emil Apfelbaum, *Maladie de famine* (Warsaw, 1946).

9. For example, leprosy disappeared from Europe in the late Middle Ages, losing its power to infect men in a moderate climate. Scarlet fever was an innocuous disease in 1700; by 1800 it was terribly virulent, returning to relative mildness again in the present century, before the introduction of antibiotics. See R. Dubos, *Mirage of Health* (New York, 1959), particularly pp. 143–49.

10. This necessarily superficial description of the plague is largely based on R. Pollitzer, *Plague* (Geneva, 1954); L. Fabian Hirst, *The Conquest of Plague* (Oxford, 1953), and "Plague," *The British Encyclopedia of Medical Practice*, ed. Lord Horder (2d ed.; London, 1952), 10, and Shrewsbury, *Bubonic Plague*. Two recent works on the plague are of great value: Jean-Noël Biraben, *Les hommes et la peste en France et dans les pays européens et méditerranéens*, Tome I, *La peste dans l'histoire* (Paris and The Hague, 1975), and Roger Schofield, "An Anatomy of an Epidemic: Colyton, November 1645 to November 1646," *The Plague Reconsidered* (*Local Population Studies* Supplement, 1977), pp. 95–126. In a brilliant analysis, Schofield shows that rat fleas rather than human fleas or lice were the insect vectors of the Colyton epidemic.

11. Shrewsbury, *Bubonic Plague*, p. 21. B. Bennassar, *Recherches sur les grandes épidémies dans de nord de l'Espagne à la fin du XVIe siècle* (Paris, 1969), pp. 15–16, shows that Spanish villages were ravaged by the disease, but the villages he mentions were large, with from 450 to 1,000 inhabitants, and he acknowledges that the disease spread from the neighboring cities.

12. Hirst, "Plague," p. 62.

13. Shrewsbury, *Bubonic Plague*, p. 8; Hirst, *Conquest of Plague*, pp. 136–37, 304–6. The "plague rat," *Rattus rattus*, was to a large extent replaced in England in the eighteenth century by *Rattus norvegicus*, the hardier, brown, "sewer" rat. Within the last fifty years, however, *R. rattus* has returned and in many cities is the predominate rat today. However, it is not now found in the countryside. See L. H. Matthews, *British Mammals* (2d ed.; London, 1968), p. 192.

14. Hirst, in *Conquest of Plague*, pp. 308–9, relates that in one modern instance, 56,000 Javanese leaving a plague-infested area were disinfected and searched for ectoparasites by the health authorities. Plenty of lice, bugs, and human fleas were discovered, but only three rat fleas.

15. Brough under Stainmore, Westmorland, recorded plague as the cause of death of eight people in 1597, of whom seven apparently were members of the same family. The parish of Shap recorded three deaths "of the infection" in 1598.

16. The devastating impact of plague on the parish of Colyton, Devon, in 1645–46 and on Eyam, Derbyshire, in 1665–66 can be traced in Roger Schofield, "An Anatomy of an Epidemic," and Leslie Bradley, "The Most Famous of All English Plagues," *The Plague Reconsidered* (*Local Population Studies* Supplement, 1977).

17. Eric Woehlkens, *Pest und Ruhr im 16. und 17. Jahrhundert* (Hannover, 1954), city plan opposite p. 56.

18. Hirst, *Conquest of Plague*, pp. 260–76. Pollitzer, *Plague*, pp. 331–32, 357–58, 372–73, doubts that *X. cheopis* was the flea responsible, but agrees that the temperature ranges given above control the number of infective fleas. But see Schofield, "An Anatomy of an Epidemic."

19. For winter incidence, see Hirst, *Conquest of Plague*, pp. 260–61; Shrewsbury, *Bubonic Plague*, pp. 157, 175–77, 191, 199, 406, 417; Woehlkens, *Pest und Ruhr*, graphs following pp. 88, 104, 120; J. Revel, "Autour d'une épidémie ancienne: la peste de 1666–1670," *Revue d'histoire moderne et contemporaine*, 17 (1970): 979–81. Bennassar, *Les grandes épidémies*, pp. 42–43, reports the same general pattern for northern Spain but with a few striking exceptions, namely villages with "continental" climates that were afflicted in midwinter.

20. In addition to these two, researchers have discovered other plague characteristics of more limited value. Hirst, "Plague," p. 61, states that the largest number of cases occurred in the 10-to-35-year age-group. He also found more cases among males than females. Revel, "La peste de 1666–1670," pp. 979–80, observed the same sex-age distribution in northern France and explained it by the increased exposure to infected fleas if one were a grain dealer or a cloth worker—trades carried on by adult males. Woehlkens, *Pest und Ruhr*, pp. 71–74, also found variations in the incidence of the disease according to occupation. Bakers and linen workers often contracted the disease; blacksmiths and woodworkers seldom, apparently because their homes were not congenial places for rats to nest. Bennassar, *Les grandes épidémies*, p. 18, writes that the disease had a predilection toward children, although his figures (p. 50) seem to contradict this

statement except in one village. Bennassar also found that more women died of the disease than men. M. F. Hollingsworth and T. H. Hollingsworth, "Plague Mortality Rates by Age and Sex in the Parish of St. Botolph's without Bishopsgate, London, 1603," *Population Studies*, 25 (1971): 135, 145, found that children had the highest mortality, men the next, and women the least. The age and sex differences, they feel, are attributable to the degree of exposure, not to any inherent resistance. With contradictory observations and inadequate records to pursue these questions, I thought it best to limit my analysis to the two characteristics discussed in the text.

21. Hirst, "Plague," p. 62. The information on pneumonic plague is drawn from the same sources as that on bubonic plague.

22. Hirst, *Conquest of Plague*, pp. 190–92.

23. M. Greenwood, *Epidemics and Crowd Diseases* (New York, 1935), p. 291.

24. R. W. Brumskill, "The Clay Houses of Cumberland," *Transactions of the Ancient Monument Society*, n.s., 10 (1962): 58–65.

25. See Appendix B for a list of all parish registers used and their places of publication or archival locations.

26. See J. C. Snyder, "The Typhus Fevers," T. M. Rivers and F. L. Horsfall, Jr., eds., *Viral and Rickettsial Infections of Man* (London, 1959), pp. 799–827; J. W. D. Megaw, "Typhus Fevers and Other Rickettsial Fevers," *The British Encyclopedia of Medical Practice*, 12: 390–414.

27. Family "reconstitution" could show us the true ages of the dead, but reconstitution is possible in only a small percentage of families, perhaps not those affected. Also, reconstitution for such a large area is beyond the capabilities of an individual historian.

28. For a list of Cumberland and Westmorland parishes affected by this and subsequent crises, see Appendix C. Howson, "Plague, Poverty and Population," p. 33, states that, "though typhus spreads very quickly in any closely packed group as in a gaol, a ship or a slum, it does not spread quickly from one group to another."

29. Drake, *Historical Demography*, p. 99.

30. Peter Bowden, "Statistical Appendix," in Joan Thirsk, ed., *The Agrarian History of England and Wales. IV, 1500–1640* (Cambridge, 1967), pp. 818–19. See also W. G. Hoskins, "Harvest Fluctuations and English History, 1480–1619," *Agricultural History Review*, 12 (1964): 37.

31. *Border Papers*, 1: 255, 258, 265–66. BL, Lans. 52, fols. 122–23, confirms that, in May 1587, prices in Cumberland were very high.

32. Bowden, "Statistical Appendix," pp. 842–43.

CHAPTER EIGHT

1. CRO, Mounsey-Heysham 1/130–32. See also J. Hughes, "The Plague at Carlisle 1597/98," *Transactions of the Cumberland and Westmorland Antiquarian and Archaeological Society*, 71 (1971): 53, for a different death total. In Carlisle, Penrith, and Kendal the plague began in the autumn of 1597 but became dormant during the winter, only to flare up again in the

summer of 1598. The great majority of the deaths occurred in the summer and fall of 1598.

2. See note 15, Chapter Seven.

3. CRO, Mounsey-Heysham 1/65ff. See also the registers of Kendal and Penrith.

4. W. G. Hoskins, "Harvest Fluctuations and English History, 1480–1619," *Agricultural History Review*, 12 (1964): 38–39; Peter Bowden, "Statistical Appendix," in Joan Thirsk, ed., *The Agrarian History of England and Wales*. IV, *1500–1640* (Cambridge, 1967), pp. 818–19.

5. Hoskins, "Harvest Fluctuations, 1480–1619," p. 46. "Normal" is here defined as Hoskins' 31-year moving average price of wheat.

6. *Ibid.*, pp. 40–41; Bowden, "Statistical Appendix," pp. 818–20, 836–37, 842–44. For the diet of the rural poor, see A. Everitt, "Farm Labourers," in Thirsk, *Agrarian History of England and Wales*, pp. 450–52.

7. *Cecil Papers*, 7: 295–96.

8. Quoted in E. M. Leonard, *The Early History of English Poor Relief* (Cambridge, 1900), p. 125.

9. *CSP,D, 1595–97*, pp. 347–48.

10. *Ibid.*, p. 420.

11. *Border Papers*, 2: 446.

12. *Ibid.*, 2: 234.

13. *Ibid.*, 2: 285, 374, 408.

14. Peter Bowden, "Agricultural Prices, Farm Profits, and Rents," in Thirsk, *Agrarian History of England and Wales*, p. 620.

15. The port books for Cumberland for this period have not survived.

16. *Tamworth Parish Register* (Staffordshire Parish Register Society, 1917), p. 163. "Danske" refers here to Danzig, not Denmark.

17. Peter Laslett, *The World We Have Lost* (London, 1965), p. 113.

18. Pierre Goubert, "The French Peasantry of the Seventeenth Century: A Regional Example," in Trevor Aston, ed., *Crisis in Europe, 1550–1660* (New York, 1967), pp. 167–69.

19. As in Colyton, Devon, in 1645–46 (E. A. Wrigley, "Mortality in Pre-Industrial England: The Example of Colyton, Devon, over Three Centuries," *Daedalus*, 97 (1968): 556–57), and in Loughborough, Leicestershire, in 1610 and 1631. Perhaps it is worth mentioning that conceptions did not fall more than 30 percent in these Loughborough plagues, as contrasted with a decline of over half in the famines of the north. A numerical abstract of the Loughborough registers is available at the Cambridge Group.

20. See F. J. Fisher, "Influenza and Inflation," pp. 120–29, and R. S. Roberts, "A Consideration of the Nature of the English Sweating Sickness," *Medical History*, 9 (1965).

21. Thomas Francis, Jr., "Influenza," in T. M. Rivers and F. L. Horsfall, Jr., eds., *Viral and Rickettsial Infections of Man* (London, 1959), pp. 652–53: "The classic features of influenza are its occurrence in epidemics which arise abruptly and spread rapidly but irregularly over a region. . . . In an area the peak [of an epidemic] may be reached in three weeks, and the course essentially completed in another three to four weeks. There is a high morbidity and low mortality. . . . In the majority of epidemics case fatality scarcely exceeds 1 per 10,000." I have not studied the duration of the

epidemic of 1557, but if mortality was great enough to stabilize prices for over a decade, as F. J. Fisher suggests in "Influenza and Inflation," perhaps the "fevers" followed by "quartan agues" were not influenza but some other disease.

22. C. W. Dixon, *Smallpox* (London, 1962), pp. 192–97; M. Greenwood, *Epidemics and Crowd Diseases* (New York, 1935), pp. 226–27; Charles Creighton, *A History of Epidemics in Britain* (2 vols.; Cambridge, 1894), 1: 463–67; 2: 434–43, 556.

23. Creighton, *ibid.*, 2: 534.

24. Pierre Goubert, "Recent Theories and Research in French Population Between 1500 and 1700," in D. V. Glass and D. E. C. Eversley, eds., *Population in History* (London, 1965), p. 471.

25. In "Plague, Poverty and Population in Parts of North-West England, 1580–1720," (*Transactions of the Historical Society of Lancashire and Cheshire*, 112 [1961]: 33), W. G. Howson attributes the 1623 mortality to plague and, in some parishes, starvation. For reasons I have given in the text, I think he is mistaken about the plague.

26. Bowden, "Statistical Appendix," pp. 820–21.

27. David Masson, ed., *Register of the Privy Council of Scotland, 1622–25* (Edinburgh, 1896), pp. 257–60. See also pp. 203–4, 287–90, 329. The effects of the 1623 famine in Scotland are briefly discussed in Chapter 9.

28. *APC,E, 1623–25*, p. 155.

29. Wool prices for the harvest year of 1622 were at their lowest point between 1587 and 1648. Bowden, "Statistical Appendix," pp. 843–45.

30. CRO, Ca/4/139/p. 92.

31. Crosthwaite parish registers.

32. CRO, PR/74/1.

33. St. Bees register.

34. W. G. Hoskins, "Price Fluctuations and English Economic History, 1620–1759," *Agricultural History Review*, 16 (1968): 29. The prices are, as usual, national rather than local and may not have reflected adequately northern price movements.

35. J. Heysham, *An Account of the Jail Fever or Typhus Carcerum: As It Appeared at Carlisle in the Year 1781* (London, 1782), pp. 2, 3, 6n, 7n.

36. *Ibid.*, pp. 5, 31, 33.

37. *Ibid.*, pp. 3n, 31.

38. Registers of Holy Trinity Church, Whitehaven, CRO, PR/84/1. From 1751, the age at death and the cause of death are given.

39. Quoted in J. Meuvret, "Demographic Crisis in France," in Glass and Eversley, *Population in History*, p. 510.

40. Particularly, see A. Keys et al., *The Biology of Human Starvation* (2 vols.; Minneapolis and London, 1950), 1: xv, 20, 448–53; 2: 1009–40.

41. *Ibid.*, 2: 1011. On the Warsaw ghetto—an ugly chapter in human history—see also Emil Apfelbaum, *Maladie de famine* (Warsaw, 1946); L. Tushnet, *The Uses of Adversity* (New York and London, 1966); F. Hocking, *Starvation* (Sydney, 1969). For the view that malnutrition increases the virulence of infectious disease, see N. S. Scrimshaw, C. E. Taylor, and J. E. Gordon, *Interactions of Nutrition and Infection* (Geneva, 1968).

42. Some half-million people were crowded into nine square miles of a

dilapidated part of Warsaw. They averaged 13 to a room. The official ration set by the Germans in October 1941 was 300 calories a day, which was somewhat supplemented by smuggled rations. See Hocking, *Starvation*, p. 13.

43. Keys et al., *Biology of Starvation*, 2: 1010.

44. For a discussion of the relationship between malnourishment and epidemic disease, see A. B. Appleby, "Nutrition and Disease: The Case of London, 1550–1750," *The Journal of Interdisciplinary History*, 6 (1975), *passim*.

CHAPTER NINE

1. Pierre Goubert, "Recent Theories and Research in French Population Between 1500 and 1700," in D. V. Glass and D. E. C. Eversley, eds., *Population in History* (London, 1965), p. 465.

2. Quoted in Gustaf Utterström, "Climatic Fluctuations and Population Problems in Early Modern History," *The Scandinavian Economic History Review*, 3 (1955): 27–28.

3. I am indebted to M. W. Flinn and T. C. Smout of the University of Edinburgh for the information on the famine of 1597 and 1623, forthcoming in *Scottish Population History from the Seventeenth Century to the 1930s*, ed. M. W. Flinn (Cambridge University Press, 1977).

4. W. G. Hoskins, "Harvest Fluctuations and English History, 1480–1619," *Agricultural History Review*, 12 (1964): 38.

5. B. Bennassar, *Recherches sur les grandes épidémies dans le nord de l'Espagne à la fin du XVIe siècle* (Paris, 1969), pp. 32–33, 51; Jorge Nadal, *La Poblacion Española (Siglos XVI a XX)* (Barcelona, 1973), p. 24.

6. L. Del Panta and M. Livi Bacci, "Cronologia, Intensitá e Diffusione delle Crisi di Mortalitá in Italia, 1600–1850," paper presented to the International Colloquium of Historical Demography, Montreal, 1975. Their data are drawn from cities and may not reflect conditions in the rural countryside.

7. Michael Drake, *Historical Demography, Problems and Projects* (Milton Keynes, 1974), pp. 98–99.

8. David Palliser, "Dearth and Disease in Staffordshire, 1540–1670," in C. W. Chalklin and M. A. Havinden, eds., *Rural Change and Urban Growth, 1500–1800* (London, 1974), pp. 61–62, 69–70.

9. W. G. Hoskins, *Old Devon* (London, 1971), p. 151.

10. I wish to express my thanks to the Cambridge Group, which kindly supplied me with these figures.

11. Peter Bowden, "Statistical Appendix," in Joan Thirsk, ed., *The Agrarian History of England and Wales*. IV, *1500–1640* (Cambridge, 1967), pp. 819–21.

12. Hoskins, "Harvest Fluctuations, 1480–1619," p. 40.

13. I have used the estimate of E. A. Wrigley, "A Simple Model of London's Importance in Changing English Society and Economy, 1650–1750," *Past and Present*, no. 37 (1967): 44.

14. David Glass, ed., *London Inhabitants Within the Walls, 1695* (London Record Society Publication, 1966), p. xxi.
15. T. C. Dale, ed., *The Inhabitants of London in 1638* (London, 1931), *passim.*
16. *Ibid.*, pp. 144–45.
17. For example, St. Botolph without Bishopsgate; *ibid.*, pp. 225–29.
18. The parish registers of all nine parishes—St. Michael, Cornhill; St. Peter's, Cornhill; All Hallows, Bread Street; St. Dionis, Backchurch; St. Mary le Bow, Cheapside; St. Mary Aldermary; St. Mary Somerset; St. James, Clerkenwell; and St. Martin in the Fields—have been published by the Harleian Society, London.
19. *CSP,D, 1595–97*, p.421.
20. L. T. Smith, ed., *The Maire of Bristowe is Kalendar* (Camden Society, 1872), n.s., 5: 62–64.
21. Paul Slack, "Poverty and politics in Salisbury 1597–1666," in Peter Clark and Paul Slack, eds., *Crisis and order in English towns 1500–1700* (London, 1972), pp. 196, 169.
22. George Abbot, *An Exposition upon the Prophet Jonah* (London, 1600), p. 204. Abbot became Archbishop of Canterbury in 1611.
23. *Ibid.*, pp. 365–66.
24. Henry Arthington, *Provision for the Poore* (London, 1597), no pagination.
25. *Cecil Papers*, 7: 526.
26. *APC, E, 1596–97*, pp. 374–75.
27. *APC,E, 1595–96*, pp. 25–27, 87–88, 164–65; *APC,E, 1596–97*, pp. 112–13, 116–17, 152–53, 269, 323, 335, 383–86, 505–6, 516–17; *APC,E, 1597*, pp. 15–16, *APC,E, 1597–98*, pp. 69, 144–45, 180–81, 315–16; *Cecil Papers*, 6: 534–35; *CSP,D, 1595–97*, pp. 126, 384, 401.
28. *APC,E, 1596–97*, p. 523.
29. *APC,E, 1595–96*, pp. 43–44.
30. *CSP,D, 1595–97*, pp. 161–62.
31. *APC,E, 1595–96*, p. 334.
32. *CSP,D, 1595–97*, pp. 316–20, 342–45; *APC,E, 1596–97*, pp. 365–66, 373–74.
33. *Cecil Papers*, 7: 148.
34. *APC,E, 1597*, pp. 55–56.
35. *APC,E, 1597*, pp. 88–89; *CSP,D, 1595–97*, p. 401.
36. Norman S. B. Gras, *The Evolution of the English Corn Market* (Cambridge, Mass., 1915), pp. 236–40.
37. *APC,E, 1595–96*, pp. 25–27; *APC,E, 1596–97*, p. 81; *APC,E, 1597–98*, pp. 29–31; *Cecil Papers*, 7: 410, 497.
38. *APC,E, 1596–97*, pp. 152–53.
39. *APC,E, 1596–97*, p. 81.
40. *APC,E, 1596–97*, p. 152.
41. *APC,E, 1597*, pp. 359–60.
42. Paul L. Hughes and James F. Larkin, eds., *Tudor Royal Proclamations*. III, *The Later Tudors (1588–1603)* (New Haven, 1969), pp. 193–95.
43. *APC,E, 1595–96*, p. 21; *APC,E, 1596–97*, pp. 149, 152–53, 154, 327, 335, 429, 539–40.
44. *APC,E, 1597–98*, pp. 291–92.

45. *APC,E, 1596–97*, pp. 112–13, 116–17, 269, 534–35; *APC,E, 1597*, pp. 15–17; *APC,E, 1597–98*, pp. 69, 144–45, 180–81, 315–16, 321.
46. *APC,E, 1596–97*, pp. 393–97, 445–46, 454–55, 550–51; *APC,E, 1597–98*, p. 8.
47. *APC,E, 1597–98*, pp. 181–82, 189–90, 438–40.
48. *APC,E, 1596–97*, pp. 94–96, 383–86.
49. *APC,E, 1596–97*, pp. 380–82.
50. *APC,E, 1596–97*, pp. 383–86.
51. Hoskins, "Harvest Fluctuations, 1480–1619," p. 46.
52. E. H. Phelps-Brown and Sheila V. Hopkins, "Seven Centuries of the Prices of Consumables, Compared with Builders' Wage-Rates," in E. M. Carus-Wilson, ed., *Essays in Economic History* (London, 1962), 2: 189, found that in 1597 the real wages of builders in England were at their lowest point between 1260 and 1954. These authors also suggested that the crisis of the 1590's was "a Malthusian crisis, the effect of a rapid growth of population impinging on an insufficiently expansive economy."
53. E. Kerridge, *The Agricultural Revolution* (New York, 1968), *passim.*
54. A. B. Appleby, "Disease or Famine? Mortality in Cumberland and Westmorland, 1580–1640," *Economic History Review*, 2d ser., 26 (1973): 403–32.
55. See note 3 above.
56. Colin D. Rogers, *The Lancashire Population Crisis of 1623* (Manchester, 1975).
57. *Ibid.*, p. 10. The actual multiple was 2.88. Including the burial totals for 1623 in the base gives a multiple of 2.63. All dating for Lancashire is old style.
58. *Ibid.*, pp. 26–27.
59. For the names of all these parishes and the location of the registers, see Appendix D.
60. The base in each of these calculations was the 11-year span 1618 through 1628, including the crisis year of 1623. This base was adopted to conform to the designation of crisis used by the Cambridge Group. It is not the same base used in either the Cumberland-Westmorland data or the Lancashire data and thus the comparisons are not as strict as one would wish. No definition of "crisis" is as yet agreed upon by all researchers; until a common system of measurement is adopted, comparisons will remain approximate. To make matters worse, researchers sometimes choose new-style years, as I have done, and sometimes old-style or even harvest years.
61. I am indebted to Professor Michael Drake for these figures. The dating is old style.
62. Rogers, *Lancashire Population Crisis*, p. 11.
63. G. H. Tupling, *The Economic History of Rossendale* (Manchester, Chetham Society, 1927), n.s., 86: 57–66, 232–33.
64. *Ibid.*, pp. 76, 235; see also pp. 77–89.
65. Other instances of encroachment on the wastes by landless squatters can be found in John Porter, "A Forest in Transition: Bowland, 1500–1650," *Transactions of the Historical Society of Lancashire and Cheshire*,

225 (1975): 40–60; and Martha J. Ellis, "A Study in the Manorial History of Halifax Parish in the Sixteenth and Early Seventeenth Centuries," *Yorkshire Archaeological Journal*, 40 (1961): 420–41. Ms. Ellis writes that "one cannot help but wonder that there was any unenclosed moorland left, especially on Halifax moor," pp. 424–25.

66. Flinn, *Scottish Population History from the Seventeenth Century to the 1930s*.

67. A. E. Imhof and B. J. Lindskog, "Les causes de mortalité en Suede et en Finlande entre 1749 et 1773," *Annales E.S.C.*, 29 (1974): 916–17.

68. *Ibid.*, p. 916.

69. The parishes of All Saints, North Street; Holy Trinity, Goodramgate; Holy Trinity, King's Court; St. Helen, Stonegate; St. John Ousebridge; St. Margaret, Walmgate; St. Mary Bishophill, Junior; St. Saviour; St. Mary, Castlegate; St. Laurence; All Saints, Pavement; St. Michael le Belfrey; St. Martin, Coney Street; St. Olave, and St. Crux. The registers of Holy Trinity, Micklegate; St. Martin cum Gregory, Micklegate; St. Cuthbert; and St. Mary Bishophill, Senior, are incomplete or appear to be defective. York does not seem to have acted as a magnet for the rural poor. Or, if they did flock to the town, the city's charities were able to keep them from starving.

70. See Appendix D for a list of these parishes.

71. D. M. Palliser, "Epidemics in Tudor York," *Northern History*, 8 (1973): 46.

72. The mortality figures for Lowther, Newbiggen, and Newton Reigny are based on old style years.

CHAPTER TEN

1. *APC,E, 1630*, p. 72. The most convenient source for price movements is W. G. Hoskins, "Harvest Fluctuations and English Economic History, 1620–1759," *Agricultural History Review*, 16 (1968); these prices, of course, are predominately from the south and may not have reflected northern grain price movements.

2. Joan Thirsk and J. P. Cooper, eds., *Seventeenth Century Economic Documents* (Oxford, 1972), pp. 51–52.

3. *CSP,D, Addenda, 1566–79*, p. 7; William Hutchinson, *History of the County of Cumberland* (Carlisle, 1794), 2: 48.

4. *Ibid.*, 2: 49.

5. CRO, D/Lons/W/Commonplace Book beginning "Mr. Drydens . . . ," p. 7.

6. *CSP,D, Addenda, 1566–79*, p. 6.

7. J. U. Nef, *The Rise of the British Coal Industry* (London, 1932), 1: 70–71.

8. CRO, Mounsey-Heysham 1/130–32.

9. CRO, D/Lons/W/Commonplace Book beginning "Mr. Drydens . . . ," p. 8.

10. PRO, E179/90/76, fols. 54–57.

11. Kendal Corporation Mss. A3 1606 (1–10).

12. PRO, E179/195/73 and E179/348.

13. CRO, D/Lons/W/Commonplace Book beginning "An Abstract . . . ," p. 5.
14. PRO, E179/195/73 and E179/348.
15. *Records of Kendal*, 2: 12–13, 26, 52–55, 80–84, 102–4, 335–36; PRO, S.C. 12/31/16; S.C. 11/1000; S.C. 11/1001; S.C. 12/33/1. Also see G. P. Jones, "Decline of the Yeomanry in the Lake Counties," *Transactions of the Cumberland and Westmorland Antiquarian and Archaeological Society*, new ser., 62 (1962): 211–12.
16. H of N, C217; H of N, C611/10; H of N, C176a/6.
17. Quoted in Jones, "Decline of the Yeomanry," p. 207.
18. J. Bailey and G. Culley, *General View of the Agriculture of the County of Cumberland . . . Drawn up for the Board of Agriculture* (London, 1794), p. 11; see also pp. 214, 264.
19. William Marshall, *Review and Abstract of the County Reports to the Board of Agriculture* (York, 1818), 1: 218.
20. *Ibid.*, 1: 231.
21. *Ibid.*, 1: 214.
22. Bailey and Culley, *Agriculture of Cumberland*, p. 263.
23. J. Nicolson and R. Burn, *The History and Antiquities of the Counties of Westmorland and Cumberland* (London, 1777), 1: 9.
24. CRO, D/Lons/L/A1/2, no pagination, and CRO, D/Lons/L/A1/1, fols. 271ff. All of Sir John Lowther's agricultural improvements are taken from these sources.
25. CRO, D/Lons/L/A1/1, fols. 247–54.
26. B. H. Slicher van Bath, *The Agrarian History of Western Europe, A.D. 500–1850* (London, 1963), pp. 330–31.
27. W. G. Hoskins, "Harvest Fluctuations and English History, 1620–1759," *Agricultural History Review*, 16 (1968): 21–22, 28–31.
28. Slicher van Bath, *Agrarian History*, pp. 206–17; A. H. John, "Agricultural Productivity and Economic Growth in England, 1700–1760," in E. L. Jones, ed., *Agriculture and Economic Growth in England, 1650–1815* (London, 1967), pp. 172–73.
29. CRO, D/Lons/L/A1/1, fol. 275.
30. This is suggested in H. Todd, *Notitia Diocesis Carliolensis* (Kendal, 1890), a late seventeenth-century description of the diocese of Carlisle, p. 32.
31. E. Kerridge, *The Agricultural Revolution* (New York, 1969), pp. 277, 287; Marshall, *Review*, 1: *passim*; Bailey and Culley, *Agriculture of Cumberland*, pp. 22–27.
32. E.g. CRO, Powson, Pattinson, Pearson, Rooke, Richardson, Sutton, Symson, Merton, all 1670, Birkhed, 1669, Caipe, 1670; LRO/WRW (C), Atkinson, 1670, Muncaster, 1656.
33. H. J. Habakkuk, "La disparition du paysan anglais," *Annales E.S.C.*, 20 (1965): 657–59. Changing trends in price movements was only one of the reasons given by Habakkuk for the decline of the peasantry.
34. P. Bowden, *The Wool Trade in Tudor and Stuart England* (London, 1962), price appendixes, pp. 219–20.

35. *Ibid.*, p. 40.
36. Cf. Habakkuk, "La disparition du paysan anglais," p. 659.
37. For a general account of the history and administration of the hearth tax, see C. A. F. Meekings, ed., *Dorset Hearth Tax Assessments, 1662–1664* (Dorchester, 1951), pp. vii–xxvii, or the same editor's *Surrey Hearth Tax, 1664* (Surrey Records Society Publications, 1940), 17: ix–li.
38. Meekings, *Surrey Hearth Tax*, xii.
39. PRO, E179/195/73.
40. PRO, E179/348.
41. W. G. Hoskins, "The Rebuilding of Rural England," reprinted in Hoskins, *Provincial England* (London, 1963), pp. 139–42.
42. Margaret Spufford, *Contrasting Communities: English Villagers in the Sixteenth and Seventeenth Centuries* (Cambridge, 1974), pp. 36–41.
43. Hoskins, "The Rebuilding of Rural England," p. 136.
44. Meekings, *Surrey Hearth Tax*, pp. lxxxix–cxxxiii. No exact comparison is possible because my figures were tabulated differently than these, but clearly there were more hearths per dwelling.
45. Meekings, *Dorset Hearth Tax*, pp. 4–65, 67–100.
46. *Collections for a History of Staffordshire*, ed. The William Salt Archaeological Society (London, 1921), 21: 50–95, 106–20. This was the hearth tax of 1666.
47. Spufford, *Contrasting Communities*, pp. 41–44.
48. R. Welford, "Newcastle Hearth Tax," *Archaeologia Aeliana*, 3d ser., 7 (1911): 49–76.
49. *Collections for Staffordshire*, pp. 44–50, 99–105; Meekings, *Dorset Hearth Tax*, pp. 3–4.
50. PRO, E179/90/76, fols. 4–6. This assessment is the most complete.
51. *Ibid.*, fols. 54–56.
52. *Ibid.*, fol. 62.
53. *Ibid.*, fol. 71.
54. *Ibid.*, fol. 51.
55. *Ibid.*, fols. 53–54.
56. *Ibid.*, fols. 57–60. The communities include Dacre, Newton Reigny, Newbiggen, Blencow, Catterlen, and Laithes.
57. J. E. Thorold Rogers, *A History of Agriculture and Prices in England* (Oxford, 1882), 3: 112–17.

CHAPTER ELEVEN

1. CRO, D/Lons/L/Book of Accounts and Purchases, 1604–55, fol. 73. Perhaps it would be more accurate to say that Sir John cleared his title to the manor; the wording is ambiguous.
2. CRO, D/Lons/W/Correspondence of Sir Christopher Lowther, Bt., pp. 5, 7, 8, 9.
3. *Ibid.*, p. 11.
4. CRO, D/Lons/W/Small Memo and Account Book, fols. 7–8.
5. CRO, D/Lons/W/Bonds, assignments, accounts, loose.
6. CRO, D/Lons/W/Correspondence of Sir Christopher Lowther, Bt., pp. 77–78.
7. *Ibid.*, p. 100. See also the list of small expenses for lighterage and

portage of coal and portage and weighing of salt. Entries dated 1635 show the purchase of several barrels of blood, which was used to clarify the salt water before it was boiled down. (CRO, D/Lons/W/Account Book, no foliation.)

8. There is reference to sailcloth, planks for ship siding, and pitch in C. Lowther's inventory *post mortem* (CRO, D/Lons/W/Account Book, no foliation).

9. CRO, D/Lons/W/Sir John Lowther's Commonplace Book beginning "An abstract . . . ," p. 42, gives 8 Chas. I (March 27, 1632–March 26, 1633) as the date, but p. 133 gives 1637 as the date. There are four commonplace books; they will be identified by the words that begin each one.

10. CRO, D/Lons/W/Correspondence of Sir Christopher Lowther, Bt., pp. 57, 94, 96.

11. *Ibid.*, p. 57.

12. *Ibid.*, p. 67; CRO, D/Lons/L/Book of Accounts and Purchases, 1604–55, fol. 93, and D/Lons/W/Small Notebook, fol. 63. The ship was carrying northern woolens.

13. CRO, D/Lons/W/Account Book, no foliation.

14. *Ibid.*, fols. 131–32. The foliation begins in the middle of the book.

15. All the following import and export data are from PRO, E122/221/95.

16. R. E. Zupko, *A Dictionary of English Weights and Measures* (Madison, Wis., 1968).

17. CRO, D/Lons/W/Commonplace Book beginning "Emery & Oyl . . . ," pp. 148–51. Coal shipments were expressed in chaldrons and have been converted to tons, using two tons to the chaldron. For coal measures, see J. U. Nef, *The Rise of the British Coal Industry* (London, 1932), 2: 370.

18. CRO, D/Lons/W/Commonplace Book beginning "Mr. Drydens . . . ," p. 8.

19. CRO, D/Lons/W/Colliery Accounts, 1675–76.

20. Nef, *British Coal Industry*, 1: 19, estimates a seventeen-fold increase in Cumberland coal production between 1551–60 and 1681–90, from 6,000 tons to 100,000 tons. However, his figures for certain areas have been called guesswork, and I have not been able to substantiate his estimates for Cumberland. See J. L. Langton, "Coal Output in South-West Lancashire, 1590–1799," *Economic History Review*, 2d ser., 25 (1972): 29, note 9.

21. CRO, D/Lons/W/Colliery Accounts, 1694–98.

22. CRO, D/Lons/W/Commonplace Book beginning "An abstract . . . ," pp. 50–53.

23. CRO, D/Lons/W/Commonplace Book beginning "Mr. Drydens . . . ," pp. 192–94.

24. CRO, D/Lons/Commonplace Book beginning "An abstract . . . ," p. 96.

25. *CSP,D, Addenda, 1566–79*, p. 7; CRO, D/Lons/W/Commonplace Book beginning "Mr. Drydens . . . ," p. 7.

26. CRO, D/Lons/W/Sir John Lowther's Memoranda Books, vol. 1, p. 190.

27. C. M. L. Bouch and G. P. Jones, *A Short Economic and Social History of the Lake Counties, 1500–1830* (Manchester, 1961), pp. 129–30; CRO, D/Lec/Egremont Box 240 (various unnumbered documents); R. F. Tylecote and J. Cherry, "The 17th-Century Bloomery at Muncaster Head," *Transactions of the Cumberland and Westmorland Antiquarian and Archaeological Society*, new ser., 70 (1970); CRO, D/Lec/Petitions to the Lord, Box 265, nos. 73, 75, and 155.

28. T. Robinson, *An Essay Towards a Natural History of Westmorland and Cumberland* (London, 1709), p. 45; CRO, D/Lec/Braithwaite & Coledale, Box 81.

29. Nef, *British Coal Industry*, esp. 1: 170–84.

30. PRO, E190/1448/8. This one cargo represents over one-half of one percent of the tobacco produced annually in the Chesapeake region at that time. See James A. Henretta, *The Evolution of American Society, 1700–1815* (Lexington, Mass., 1975), p. 63.

31. CRO, D/Lons/W/Commonplace Book beginning "Mr. Dyrdens . . . ," p. 169; PRO, E190/1448/8.

32. PRO, E190/1448/8; CRO, D/Lec/Egremont Box 240.

33. CRO, D/Lons/W/Commonplace Book beginning "Mr. Drydens . . . ," p. 10. The date of this shipment, which was to Maryland, was 1685.

34. L. M. Cullen, *Anglo-Irish Trade, 1660–1800* (Manchester, 1968), pp. 32, 37–38.

35. PRO, E190/1448/8.

36. PRO, E190/1448/6.

37. *Ibid.*

38. PRO, E190/1448/8.

39. See J. E. Williams, "Whitehaven in the Eighteenth Century," *Economic History Review*, 2d ser., 8 (1956): 393–404.

40. A. R. B. Haldane, *The Drove Roads of Scotland* (Edinburgh, 1952), p. 18.

41. *Ibid.*, pp. 152–70, 178, 166; William Hutchinson, *History of the County of Cumberland* (Carlisle, 1794), 1: 95; CRO, Ca/2/140 and 154.

42. The information on the Carlisle tolls is from CRO, Ca/4/139 and 141; PRO, E134/3 Jas II/M33, and W. Nanson, "The Shire or County Tolls Belonging to the City of Carlisle," *Transactions of the Cumberland and Westmorland Antiquarian and Archaeological Society*, orig. ser., 3 (1878).

43. *CSP,D, 1663–64*, p. 24. A slightly different total is given in PRO 30/24/4/112 (Shaftesbury Mss.). I am indebted to Mr. Donald Woodward of Hull University for this latter reference.

44. CRO, Ca/2/140.

CHAPTER TWELVE

1. P. Bowden, "Price Appendix," in Joan Thirsk, ed., *The Agrarian History of England and Wales. IV, 1500–1640* (Cambridge, 1967), pp. 820–21, 842–45.

2. For a discussion of the divergence of wool and grain prices, see P. Bowden, "Movements in Wool Prices, 1490–1610," *Yorkshire Bulletin of Economic and Social Research*, 4 (1952); 118–24.

3. Bowden, "Price Appendix," in Thirsk, *Agrarian History of England and Wales*, pp. 842–45.

4. In the northwest, at least. The State Papers, however, are full of references to grain riots and shortage in southern England.

5. Bowden, "Movements in Wool Prices," pp. 122–23.

6. W. G. Hoskins, *The Midland Peasant: The Economic and Social History of a Leicestershire Village* (London and New York, 1965), pp. 176–77, 186.

7. *Ibid.*, pp. 178–79.

8. *Ibid.*, p. 176. The customary tenants, too, were protected against increases in rents and fines.

9. Hoskins does not mention any problems in 1597, which would have been the worst subsistence crisis that faced the villagers.

10. *Ibid.*, p. 189.

11. C. E. Banks, *Topographical Dictionary of 2885 English Emigrants to New England, 1620–1650* (Philadelphia, 1937) lists one emigrant from Cumberland and none from Westmorland, compared, for example, to 298 from Suffolk and 266 from Essex. H. Whittemore, *Genealogical Guide to the Early Settlers of America* (Baltimore, 1967), lists one Westmorland emigrant.

12. See A. B. Appleby, "Nutrition and Disease: The Case of London, 1550–1750," *The Journal of Interdisciplinary History*, 6 (1975): 1–19.

13. Margaret Spufford, *Contrasting Communities: English Villagers in the Sixteenth and Seventeenth Centuries* (Cambridge, 1974), pp. 77–83, 90–92.

14. David Levine and Keith Wrightson, "The Social Context of Illegitimacy in Early Modern England," forthcoming in P. Laslett, ed., *Comparative Studies in the History of Bastardy* (London).

15. Joel Samaha, *Law and Order in Historical Perspective: The Case of Elizabethan Essex* (New York and London, 1974), p. 22.

16. *Ibid.*, p. 36.

17. Peter Laslett, *The World We Have Lost* (London, 1965), p. 127.

A Note on Sources

THE FOLLOWING note is not intended as a complete guide to the sources used in this study but merely as an elaboration of the most useful sources and the major problems the reader is likely to face in using them. Sources that have been fully discussed in the text will not be dealt with here, although in some instances I shall give the names of handbooks and guides the reader may find helpful.

Throughout this book, I have made extensive use of parish registers. In 1538, Thomas Cromwell ordered that each parish in England keep a record of all baptisms, burials, and marriages. Usually the registers show merely the name of the person (in marriages the names of the persons) and the date of the event. Not all parishes immediately began to keep registers in 1538, and the registers of many that did have not survived. However, from about 1558—or perhaps a few years later in Cumberland and Westmorland—the registers provide a good picture of population change. The registers, of course, show religious ceremonies, not demographic events, but the historical demographer can safely assume that burial quickly followed death and—during the period covered by this study—baptism usually came soon after birth. In other words, the recorded religious events faithfully reflect the demographic events. For an analysis of the delay between birth and baptism, see R. S. Schofield and B. M. Berry, "Age at Baptism in Preindustrial England," *Population Studies*, 25 (1971).

It is also well known that the registers cover only part of the population. In the sixteenth and seventeenth centuries Roman Catholics and nonconformists were not always baptized, buried, or married within the Church of England. However, underregistration was not a serious problem until late in the seventeenth century. During the time of the population crises covered in this study, the registers include an overwhelming majority of the parish population, including a representative sample from all economic groups. There is no reason to suppose that the registers show a weighted sample—predominantly poor or predominantly well-off—although readers should be aware that this may be a problem in the eighteenth century.

As a glance at my appendixes will show, many registers have been printed. I have used these where possible because any errors in transcription were not great enough to affect my findings. A good many other registers are conveniently on deposit in the record office of the county where the parish lies. Still others are on deposit in local libraries or historical institutions. For a handy list of these deposited registers, see *Original Parish Registers in Record Offices and Libraries* (Cambridge, 1974). Finally many registers remain in their respective parish churches and can be inspected with the permission—not always easy to obtain—of the church authorities.

Although I have found that most registers were painstakingly kept and accurately reflect the population history of the parish, some registers are clearly worthless to the historical demographer, although they may be of interest to the genealogist. For example, the entries might be badly jumbled—June before March, December before September—or merely listed without any dates. Or it may be impossible to tell whether the event shown was a baptism or a burial. One can usually quickly tell when the register is defective.

Unfortunately, the registers are occasionally broken by gaps—pages torn from the register or perhaps an entire book of entries lost. Sometimes, these lacunae can be made good by reference to the copy, the so-called Bishops' Transcript, that every parish was ordered to send to the diocesan headquarters. Of course, if there was some interruption in the original recording of the entries—for example, the clerk may have died—the gaps cannot be filled.

Useful introductions to the registers can be found in J. C. Cox, *The Parish Registers of England* (London, 1910) and D. J. Steel, *National Index of Parish Registers* (Vol. I, London, 1967; other volumes in progress). The Steel series gives the beginning date for each extant register and indicates its location. It also indicates if the register has been microfilmed by the Church of Jesus Christ of Latter-Day Saints. If it has, the microfilm is available on order at the church's genealogical libraries located in most of the major cities of the United States. A valuable critical evaluation of the registers can be found in T. H. Hollingsworth, *Historical Demography* (London, 1969); his footnotes provide further references.

The other sources on population history—household counts, communicant lists, etc.—are also evaluated by Hollingsworth and by Michael Drake, *Historical Demography: Problems and Projects* (Open University Press, Milton Keynes, Bucks, 1974). A very useful general introduction to historical demography is E. A. Wrigley, *Population and History* (London, 1969).

A Note on Sources

The sources for the economic and social history of a region such as Cumberland and Westmorland are too lengthy for analysis here, but I have found W. G. Hoskins, *Local History in England* (London, 1959), and F. G. Emmison, *Archives and Local History* (London, 1966) to be particularly valuable guides to the extraordinary richness of local records. My own study benefited enormously from the knowledge and kindness of the archivists and staff at the Cumbria Record Office. It should perhaps be mentioned that within the last few years large collections of private papers have been given to the county record offices, as it has become impossible for many of the great English families to maintain their records at their own cost. These private collections have been (or are being) catalogued and calendared by the county record offices and provide the researcher with much evidence that previously was either unobtainable or difficult to use. Although older local histories abound for England, these new acquisitions will permit much reassessment and reevaluation of local and regional history.

However much the student today may rewrite the older histories, they still remain invaluable sources of information, and I would like to close this note by mentioning three important histories of Cumberland and Westmorland: J. Nicolson and R. Burn, *The History and Antiquities of the Counties of Westmorland and Cumberland*, 2 vols. (London, 1777); W. Hutchinson, *History of the County of Cumberland*, 2 vols. (Carlisle, 1794); and C. M. L. Bouch and C. P. Jones, *A Short Economic and Social History of the Lake Counties, 1500–1830* (Manchester, 1961).

Index

Index

Index

Index

Index